WHAT OTHER

THERE ARE FEW THINGS in today's social and political climate more relevant than the matter of interpretation. The recent overturn of Roe v. Wade has brought to the forefront the issue of how we as a nation interpret the Constitution. The Supreme Court ruled that the subject of abortion was not to be decided on the Federal level, but on the State level. For religious leaders, the question was not if this was a Federal or State issue. The question centered on the status of the unborn. These leaders have turned to the Bible for their interpretation of the rights of the unborn.

This is just one example of a practical application that the book *The Joy of Interpretation* can address. Steve Richardson's academic overview of interpretation is thorough and helpful. The book seeks to define Interpretation, its role, its relevance, and its vocabulary before delving into a look at Biblical interpretation and Constitutional interpretation.

If you are serious about your study of either the Constitution or the Bible, this book will set you on solid ground in interpreting what you study.

Faithe Thomas
Owner, Master Design Publishing
Author of the *Color Thru History* series

WE ALL PROCESS IN our minds all that we read. But how do we interpret it all? We need a baseline for the interpretation of current affairs, history, and the Word of God. Steve Richardson takes you on a very thorough walk through how to interpret our times, the Bible, and the documents that helped form our nation.

Doug Dees
Pastor, Author, *Fish Prison*

NOT MANY PEOPLE QUESTION whether they are correctly interpreting what they read, but Richardson's *The Joy of Interpretation* will have readers paying close attention to the original context, meaning, and intent of an author's work in order to avoid misinterpretation. Specifically regarding the Bible and the US Constitution, Richardson explains how easy it is to misinterpret the true meaning of these authoritative texts and thus create unintentional and potentially damaging consequences. Through this book, Richardson reveals the true joy in learning to correctly interpret what we read so that we can have faith and assurance in our understanding and application of written words to life.

Ashley Niro
Editor, Tallahassee, FL

STEVE RICHARDSON GROUNDS HIS analysis of scriptural and constitutional interpretation in a nuanced and timely consideration of whether interpretation itself is a becoming a lost art. After thinking carefully about how one might engage in the practice of interpretation, he reveals his own thoughts about how to interpret both Scripture and constitutional law. Even those who might not agree with all of Richardson's normative prescriptions will find ample food for thought in *The Joy of Interpretation*.

Laura R. Olson
Thurmond Professor,
Department of Political Science, Clemson University

AS A FORMER MAINE State Representative caught between conflicting party ideologies and as a pastor/theologian caught between heaven and earth, the call to careful interpretation of both the commands of Caesar and the words of God are most welcome. If nothing else, Steve Richardson urges caution before jumping to ill-informed conclusions concerning the kingdom of God or the nation-state. That not only keeps us centered but helps us become good listeners to the neighbor with conflicting points of view.

As I read *The Joy of Interpretation*, I was reminded of a statement regarding biblical inerrancy that came from an evangelical denomination in the 1960s: "The Bible is inerrant in all that it intends to teach." If we ask of either Scripture or civil law, "What does this intend to teach?," it pushes us to broader research and understanding of the history and intent of verse or law. With Scripture deriving from divine inspiration and civil law deriving from highest collaborative intention, rigorous interpretation can help us see more clearly the points of intersection between kingdom and nation-state while remaining faithful to Jesus' command to render separate allegiance without compromise or merger.

Rev. Stan Moody, Ph.D.
Pastor Emeritus, Columbia Street Baptist Church
Founder and President, Columbia Street Project

"COMMUNICATION PROBLEMS" ARE TOO often cited for dividing marriages, closing businesses, and starting wars. The human and financial cost is staggering. Thanks to *The Joy of Interpretation* I realized that misinterpretation is the spark of fiery relationships. Learning the science and art of interpretation as presented in this book holds great promise for living more peacefully and productively in service to the Common Good.

Kevin W. McCarthy
Author, *The On-Purpose Person*,
Making Your Life Make Sense

IN THIS ACCESSIBLE YET erudite volume the author has built a strong case for his thesis that there exist universally valid principles for interpreting texts, and that these principles make it possible for readers to apprehend the original intended meaning. Whether the text is pragmatic (lawnmower manual), legal (U.S. Constitution), or sacred (Bible), the rules of interpretation (hermeneutics) make it possible for texts to do what they were designed to do—transmit knowledge through space and time. The author defends the principles of interpretation from the alarming encroachment of philosophical nihilism and relativism which recognize no source of absolute truth. Two authoritative texts—the Constitution, which we read for our political freedom and the Bible for our spiritual freedom—have become major targets of this post-modern skepticism. This book defends against these thoroughly anti-constitutional and anti-theological activities. The author guides us to heed the eighteenth-century philosopher/theologian, Johann Martin Chladenius, who admonished us to consider "how much theology and jurisprudence depend on this discipline, then one sees how important it is that a person first thoroughly acquaint himself with hermeneutics before making this discipline his life work ... A person who is well versed in theology and jurisprudence should firmly inculcate himself with the principles of interpretation." This is the intent of this author.

Larry D. Bruce, PhD

THIS BOOK IS AN interesting read, which breaks complex subjects down into short chapters. This book may help you see the subject of "interpretation" from a different viewpoint.

Patrick Stillwell
Author, *All Things Are Fulfilled*

THE JOY
OF
INTERPRETATION

THE JOY OF INTERPRETATION

STEVE F. RICHARDSON

HIGHERLIFE
PUBLISHING & MARKETING
Oviedo, FL

Published by HigherLife Development Services Inc.
PO Box 623307
Oviedo, Florida 32762
www.ahigherlife.com

ISBN: 978-1-954533-61-5 (Paperback)
ISBN: 978-1-954533-62-2 (ebook)

Library of Congress Control Number: 2022909351

Printed in the United States of America.
10 9 8 7 6 5 4 3 2 1

DEDICATION

For Darlene, Danielle, David, Malikai,
Kamryn, Stephen, and Makayla

For Don, Greg, and Troy

For Mike and Glen

CONTENTS

CHAPTER 11

PART TWO
REGARDING BIBLICAL INTERPRETATION

CHAPTER 12

CHAPTER 13

PART THREE
REGARDING CONSTITUTIONAL INTERPRETATION

CHAPTER 14

INTRODUCTION

Think what punishment shall come on us on account of this world, when we have not ourselves loved [the gift of literacy] in the least degree, or enabled others to do so.

—King Alfred

EVERYONE INTERPRETS. IT IS an inescapable part of the reality and the order of things. However, most people interpret without stopping to consider the act itself. Whether reading the Bible, the US Constitution, a lawnmower manual, or a stop sign, interpretation is involved. But is the way we interpret clear or unclear, critical or naïve, adequate or inadequate, correct or incorrect?

I became fascinated with interpretation in the late 1970s when my business partner, Don Guidas, purchased *How to Read the Bible for All Its Worth*, by Gordon Fee and Douglas Stewart. He began sharing many of the authors' informative insights with me. I purchased my own copy. That began my perennial interest in the subject, which has now given me great joy for several decades. I am fascinated with the beauty of its principles and enchanted with the fact that writing can transmit knowledge through space and time. What an incredible thing that I can "hear" Plato, the Apostle Paul, Marcus Aurelius, Augustine, Martin Luther, Emily Dickinson,

G. K. Chesterton, Margaret Thatcher, and J. R. R. Tolkien. But that is just one side of the coin.

The other side of the coin is the misery of witnessing incorrect interpretation—false interpretations which are the results of interpretive incompetence or malfeasance. It is distressing to observe the distortion of the Parable of the Good Samaritan by allegorization, the distortion of Christian theology by medieval four-fold exegesis, and the wholesale transformation of the Bill of Rights by the Supreme Court's Doctrine of Incorporation. This book's goal is to help make us better interpreters.

Perhaps this book should be titled *Interpretive Literacy: What Every American Christian Should Know About Interpretation—But Doesn't.* This title would follow the form of other "Literacy" books such as E. D. Hirsch's *Cultural Literacy: What Every American Needs to Know* and Stephen Prothero's *Religious Literacy: What Every American Needs to Know—and Doesn't.* Hirsch and Prothero focus our attention on specific neglected subjects regarding our American experience and the deleterious results caused by these ignorances. Hirsch worries about the accumulative effects of high school students thinking that the Alamo is an epic poem of Homer and that Leningrad is a city in Jamaica. Prothero worries about religious illiteracy, such as the kind that proved deadly to Balbir Singh Sodhi. He was a Sikh who was killed at an Arizona gas station in the aftermath of September 11, 2001. A vigilante thought his turban marked him as a Muslim. As Prothero said, "What killed Balbir Singh Sodhi, who was actually a Sikh, was not simply bigotry. It was ignorance: the vigilante's inability to distinguish a Muslim from a Sikh."[1]

This book is an attempt to show the importance of interpretive literacy to Christians who read the Bible for their spiritual freedoms and to Americans who read the Constitution for their political freedoms. It attempts to improve Christians' ability to recognize biblical errors and Americans' ability to recognize constitutional errors. We need to improve our skills in recognizing error patterns in interpretation. This book will address the nature and structure of interpretation, how it bares on history and current affairs, its relevance to Christians and Americans, and prescribe the universally valid principles for interpreting the various genres which readers encounter.

---

1   Stephen Prothero, *Religious Literacy: What Every American Needs to Know—and Doesn't*, (New York: HarperCollins, 2007), 2-3.

PART ONE
WHAT IS INTERPRETATION?

CHAPTER 1

THE WORST INTERPRETATION
I'VE EVER HEARD

I BECAME A CHRISTIAN ON December 9, 1970, as the Jesus Movement swept America. Mary Goodwin, with the help of her husband D. O., purchased a small, abandoned concrete building directly across from Rutherford High School where I attended. The building had been used as a snack shop for the students. They converted it into a chapel to minister to the students. One day after school a friend and I were drawn into the chapel by the music inside. Mike Littleton was playing a Gibson electric guitar as Glen Henderson came over and presented the gospel to us. That was the beginning of my Christian life.

I was fifteen years old, zealous for the Lord, and attending a small young people's church. Our pastor, Glen, was twenty years old, and the music minister, Mike, was twenty-one. We met for church in any old building we could afford to rent. Without a formal name, our church was referred to simply as The Building. We were long on zeal, short on organization, weak on wisdom, but we won a lot of hippies and rednecks to the Lord.

Hal Caldwell was a church brother who was a couple of years older than many of us. He owned a car and provided us with a lot of transportation. We heard of a man who sold gospel tracts from his home. On arriving, we found a very elderly man living in a dilapidated cottage with his elderly wife. There were dozens of large cardboard boxes scattered throughout his house, all filled with gospel tracts. Most of the tracts did not suit our tastes, but the boxes were cheap and we found some of them useful. (This was a time before we had heard of Chick tracts—small comic-book type tracts which we came to rely on in our evangelism.)

On a return trip to purchase more tracts, the old man said to me, "Steve, there are graveyards in heaven!" I asked him how he knew that, and he said, "The Bible says, 'on earth as it is in heaven!' If something is on earth then it is also in heaven." Somehow I knew, even at fifteen years of age, that his interpretation of that phrase in the Lord's Prayer, found in Matthew 6:10, was spurious. I did not challenge his exegesis for two reasons. First, I felt it would be disrespectful to someone who was seventy years my elder. Second, at that time I was not in possession of the interpretive theories and the accompanying vocabulary that were needed to explain his error. Armed only with an elementary common sense hermeneutic, I left there knowing he was wrong but could not have explained why.

During this same time, we encountered a similar interpretive problem back at the Rutherford Student Chapel. A recent convert was upset and was strongly considering literally obeying Jesus' instructions in Matthew 18:9, which says, "And if your eye causes you to stumble, gouge it out and throw it away." I knew Jesus did not literally mean for us to gouge out an eye, but, again, I couldn't convincingly explain why. Mary Goodwin and a couple other adults counseled him as best they could through his interpretive anxiety, convincing him that Jesus' point would not be achieved through literal physical mutilation.

I knew nothing at that physical and spiritual age about hermeneutics, context, exegesis, figurative language, genre, similes, metaphors, hyperbole, or any of the other subjects needed for systematically understanding and explaining biblical texts. I knew the Bible was important and was authoritative, and sensed that the ability to explain it was going to be necessary. Yet, I had no idea how that ability was going to be acquired. It appeared to me that it would be picked up piecemeal through continued discipleship. I could not have seen that a pursuit of systematically understanding and explaining biblical texts, and other texts, would become so interesting to me and such an important part of my life experience.

CHAPTER 2

THE NATURE AND STRUCTURE OF INTERPRETATION

READING AND INTERPRETATION ARE existentially linked and in many ways are synonyms for each other. For example, "How do you read this text?" can also be stated as "How do you interpret this text?" Therefore, this chapter addresses reading and interpretation and the interconnected subjects surrounding them.

Before directly addressing interpretation, let's begin with the nature of literacy and its twin disciplines, reading and writing.

FIRST, WHAT IS LITERACY?

Children are sent to school for two basic reasons: to become numerate and literate. Numeracy is the ability to successfully manipulate numbers and literacy is the ability to successfully manipulate words. Literacy is the ability to read and write a language's vocabulary, grammar, and syntax. It is the ability to communicate, understand, interpret, and create using written materials found in various textural forms. Through literacy, we are able to escape from the here and now of our personal experiences. It allows us to "think thoughts others have already thunk." Through reading, we are able to learn from those who are separated from us by time and geography. Reading allows us to experience the dead as if they were alive. Through writing, we can teach our contemporaries and those in our future and those separated from us by geography. The texts we read and write transmit knowledge through time and space. Literacy enables us to render near what is far. It enables us to access the archives of discourse.

SECOND, WHAT IS ILLITERACY?

Illiteracy is the inability to communicate, understand, interpret, or create using written materials found in various textual forms. Illiteracy traps disadvantaged children in the same educational and social circumstances as their parents. The illiterate are denied economic opportunity. They cannot comprehend or claim their inheritance as members of Western Civilization and the American democratic experiment. A lot has been said about illiteracy, and hardly a Miss America contest goes by without at least one contestant pledging to fight illiteracy. While America has a high literacy rate, we should continue efforts against illiteracy. However, a more severe problem is aliteracy.

> I digress: America's literacy rate is approximately 99%. It has been lauded in many circles that Cuba's communist government has achieved a literacy rate of 99.8%. We will have to "trust" the communist government's claim,

since they are a closed society and we have no way of independently verifying it. However, even if the claim is true, so what? As Anthony Daniels in *The Wilder Shores of Marx* asked, is it "better to be illiterate with something to read, or literate with nothing to read?"[1]

He posed this question after visiting several bookstores in Havana in 1990. What he found was *The Memoirs of Leonid Brezhnev* but not *The Great Gatsby*, *Bulgarian Journalists on the Path of Leninism* but not *Huckleberry Finn*, *The Speeches of Konstantin Chernenko* but not *The Divine Comedy*. I also witnessed this while on a humanitarian trip to Havana a number of years ago. In new and secondhand bookstores and in an outdoor book "festival" in Plaza De Armas, there was an *ad nauseam* supply of Vladimir Lenin, Che Guevara, Fidel Castor, and Karl Marx, but no George Orwell, Ray Bradbury, Jane Austin, C. S. Lewis, or Aleksandr Solzhenitsyn.

"I pleaded with Castro and his government," said Ray Bradbury, author of *Fahrenheit 451*, "to immediately take their hands off the independent librarians and release all those librarians in prison."[2] He said this in the American Library Association's 2005 annual

---

1   Anthony Daniels, *The Wilder Shores of Marx: Journey in a Vanishing World* (London: Hutchison, 1991), 30.
2   Humberto Fontova, *Exposing the Real Che Guevara—and the Useful Idiots Who Idolize Him* (New York: Penguin, 1991), 118.

THE JOY OF INTERPRETATION

convention because sixteen librarians were serving twenty-five year sentences for stocking Orwell's *Animal Farm*, the UN Declaration on Human Rights, and Martin Luther King's "I Have a Dream" speech. The Castor-Che regime's first official act on entering Havana after the revolution was a massive burning of more than three thousand books and the signing of death warrants for many authors.

Did you see Robert Redford's movie about those sixteen Cuban librarians who unjustly suffered for years in Castro's prisons? Of course, you didn't. Redford never made such a movie because he was too busy paying homage to Che by making a laudatory biopic called *Motorcycle Diaries*. You can tell where the Left's fealties lie not only by the movies they make, but also by the movies they don't make.

I was thirteen in 1969 when I first heard of Che. After making my weekly motorcycle payment of $3.00 to the Harley Davidson shop on Harrison Ave. in Panama City, Florida, I then drove to the Martin Theatre. I bought a ticket for *Che!*, a movie I knew nothing about. After the movie, being young and naïve, I was perplexed that an anti-democratic and anti-American hero would be eulogized by an American film. Only twenty-one months had elapsed between Che's death and the release of

8

> the movie, which was filmed in Malibu Creek State Park, California.
>
> Cuba is an island of eleven and a half million literate people with nothing to read. Fidel, man does not live by "being able to read" only.

FINALLY, WHAT IS ALITERACY?

While the literacy rate in the US is high, and we need to continue the struggle against illiteracy, a more critical problem is the rise in aliteracy—being able to read, but never doing it. Aliterate people do read for utilitarian purposes, such as earning a living, finding their way around by reading traffic signs, reading related to bill paying, etc. But that is a "bread only" approach to reading. As Gene Edward Veith, Jr. said in *Reading Between the Lines*,

> If we cultivate reading—if we read habitually and for pleasure, reading the Bible, newspapers, the great works of the past and the present, the wide-ranging 'promiscuous reading' advocated by the Christian poet Milton—we will reinforce the patterns of the mind that support Christian faith and lead to a healthy and free society.[3]

In another place Veith says,

> The habit of reading is absolutely critical today, particularly for Christians. As television

---

3   Gene Edward Veith, *Reading Between the Lines: A Christian Guide to Literature* (Wheaton: Crossway Books, 1990), 25.

9

turns our society into an increasingly image-
dominated culture, Christians must continue
to be people of the Word. When we read, we
cultivate a sustained attention span, an active
imagination, a capacity for logical analysis and
critical thinking, and a rich inner life. Each of
these qualities, which have proven themselves
essential to a free people, is under assault in
our TV-dominated culture. Christians, to
maintain their Word-centered perspective in
an image-driven world, must become readers.[4]

While drinking from a large Cornish-ware cup and reading *Bleak House*, C. S. Lewis exclaimed, "You can't get a
cup of tea large enough or a book long enough to suit me."[5]
Is the church and are Americans allowing this remark to
become "You can't get a cup of tea large enough or a movie
long enough to suit us"?

The church, "the People of the Book," and Americans,
"the People of the Constitution," must be aware of aliteracy
and struggle against it. We must be cognizant of both ex-
tremes which can befall a literate society. George Orwell's
dystopian novel, *1984*, warned us that an externally imposed oppression could ban books. At the other extreme,
Aldous Huxley's dystopian novel, *Brave New World*, warned
us that we could become a trivial and passive society where
there is no need to ban books because no one wants to read
them. Aliterate *Brave New World* citizens have dispensed

---

4 Ibid., xiv.
5 C. S. Lewis, *On Stories: and Other Essays on Literature* (San
   Diego: Harcourt, 1982), ix.

with the slow-moving printed word and have embraced image-based technologies which have drowned them in a sea of amusements and irrelevance. Neil Postman, in *Amusing Ourselves To Death*, said Huxley warned us that

> the civil libertarians and rationalists who are ever on the alert to oppose tyranny 'failed to take into account man's almost infinite appetite for distractions.' In *1984*, Huxley added, people are controlled by inflicting pain. In *Brave New World*, they are controlled by inflicting pleasure. In short, Orwell feared that what we hate will ruin us. Huxley feared that what we love will ruin us.[6]

We are much more prepared to discern the rising of an Orwellian world than to discern a Huxleyan world. A precursor of these warnings can be found in Jesus' Parable of the Sower. In it, the seed can be made unfruitful by things we hate (persecution, tribulation) and by what we love (riches, materialism).

---

6   Neil Postman, *Amusing Ourselves to Death: Public Discourse in the Age of Show Business* (New York: Penguin, 1985), viii.

CHAPTER 3

THE LITERACY LADDER

BECOMING LITERATE IS LIKE climbing a ladder. The first step on the "Ladder of Literacy" is orality—learning a language through hearing and speaking. Children should be immersed in language from birth. They need exposure to language, and lots of it, from both normal conversation and from being read to. Kids who hear a lot of language do better in school, and being read to is one of the best ways to hear language. Kids who are not read to enter kindergarten having heard about 1.5 million fewer words than kids who were read to. This million-and-a-half-word gap could explain some of the differences in reading development.

The next step on the ladder is the alphabet. Kids are taught the ABCs, the letters being the building blocks of words. On the next step of the ladder, kids are taught that letters can be combined to make words. Continuing to ascend the ladder, they are taught that words can be strung together to make sentences, then sentences into paragraphs, paragraphs into chapters, and chapters into books.

Eventually, as these students ascend the ladder, they master a sufficient amount of reading techniques, are given diplomas and certificates, and are deemed "literate." They have reached the top step on the Ladder of Literacy and can dispense with the struggle. But have they? In reality, we never reach a top step—a place where we no longer need to struggle with the issues of becoming a better reader. In fact, the certificate we get saying we can now stop the struggle is a death certificate.

Continuing to climb the ladder involves the pursuit of many issues. Here are some: what is reading? What is a text? What is an author? What does it mean to write? What does it mean to interpret? Have people always interpreted the way we do today? How did "Congress shall make no law" become "Georgia shall make no law"? What role do my virtues and vices play in my ability to be a good reader? What is a willful reader? Why did Jesus use parables? What is grammatical-historical hermeneutics? What is deconstruction?

BEYOND JUST MASTERING THE MECHANICS OF READING

These are a few of many issues related to becoming ever more literate and a more informed interpreter. Unfortunately, many of these foundational and philosophical issues are never taught or studied. These issues have great relevance to Christians who read the Bible for their spiritual freedom and to Americans who read the US Constitution for their political freedom. Why do our churches not offer, as part of their Sunday school curriculum, classes on interpretation? Why do we not teach systematically how to do what we are there doing—interpreting the Bible? Classes on interpretation/hermeneutics are offered in our seminaries and Bible colleges, but I know of none

offered to laity other than the one I have developed. My
class, "Introduction to Biblical Interpretation," is about a
thirteen-week class I teach in churches and faith-based
prison ministries. The first time I approached our Sunday
school superintendent about teaching my class, he said the
subject should be left to our Bible colleges.

The universally valid principles of reading and writing
which should be promoted and prescribed to Bible-study-
ing Christians are applicable to Americans who pursue a
greater understanding of the US Constitution and of US
Supreme Court behavior. In the 19th century, the theologian John Henry Newman wrote *An Essay on the Development of Christian Doctrine*. It was a guide to biblical interpretation and to the development of Christian doctrine.
Jaroslav Pelikan, in *Interpreting the Bible and the Constitution*, tells us,

> Newman's *Essay on Development* has also
> proved to be of use to the study of constitutional
> law. Therefore 'development of doctrine' is no
> longer confined to the history of Christian
> doctrine, where it arose, but seems to have also
> established itself as a quasi-technical term in
> the Constitution. Together with such a term as
> 'evolving doctrine,' it serves as a more 'organic'
> metaphor to describe doctrinal change, which
> is also the function it performs for the history
> of Christian doctrine.[1]

---

1   Jaroslav Pelikan, *Interpreting the Bible and the Constitution* (New
    Haven: Yale University Press, 2004), 120.

The principles which inform faithful development in theology also inform it in jurisprudence. Newman prescribes principles which help discriminate between good doctrinal growth and bad. We know some forms of growth are good, as when we exercise to stimulate muscle growth. But we must remember that cancer is also growth. If there are no universally valid interpretational principles, then Newman's essay is useless sophistry, because in the end there are no objective methods for distinguishing sacred and legal orthodoxy from heterodoxy. In the absence of valid principles, anyone's interpretation is as good as everyone else's, and hermeneutics, understood as the "science" of interpretation, would have no more legitimacy than alchemy or astrology.

While I have been frustrated at the church's neglect of interpretive training, Antonin Scalia expressed similar frustration at the legal community's neglect of interpretive training. In *A Matter of Interpretation*, he says,

> The state of the science of statutory interpretation in American law is accurately described by a prominent treatise on the legal process as follows: 'Do not expect anybody's theory of interpretation, whether it is your own or somebody else's, to be an accurate statement of what courts actually do with statutes. The hard truth of the matter is that American courts have no intelligible, generally accepted, and consistently applied theory of statutory interpretation.' Surely this is a sad commentary: We American judges have no

intelligible theory of what we do most. Even sadder, however, is the fact that the American bar and American legal education, by and large, are unconcerned with the fact that we have no intelligible theory. Whereas legal scholarship has been at pains to rationalize the common law—to devise the *best* rules governing contracts, torts, and so forth—it has been seemingly agnostic as to whether there is even any such thing as good or bad rules of statutory interpretation. There are few law-school courses on the subject, and certainly no required ones; the science of interpretation (if it is a science) is left to be picked up piecemeal.... There is to my knowledge only one treatise on statutory interpretation that purports to treat the subject in a systematic and comprehensive fashion.... Despite the fact that statutory interpretation has increased enormously in importance, it is one of the few fields where we have a drought rather than a glut of treatises.[2]

Christians and Americans owe a debt of gratitude to those hermeneuticists who, throughout history, have labored to defend these documents of ultimate authority—the Bible and the Constitution—from a constant intrusion from theoretical and practical threats. These threats can come from hostile antagonists who see in these documents too little meaning and from over-zealous proponents who see

---

2   Antonin Scalia, *A Matter of Interpretation: Federal Courts and the Law* (Princeton: Princeton University Press, 1997), 14-15.

in them too much meaning—those who see in them a dearth of meaning and those who see a never-ending cornucopia of meaning. Wilhelm Dilthey, in *The Development of Hermeneutics*, warns us that

> The function of hermeneutics is to establish theoretically, against the constant intrusion of romantic whim (seeing too much meaning) and skeptical subjectivism (seeing too little meaning) into the domain of history, the universal validity of interpretation, upon which all certitude in history rests.[3]

In a letter written June 12, 1823, Thomas Jefferson said,

> On every question of construction [interpretation/doctrinal growth], carry ourselves back to the time when the Constitution was adopted, recollect the spirit manifested in the debates, and instead of trying what meaning may be *squeezed* out of the text, or *invented* against it, conform to the *probable* one in which it was passed.[4] (emphasis added)

Jefferson's hermeneutical guidance can apply to the interpretation of the Bible as well as the Constitution. There will always be those who will be squeezing and inventing against these documents of ultimate authority, because

---

3   Wilhelm Dilthey, *Selected Writings*, trans. H. P. Rickman (Cambridge: Cambridge University Press, 1976), 248.

4   Thomas Jefferson, *Jefferson Writings*, Merrill D. Peterson, ed., (New York: Literary Classics of the United States, Inc., 1984), 1475.

they have ideological, financial, moral, or political ambitions which are impeded by these documents.

The Ladder of Literacy is tall and has many more steps than most people imagine. The continuation of the climb is rewarding, fascinating, and sometimes frustrating, but is worth the effort.

CHAPTER 4

THE PURSUIT OF "GETTING INTERPRETATION RIGHT"

THE RELIGIOUS IMPETUS

The pursuit of "getting interpretation right" has developed stronger in Western Civilization than in Eastern Civilization for a number of reasons. First, there is the religious impetus. In Western Civilization, Jews and Christians have a long tradition of viewing their sacred books, the Torah and the Bible, as inspired by God. Because God is the ultimate author, the importance of these books cannot be overstated and they serve as documents of ultimate authority for their beliefs and behaviors. In Eastern Civilization, the three major Yogic religious traditions of Buddhism, Confucianism, and Hinduism have sacred books, but do not claim they were authored by God or gods. They believe the books were written by brilliant and virtuous men. Because they are not viewed as "written by the finger of God," they do not carry the same authority nor demand the high degree of exegetical accuracy which Christians and Jews assume is needed for interpreting their sacred texts. Eastern sacred texts do not prescribe orthodoxies and orthopraxis as explicitly as Western sacred texts. There is not the strong imperative to "rightly divide" the Word of Truth (2 Timothy 2:15) nor the warning and penalties of adding or taking away (Revelation 22:18-19).

THE POLITICAL IMPETUS

The second "getting interpretation right" motivation is the political impetus. When it comes to governance, Eastern Civilization's social orders are less informed and guided by written constitutions. A written instrument is required for a constitutional form of government. It helps to objectify the principles and rules that constitute the legal basis of a government. Western Civilization has a longer and deeper history of constitutional governance which helps to codify political freedoms and protect civil liberties and civil rights. Constitutions can serve to limit the capricious nature of authoritarian forms of government such as dictatorships, theocracies, and despotisms. The existence of constitutional governance has fostered the need for an interpretive legal magisterium which is guided by, or should be guided by, the universally valid principles of writing and reading. The United States Supreme Court is the commonly acknowledged legal magisterium regarding the interpretation of the US Constitution. It is mostly their responsibility to "rightly divide" the legal scriptures of the US Constitution.

THE PHILOSOPHICAL IMPETUS

The third motivation is the philosophical impetus. Eastern Civilization's religious and philosophical traditions embrace contradiction. They believe that reality is contradiction. Their first principle—their primary, bedrock philosophical presupposition—begins with the rejection of the law of non-contradiction. They hold that two contradictory propositions can both be true at the same time. Stated abstractly, "A can be non-A."

Not so in Western Civilization. "In Western logic," says Mortimer Adler in *Truth in Religion,*

> the laws governing the opposition of incompatible propositions are unquestioned. They are self-evident because the opposite is unthinkable. Two propositions that are contrary to each other cannot both be true though both can be false. The pursuit of truth in mathematics, science, and philosophy is governed by freedom from contradiction. Now that mathematics and science have become transcultural, one might suppose that the logic of incompatible propositions would also have become transcultural. But that is not the case. Some, if not all, of the Far Eastern cultures do not accept this rule of thought with respect to incompatibles, nor do they accept the underlying view of reality that it presupposes. It is not self-evidently true for them.[1]

---

1   Mortimer Adler, *Truth in Religion: The Plurality of Religions and*

The East's rejection of the law of non-contradiction has attenuated their pursuit of truth in philosophy and in the hard sciences, such as chemistry, geology, biology, and astronomy, and in the soft sciences of psychology, sociology, political science, and anthropology. All the sciences and technologies have a difficult time taking root in the soil of cultures which embrace contradiction. It is no accident that science and technology developed in the fertile soil of the Christian West, which has rejected contradiction. In the East the pursuit of "getting interpretation right" was, and still is, hampered by their philosophical mistake of embracing contradiction. In the end, it was for religious, political, and philosophical reasons that the development of hermeneutics languished in the East.

---

the *Unity of Truth*, (New York: Macmillian Publishers, 1990), 72.

CHAPTER 5

KIERKEGAARD'S PARABLE: THE CRITICAL APPARATUS

Imagine a country. A royal command is issued to all the office-bearers and subjects, in short, to the whole population. A remarkable change comes over them all: they all become interpreters, the office-bearers become authors, every blessed day there comes out an interpretation more learned than the last, more acute, more elegant, more profound, more ingenious, more wonderful, more charming, and more wonderfully charming. Criticism which ought to survey the whole can hardly attain a survey of this prodigious literature, indeed criticism itself has become a literature so prolix that it is impossible to attain a survey of criticism. Everything became interpretation—but no one reads the royal command with a view to acting in accordance with it. And it was not only that everything became interpretation, but at the same time the point of view for determining what "seriousness" is was altered, and to be busy about interpreting became real seriousness. Suppose that this king was not a human king—for though a human king would understand well enough that they were making a fool of him by giving the affair this turn, yet as a human king he is dependent, especially when he encounters the united front of office-bearers and subjects, and so would be compelled to put the best face on a bad game, to let it seem as if all this were a matter of course, so that the most elegant interpreter would be rewarded by elevation to the peerage, the most acute would be knighted, &c.—Suppose that this king was almighty, one therefore who is not put to embarrassment though all the office-bearers and all the subjects play him false. What do you suppose this almighty king would think about such a thing? Surely he would say, "The fact that they do not comply with this commandment, even that I might forgive; moreover, if they united in a petition that I might have patience with them, or perhaps relieve them of this commandment which seemed to them too hard—that I could forgive them. But this I cannot forgive, that they entirely alter the point of view for determining what seriousness is." [1]

---

1   Soren Kierkegaard, "The Critical Apparatus," in *Parables of Kierkegaard*, ed. Thomas C. Oden (Princeton: Princeton University Press, 1978), 12–13.

Kierkegaard's point is to be doers of the word and not interpreters only.

CHAPTER 6

WHAT IS INTERPRETATION?

ALL READING INVOLVES INTERPRETATION to one degree of intensity or another. But what is interpretation? The primary goal of interpretation is the fixing of meaning (content) to symbols. Interpretation is the opposite of abstraction. The more interpreted a set of symbols is, the less abstract they are. The more abstract a set, the less interpreted. These two have an inversely proportional relationship—the more of one, the less of the other. Remember, in a directly proportional relationship, the more of one, the more of the other. For example, "the more you work the more you earn" is a directly proportional relationship. On the other hand, "the more you work the less poverty you will have" is an inversely proportional relationship.

But what is abstraction? The primary goal of abstraction is the removal of meaning (content) from symbols. As the process of abstraction progresses, more and more content is being removed from a set of symbols, and, as a result, the more that form is exposed. Form is exposed when propositions become denuded of the clutter of content.

LiDAR (light detection and ranging) is somewhat comparable to the process of abstraction. From airplanes, it directs millions of pulses of light toward the ground and provides users the ability to capture extraordinarily accurate, high-resolution, 3D data. The different wavelengths can be filtered to eliminate the foliage and display the ground features. This technology has revolutionized archaeology, making it possible to measure and map objects and structures that might otherwise be hidden. Archaeologists can see through forest canopies to discover sites scattered across thousands of square miles. What would have taken thousands of archaeologists many decades to find can now be done in a matter of days. Vast numbers of Mayan archaeological sites are being discovered now that the clutter of dense tropical jungle can be seen through. LiDAR exposes underlying architectural forms—abstraction exposes underlying categorical forms.

CHESTERTON ADDRESSES FORM

G. K. Chesterton alluded to form in a disagreement he had with H. G. Wells when Wells said, "All chairs are quite different." Chesterton responded, "he utters not merely a misstatement, but a contradiction in terms. If all chairs were quite different, you could not call them 'all chairs.'"[1] Wells had been insisting that every separate thing is "unique," therefore, there would be no such thing as categories (forms). The thing which all chairs have in common is "chairness." However, the recognition of forms is one of

---

1   G. K. Chesterton, *Orthodoxy: The Romance of Faith* (New York: Doubleday, 1959), 35.

the resplendent characteristics of the human mind as God created it.

In the same vein, Aristotle said regarding form, "The greatest thing by far is to have a command of metaphor. This alone cannot be imparted by another, it is the mark of genius, for to make good metaphors implies an eye for resemblances."[2] The existence of form makes resemblances possible. A metaphor is the product of someone who has a metaphorical eye—seeing form in things which appear on the surface to be "unique."

A MATHEMATICAL EXAMPLE OF INTERPRETATION AND ABSTRACTION

The following is a mathematical example of interpretation, abstraction, and their relationship. In mathematical pedagogy, children are introduced to math through a highly interpreted approach. Many physical manipulatives are used in the teaching—5 ducks, 2 bears, 4 apples, etc. Teachers feel a sense of accomplishment when their young students finally comprehend 3 apples + 1 apple = 4 apples. Next, the students are introduced to a higher level of mathematics when one layer of interpretation is removed. Teachers remove the manipulatives—ducks, bears, apples—and the students are taught that 3 + 1 = 4. The students may ask, "4 what?," to which the teacher responds, "4 anything!" When the students have sufficiently digested this mathematical reality, this level of abstraction, the teacher then

---

2   Aristotle, *The Poetics of Aristotle*, trans. S. H. Butcher (New York: Macmillan, 1907), 87.

removes more content by introducing the next level of abstraction. At this level, the content, 3, 1, and 4 are removed and the students are taught a + b = c. At this level, all content (meaning) has been removed and the students are left with bare form—a mathematical proposition denuded of all content.

Plato says, "Arithmetic has a very great and elevating effect, compelling the soul to reason about abstract number, and rebelling against the introduction of visible or tangible objects into the argument."[3] The human brain was designed by God to feed on abstraction.

When we don't know the definition of a word, we turn to a dictionary. In this act we are taking a symbol that has no content for us and finding the content that belongs to that symbol. The word then goes from merely an abstraction to being interpreted. The word "concupiscence" found in 1 Thessalonians 4:5 in the King James Version is an archaic word to us, and is translated in the New International Version as "lust." Concupiscence was not abstract to seventeenth-century readers, but four centuries later, it has become abstract to modern readers.

The word "establishment" in the Establishment Clause of the First Amendment has become an abstraction to modern constitutional jurisprudence. The meaning of the word which the Founding Fathers intended has decayed because of the accumulation of judicial mistakes and interpretive embarrassments. The founders' use of "establishment" meant something specific: the process of founding

---

3   Plato, *The Republic of Plato*, trans. Benjamin Jowett (Oxford: Clarendon Press, 1881), 221.

of a church, setting the procedures for choosing clergy, defining the rules of conduct for clergy and the laity, defining the penalties for impiety, and deciding how the church is to be funded. Now the disciples of "Living Constitutionalism" define establishment to mean that it is a violation of the Establishment Clause and therefore unconstitutional for a kindergartner to ask during a school assembly whose birthday is celebrated on Christmas (*Florey v. Sioux Falls School District*, 1979). Also, if a student prays over lunch, it is unconstitutional for him to pray aloud (*Reed v. van Hoven*, 1965).

THE LOGICAL FORM OF WRITING AND READING

Here is the logical form of writing and reading: a creator with some type of intent uses symbols on a medium which is read by an exegete (Creator + Intent + Symbols + Medium + Exegete = Meaning). But this logical form is also shared by other context-dependent activities such as archaeology, criminology, and art.

	Writing	Criminology	Archaeology	Art
Creator	author	criminal	inhabitant	painter
Intent	reveal	conceal	neutral	reveal
Symbols	words	clues	artifacts	paint
Medium	text	scene	site	canvas
Exegete	reader	detective	archaeologist	viewer

THE LOGICAL FORM AS FOUND IN WRITING

In writing, the intent of a creator (author) is to reveal some type of information to an audience. It may be didactic, poetic, historical, or some other type of information, but an author is trying, successfully or not, to communicate something to his audience. The symbols he uses are words. The text may be paper, parchment, a scroll, a stone temple wall, a traffic sign, or a computer screen, but the combination of words fixed on some kind of medium is the text. No author writes without some type of audience in mind. The choice of that audience gives focus to the author. But, finally, that audience becomes the exegetes—the interpreters of the text, for good or bad, right or wrong, faithfully or willfully—who judge meaning.

THE LOGICAL FORM AS FOUND IN CRIMINOLOGY

In criminology, the intent of the creator (criminal) is to conceal information—the clues (symbols) of his crime scene. In committing the crime, he has "written a text," one that he hopes an exegete (detective) either cannot read or will read incorrectly. He removes the incriminating clues or plants misleading clues to protect himself from arrest and prosecution. The symbols he writes on the text (crime scene) with are items such as a bloody knife, a gun, an overturned table, a piece of clothing, etc. Detectives hope to arrive at a "virgin" crime scene before it is "rewritten" by careless policemen, or a mitigation company, or curiosity seekers, or any other source which could disturb the text, and, therefore, contribute to inaccurate exegesis.

Retired master sergeant Hayden B. Baldwin began his career in law enforcement after graduating from the Illinois State Police Academy in 1970. He spent eighteen years in crime scene investigation, the last eleven years as a supervisor. He is a member of International Association for Identification, Association for Crime Scene Reconstruction, and International Crime Scene Investigators Association, and has written articles and books on crime scene investigation. He was responsible for the training of the Illinois State Police Crime Scene Investigators and has codeveloped their training manual and training program.

In an article titled "Crime Scene Interpretation," what Hayden says illustrates the link between literary interpretation and crime scene interpretation:

> The reconstruction of crime scenes is a misnomenclature. You are in reality *interpreting* the information that you find by examining and processing the scene for evidence. This evidence will then permit you to make factual statements in regards to your findings. For instance, examining a footwear impression left at a scene you will be able to determine what direction the person was walking when that impression was made. Therefore, you are *interpreting* the information you discovered to develop a factual reconstruction. In other words, you are placing your *interpretation* in a logical order to reconstruct what has taken place in the crime scene. This will apply to all crime scenes that are left intact and are not disturb [sic] by the victims, paramedics or

police officers. Without this *"virgin"* crime
scene the *interpretation* could be altered and
may not be as it was when the suspect(s) were
there. Never, never assume or guess at the
reconstruction without all the facts from the
interpretation.... The testimonial evidence
is the *interpretation* of the facts in the crime
scene.[4] (emphasis added)

THE LOGICAL FORM AS FOUND IN ARCHAEOLOGY

In archaeology, the native (author) who created the archaeological site (text) has no intent when contributing to the creation of that site—he is neutral in intent, neither trying to create one nor obscuring it. The native many centuries ago was not aware that he was creating a site by killing an animal, cooking it, and discarding the bones into his fire pit. However, an archaeological text was written by this activity. Are we aware that our activities are creating such texts which might sometime in the future be "read" by archaeologists? The native's symbols used to "write" with are artifacts—the bones, lithic debitage, coals, tools, etc. (An artifact is an object which has some type of human design, as opposed to an ecofact which has none. An animal bone which has been shaped into a tool is an artifact, whereas one found in nature without human design is an ecofact.) The medium is the site composed by the spatial (horizonal) dimension and the temporal (vertical)

---

4   Hayden Baldwin, "Crime Scene Interpretation," Hayden
     Baldwin, accessed June 3, 2021, http://www.feinc.net/cs-int.htm.

dimension. If the native used the site for many years then a temporal dimension to the text is created each time he adds another layer to that site. These layers are stratigraphy, which resemble the pages of a book. Like the detective hoping for an undisturbed "virgin" crime scene, an archaeologist hopes for an undisturbed site. If the context—the arrangement of the artifacts and the stratigraphy in which they were originally deposited—has not been disturbed, an accurate "reading" is much more possible. But, just like a crime scene, the integrity of the text can be compromised by disturbances. Erosion, plowing, looters, and burrowing animals are some of the disturbances which can diminish the context of a site. The exegete's "reading" of an undisturbed site is more conclusive than from a disturbed site.

When I took some archaeology classes at Florida State University, I was amazed by the feeling that I was sitting in a hermeneutics class. Almost all of the instructions were a slight variation of what I had been taught in my Trinity Seminary's hermeneutics class. Our FSU instructor, Stephen Hale, warned us against imposing our views when interpreting the data collected from archaeological sites. He constantly stressed the issue of context, saying that what location, location, location is to real estate, context, context, context is to archaeology. Yes, the artifacts from a site are important. However, a massive amount of information is lost when the artifacts are divorced from their context. To stress the importance of context, he posed the following scenario: if a fire occurred in your archaeological research laboratory and you could save either the artifacts from a dig or your fieldnotes with all the information about those artifacts and their spatial and temporal context, which should you save? The correct choice is to save the field-notes. In the days before archaeology matured, when it was little more than antiquarianism and treasure hunting, the emphasis was on the artifacts themselves. Treasure hunters were only seeking valuable artifacts and had no regard for the information that could have been gained from recording the context. Indiana Jones wanted treasure—Stephen Hale wanted burnt corn cobs. Stephen's research goal was to determine when Florida natives began cultivating and eating corn. Old burnt corn cobs would not bring much at a Sotheby's auction, but they can bring a great deal of information about early Native Americans.

In the late 1980s, I was part of the Marine Archaeological Divers Association. MADA was a voluntary group of scuba divers who were amateur archaeologists. In 1988 we cooperated with Jim Dunbar at Florida State University's Department of Anthropology. Jim asked our group to dive a portion of the Aucilla River from the Gulf of Mexico north to Hwy 98, a distance of about three quarters of a mile. Jim, the FSU archaeological department and National Geographic were excavating underwater sites on the Aucilla River just north of Highway 98. They were professional archaeologists with the training and finances to properly excavate those high-value sites. The sites were high-value because they were undisturbed "virgin" sites with intact stratigraphical integrity. The artifacts and their context were found in the original arrangements in which they had been laid down. Our underwater task was to collect artifacts and ecofacts from the bottom of the river and to deliver to them a report of what was found and from where on the river it came. I was the project director and wrote our report, which was published in *The Florida Anthropologist* (41[4] [December 1988]). They were hoping that our findings could help locate intact sites which they could professionally excavate. We had collected artifacts that had been very disturbed from their original contexts. These artifacts were of much lower value to the professionals because they lacked most of their context.

The following is a grammatical illustration of artifacts which have lost most of their contexts and those with their context. Here is a familiar passage without its context:

> how we . , there something wish " sat ! with
> had . We two , said I Sally " do there sat I to
> And I We.

Here is Dr. Seuss' passage in its proper context:

> I sat there with Sally. We sat there we two. And
> I said, "I wish we had something to do!"

While both "passages" contain the same vocabulary and punctuation, the first is lacking grammatical context. Artifacts without their context are analogous to this.

John Bower, in *In Search of the Past: An Introduction to Archaeology*, says:

> When the primary context of a site is destroyed, the material may be so displaced as to lose most, if not all, of their archaeological information. Or they may be redeposited in such a way as to preserve at least some of their context. While material in secondary

context is not well suited for detailed studies of behavior in the past, it may at least serve in the reconstruction of cultural history, environment, and a few aspects of ancient lifeways, notably technology and stylistic or aesthetic standards.[5]

Also, declared Martha Joukowsky in *A Complete Manual of Field Archaeology*, "Once an artifact or feature such as a hearth is moved out of its context, its pattern within the site is broken and a vital context is, therefore, destroyed."[6]

Archaeology, like writing and crime scene investigation, is existentially linked to interpretation. Perusing any book on archaeology will reveal that link. Interpret, interpretation, interpreted, and interpreting are words you will quickly encounter. Joukowsky uses these tenses ten times in her seven-page introduction and eleven times in chapter 9 ("Fieldwork: Recording and Measuring"). She begins chapter 9 with, "The accurate interpretation of features and artifacts depends in many respects upon the information shown in the square/trench supervisor's field notebook."[7]

The correlation between reading and archaeology was acknowledged by Alberto Manguel in *A History of Reading*. He says, "The readers, like imaginative archaeologists, burrow their way through the official literature in order to rescue from between the lines the presence of their fellow

5   John Bower, *In Search of the Past: An Introduction to Archaeology* (Chicago: Dorsey Press, 1986), 97.
6   Martha Joukowsky, *A Complete Manual of Field Archaeology: Tools and Techniques of Field Work for Archaeologists* (Englewood Cliffs: Prentice-Hall, 1980), 220.
7   Ibid., 200.

outcasts, to find the mirrors for themselves in the Clytem-
nestra, of Gertrude, of Balzac's courtesans."[8]

THE LOGICAL FORM AS FOUND IN ART

In art, the intent of the creator (artist) is to reveal some
sense of emotion or statement to an audience. The symbols he uses are shapes, colors, and textures. The mediums
he creates his texts on are canvas, stone, metal, wood, and
paper, to name a few. The exegetes are his viewers who experience and interpret his work.

Of course, not all art is intended to say something.
Art is not required to serve some pragmatic or utilitarian purpose, and I'm certainly not attempting to unleash
the didactic dragons who might gobble up the art. However, much of art does, in fact, say something, and viewers should have some means whereby art can be critically
interpreted. To help with this, in 1970, Professor Edmund
Feldman of Georgia University proposed a four-step technique for critiquing art. His technique has been widely
used. It is as follows:

- Description: What can be seen in the artwork?
- Analysis: What relationships exist with what is
  seen?
- Interpretation: What is the content or meaning,
  based on steps 1 and 2?
- Judgment: What is your evaluation of the work,
  based on steps 1, 2, and 3?

---

8   Alberto Manguel, *A History of Reading* (New York: Penguin
     Group, 1996), 233.

While Professor Feldman's four-step technique is a helpful introduction to critiquing and interpreting art, it is included here to show that art and interpretation are undeniably linked.

The German philosopher, Martin Heidegger, wrote a beautifully interpreted and beautifully expressed interpretation of Vincent van Gogh's painting, *A Pair of Worn Shoes*. In his essay titled "The Origin of the Work of Art" (1935), he wrote:

> From out of the dark opening of the well-worn insides of the shoes the toil of the worker's tread stares forth. In the crudely solid heaviness of the shoes accumulates the tenacity of the slow trudge through the far-spreading and ever-uniform furrows of the field swept by a raw wind. On the leather lies the dampness and richness of the soil. Under the soles slides the loneliness of the field-path as the evening falls. In the shoes there vibrates the silent call of the earth…. But perhaps it is only in the picture that we notice all this about the shoes. The peasant lady, by contrast, merely wears them.[9]

These lines foster in us a brooding empathy for Heidegger's peasant lady. Sadly though, virtually every one of his statements are wildly wrong. The shoes were Van Gogh's, not a peasant lady's.

---

9   Martin Heidegger, *"The Origin of the Work of Art"* in *Off the Beaten Track*, trans. Julian Young and Kenneth Hayes (Cambridge: Cambridge University Press, 2002), 14.

We know the shoes are Van Gogh's because he told his intent for painting them to Paul Gauguin, the French post-Impressionist painter, who shared a room with him in Arles, France, in 1888. Van Gogh told Gauguin that these were the shoes he had worn during some significant episodes of his life. Heidegger's highly speculative and unbridled interpretation could have been avoided by some historical consideration of Van Gogh's intent and biographical history. Heidegger's interpretation may have been elegant, it may have been profound, it may have been ingenious, it may have been wonderful, it may have been charming, and it may have been more wonderfully charming. Yet, it was wrong. He had fallen victim to a temptation which we all, as interpreters, encounter—the temptation to appear profound at the expense of truth.

Socrates admonished Phaedrus when he said,

> You know, Phaedrus, that's the strange thing about writing, which makes it truly analogous to painting. The painter's work stands before us as though the paintings were alive, but if you question them, they maintain a most majestic silence. It is the same with written words; they seem to talk to you as though they were intelligent, but if you ask them anything about what they say, from a wish to know more, they go on telling you the same thing over and over again forever.[10]

---

10   Plato, *Phaedrus*, in *The Collection Dialogues*, ed. Edith Hamilton and Huntington Cairns (Princeton: Princeton University Press, 1961).

In summary, writing, crime scene investigation, archaeology, and art are all context-dependent activities. They share a common logical form. They are, therefore, analogous to each other. They are all existentially linked to interpretation. They benefit from advances in interpretive theory. They also suffer from the cancerous effects of interpretive nihilism, which sees in interpretation a dearth of meaning, and from interpretive romanticism, which sees in interpretation a plenitude of meaning. Somewhere between nihilism and romanticism exists an objective set of universally valid principles of interpretation. If these principles do not exist, then we have no objective means to distinguish between fact and fiction, or between history and myth. If they do not exist, then the discipline of interpretation is no more objective or scientific than alchemy or astrology. E. D. Hirsch, Jr., in *Validity in Interpretation*, stated,

> The wider implications of such [interpretive] skepticism are usually overlooked by its adherents. At stake ultimately is the right of any humanistic discipline to claim genuine knowledge. Since all humanistic studies, as Dilthey observed, are founded upon the interpretation of texts, valid interpretation is crucial to the validity of all subsequent inferences in those studies.[11]

---

11   E. D. Hirsch, *Validity in Interpretation* (New Haven: Yale University Press, 1967), viii.

CHAPTER 7

WHAT RELEVANCE DOES INTERPRETATION HAVE TO US?

IS INTERPRETATION (HERMENEUTICS) AN irrelevant subject better left to the esoteric interest of Bible scholars cloistered in a Bible college or the black-robed justices of our judiciary? Some philosophers of mathematics will be offended when I say that if plenitudinous platonism turns out to be a more solid foundation for mathematics than the traditional versions of mathematical platonism, that determination will not have much of an impact on the life of an average person. However, the subject of interpretation is not like that. Interpretation is at the heart of the frantic hysteria surrounding Supreme Court judge appointments. It is at the heart of global Islamic jihadism. It was, and still is, at the heart of the Protestant Reformation. These three are interpretation-oriented issues, and how interpretation is, or was, conducted presses heavily on our lives.

THE RELEVANCE OF SUPREME COURT INTERPRETATION

Supreme Court appointments have not always been as contentious as they are now. In the past, appointments usually occurred with the general public barely aware of them. The political battles and the media frenzy which now surround Supreme Court appointments are a recent development. This fervor boils down to this: how will the nominee interpret the Constitution? Too often, the Supreme Court and federal courts have given in to the temptation to politicize the judicial branch, and this politicization occurs when judges render "interpretations" which flow more from their public policy preferences rather than the limiting language of the Constitution.

The domain of jurisdiction for the Supreme Court was originally small, limited to those specific areas which the enumerated powers and the Bill of Rights granted them. The domain of federal powers was defined in Article I, section 8 of the Constitution and in the Bill of Rights. The Enumerated Powers Doctrine holds that the federal government has no unexpressed or general powers. Fearing the undermining of this structure of the federal system, James Madison said that a broad reading of Article I, Section 8 "would have the effect of giving to Congress a general power of legislation instead of the defined and limited one hitherto understood to belong to them."[1] Knowing the Constitution listed specific congressional powers, it would

---

1   James Madison, "Veto of federal public works bill," accessed
     March 31, 2022, https://constitution.org/1-History/Founders/
     jm/18170303_veto.htm.

follow that Congress must not have a general power to do whatever it wanted to. It would make no sense for the Constitution to say, "Congress may only do A, B, and C, plus whatever else it wants." The Bill of Rights was also a restriction on the federal government's jurisdictional domain. It states as explicitly as possible what issues "Congress" could not do. In an upcoming chapter I will explain how "Congress shall make no law" was transformed into "the states shall make no law," and address if the transformation was hermeneutically legitimate and justifiable.

Now that the Supreme Court's domain of jurisdiction has been allowed to illegitimately sprawl out of defined constitutional restraints and into almost all areas of the public square, we find ourselves fearful with each change of membership on the Court. Interpreting the Constitution as the Founders intended and in the way courts had interpreted it for one hundred and fifty years would have restricted the courts' ability to protect pornography, redefine marriage and the family, limit school discipline, banish religion from public life, frustrate the prosecution of obscenity, coerce participation in the Sexual Revolution, persecute the Little Sisters of the Poor, and invent the right to abortion. This change in jurisdictional domain, which has occurred mostly in the last sixty years, has allowed the Supreme Court to become a revolutionary force in remaking America's culture and politics. As Robert Bork has said, the courts prescribe

> new constitutional law that is much more
> egalitarian and socially permissive than either
> the actual Constitution or the legislative

opinion of the American public. *That, surely, is the point of their effort.*[2] (emphasis added)

Hopefully, there could come a time when the courts are forced to returned to their constitutionally legitimate domain. We need a Constitutional Reformation analogous to the Protestant Reformation—we need the effects of *sola constitutio* the way the church needed *sola scriptura*. As for now, the Supreme Court maintains more relevance in Americans' lives than it should.

THE RELEVANCE OF ISLAMIC INTERPRETATION

Interpretation had a brutal relevance on the life of Vincent van Gogh's grandson, Theo van Gogh. Ayaan Hirsi Ali, in her book *Infidel*, tells us that

> One November morning in 2004, Theo van Gogh got up to go to work at his film production company in Amsterdam. He took out his old black bicycle and headed down a main road. Waiting in a doorway was a Moroccan man with a handgun and two butcher knives. As Theo cycled down Linnaeusstraat, Muhammad Bouyeri approached. He pulled out his gun and shot Theo several times. Theo fell off his bike and lurched across the road, then collapsed. Bouyeri followed. Theo begged, 'Can't we just talk about this?' but Bouyeri shot him four more times. Then he took out one of his butcher knives and sawed

2   Robert Bork, *The Tempting of America: The Political Seduction of the Law* (New York: The Free Press, 1990), 6.

into Theo's throat. With the other knife, he stabbed a five-page letter onto Theo's chest. The letter was addressed to me.[3]

She was threatened because two months earlier she had made a short film called *Submission, Part 1* with Theo, which criticized Islam's treatment of women. Bouyeri's method of Koranic interpretation was the motivation for his actions.

I'm not going to treat the issue of whether Bouyeri's hermeneutic is the correct method of Koranic interpretation for representing authentic Islam. My point here is to show that his hermeneutic, which is embraced by millions of Muslims, impacts all of our lives. If this was the hermeneutic of just one individual, then we would have little to be cautious about from this school of Koranic exegesis, but the prevalence of this hermeneutic makes it extremely relevant to non-Muslims and to Muslims who embrace more peaceful and tolerant interpretations of the Koran. His interpretational method was the motivation for 9/11, for the riots in Nigeria because Christians rejected the imposition of Islamic law, for grenades being tossed into a Pakistani church one Sunday morning, for the beheading of a Christian in Saudi Arabia who had converted from Islam to Christianity, for two million killed, mostly Christians, in Sudan, and for the beheading of twenty-one Copts in Libya, just to name a few.

I hope Bouyeri's hermeneutic is wrong. I wish his method could be proved invalid. I would be thrilled, as well as

---

3   Ayaan Hirsi Ali, *Infidel* (New York: Free Press, 2008), xxi.

feel safer, to see a less violent and less conquest-oriented form of Koranic interpretation prevail, one open to democracy and religious tolerance. However, we must remind ourselves that valid and proper methods of interpreting any document of ultimate authority is not based on whether the interpretation produces ideas or imperatives that we prefer or are advantageous to our preferences. Since, as a Christian, I do not believe the Koran to be divinely inspired or theologically true, the Koran is not a document of ultimate authority to me. But to approximately one and a half billion Muslims, it is. When there exists an interpretive community of that size, their hermeneutic, correct or not, will in some way impact the lives of those outside that community.

I hope the "Davos" Muslims' hermeneutic prevails. The phrases "Davos Man" and "Davos Woman" are credited to the political scientist Samuel P. Huntington. Father Richard John Neuhaus describes these "Davos" Muslims by saying,

> As for conferences, it is not hard to get 'Muslim spokespersons.' There are teams of them flitting from conference to conference all over the world. They are part of the "Davos people" so brilliantly described by Huntington in his book. I have met them in Davos, Switzerland, where top CEOs and heads of state annually gather with select intellectuals to chatter about the state of the world in the Esperanto of an internationalese that is not spoken by real people anywhere. The Muslims in such settings are for the most part westernized,

secularized academic intellectuals who are there to 'represent the Muslim community viewpoint' but have little more connection with living Islam than many Christians and Jews. The unhappy fact is that Muslim thinkers who can speak out of the heart of authentic Islam and especially of resurgent Islamism, either do not want to talk with us or are prevented from doing so under the threat of very real injury to themselves or their families.[4]

Most of these westernized Islamic apologists interpret the Koran in a method which presents jihad as being only a personal inward spiritual struggle, and that Islam, properly understood, is compatible with Western-style democracy, religious tolerance, and human rights. I prefer this view, but I doubt these Oxford-educated, westernized Muslims actually represent authentic Islam. Their method of interpretation appears to have done to the Koran what liberal theologians have done to the Bible and what liberal judges have done to the Constitution.

Abdullah Saeed, the Sultan of Oman Professor of Arab and Islamic Studies at the University of Melbourne, Australia, advocates that religious liberty is an organic part of the Koran, the hadith, and Islamic history. He states,

> The words of the Qur'an and hadith contain rich resources for supporting the democratic order. If Muslims are to embrace modernity, including life in a pluralistic, democratic

---

4   Richard John Neuhaus, "The Approaching Century of Religion," *First Things*, no. 76 (October 1997):79.

society, without abandoning their faith, they must take up the argument for religious liberty that is embedded in their history and that stands at the center of their most sacred texts.[5]

Perhaps Saeed's optimism is warranted, but his concluding remarks seem to reveal the state of actually existing Islam. He concludes,

Sadly, the implementation of this [method of interpretation] continues to be painfully slow because of certain trends within Islam. At a time when a number of ultraconservative voices appear to be dominating the discourse in many parts of the Muslim world, Muslim scholars who advocate for religious liberty are fiercely opposed. They are often labeled as stooges for the West or accused of being apostates or heretics. Many such scholars in Muslim nations are imprisoned for their views or have their publications banned. My book *Freedom of Religion and Apostasy in Islam* was banned in the Maldives in 2008 after a targeted campaign against my coauthor (and brother) Hassan Saeed by certain politicians and an ultraconservative group.[6]

Again, and I cannot stress this enough, I hope Saeed's hermeneutic is correct, but the ubiquity of religious intolerance

---

5   Abdullah Saeed, "The Islamic Case for Religious Liberty," *First Things*, no.217 (November 2011):33.
6   Ibid., 36.

throughout the Islamic world causes me to doubt that it is he who represents authentic Islam. In reality, any substantive decisions regarding Islamic interpretive theory will have to come from Islamic exegetes in the Middle East, Mecca, and the world surrounding Islam's sacred story.

Proper exegetical procedures aside for a moment, a document of ultimate authority's orthodoxy can be fairly accurately inferred from its orthopraxy. For example, even without knowing anything about the game of baseball and without having access to its rule book, the rules of baseball could be inferred by observing the conduct of the players and referees over the course of several games. Patterns of behavior would lead to the understanding of what strikes and balls are, and the consequences of three strikes and four balls, and that base runners proceed in a counter-clockwise direction, and so on and so forth. You will know a tree's orthodoxy by the orthopraxy fruit it bears. Observing Islam's behavior can produce a lot of circumstantial evidence about what its orthodoxy is.

The claims that Islam, properly understood, supports democracy and that the Koran, properly interpreted, supports religious tolerance and civil liberties is hard to reconcile with what can be observed throughout the world. Of the approximately forty-five traditional Muslim countries in the world, none are liberal democracies. Of the top ten refugee-producing countries, seven are Muslim. It should be noted that Muslim refugees from the Middle East and Africa are going into Europe, and are not fleeing to the Gulf States. Most Muslim countries refuse to accept these refugees, even though they are fellow Muslims. Israel's

GDP is twenty times that of impoverished Egypt. Turkey, a nation of sixty-four million people, has a GDP that is twenty-third in the world, which ranks them between Denmark and Austria, each with about five million people. As far the translation of books, the Arab world translates slightly more than three hundred books a year, which is one-fifth the number translated by Greece. Muslims, who comprise approximately 22% of the world's population, have been awarded 1.4% of the Nobel prizes, while Jews have received 20% and have 0.2% of the world's population. There are more mosques in Jackson, Mississippi (population 164,00) than there are churches in Saudi Arabia (population 33,700,000). Jackson has two mosques; Saudi Arabia has zero churches. Of course, such earthly situations do not ultimately determine heavenly truth, but these situations do make it extremely difficult to believe the claims of the "Davos" Muslims' apologetic that the Koran is compatible with Western-style democracy and religious tolerance. It is much more likely that Islam is as Islam does.

THE RELEVANCE OF BIBLICAL INTERPRETATION

Concisely, the historical period known as the Renaissance was an attempt to return Western Civilization back to its classical Greek roots. It was a revival of classical knowledge and a reminder that we are, in many ways, Aristotle's children. Another transformative period was the Protestant Reformation, and it was an attempt to return Western Civilization back to its biblical roots. The Reformation reminded us that we are, spiritually, Abraham's children.

No survey of the history of Western Civilization could be complete without including the Protestant Reformation. It does not matter if you are Catholic, Protestant, atheist, Marxist, or agnostic, knowledge of this period is a part of the stock knowledge required for being culturally literate in the West. It was a tectonic collision of religion and public life, and led to changes, not only for those religious, but also for government, civil rights, literacy, individualism, church-state relations, education, and for the idea of questioning authority.

The Protestant Reformation was essentially the debate, or battle, over how the Bible should be interpreted. There were two maxims which became the rallying-cry of the Reformation: *sola fide* (only faith) and *sola scriptura* (only scripture). *Sola fide* is the biblical truth that was rediscovered—*sola scriptura* was the *method* by which that truth was rediscovered. The course of Western Civilization was impacted by the issue of interpretation.

When Martin Luther posted his now famous Ninety-five Theses on the door of the Castle Church in Wittenberg, Germany, on October 31, 1517, the Protestant Reformation began. Though he is the father of the Reformation, many people before him helped set the stage for it. In the fourteenth century, men such as Pierre d'Ailly, John Wyclif, Jean Gerson, and John Hus had advocated for reforms similar to those Luther successfully set in motion. Though *sola scriptura* was the formal principle of the Reformation, a number of Catholic writers had stressed it prior to Luther. A group known as the Brethren of the Common Life had called for a new emphasis on Bible reading. The Dutch scholar, Desiderius Erasmus Roterodamus, and others began to realize that the early church was radically different from the Roman Catholic Church of their time. Erasmus advocated for a revival of Hebrew, Greek, and Latin so that the Roman Church could be examined in light of early Christianity.

When Luther was ordained to the priesthood in 1507, he was the recipient of a body of theology which had been subjected to fifteen centuries of ecclesiastical commentaries, papal bulls, ecumenical councils, general councils, theological inferences drawn from theological inferences, and various specious interpretive schemes. The emphasis on the text of the Bible had been so neglected that Luther was working to finish a degree in theology, yet he had not read the New Testament. Luther came to see the need to abandon the medieval method of interpreting the Bible. That method was a major contribution to the biblical distortions which had masked authentic biblical truth. In essence, he engaged in some Bible archaeology, and began digging down through the layers of fifteen centuries of accumulated theological debris, allegorical speculation, and interpretive embarrassments.

The interpretive method which Luther rejected is known as medieval four-fold exegesis. The method claimed that the Scriptures contained four separate meanings for each statement in Scripture. In a later chapter, "The History of Biblical Interpretation," I will further discuss Luther's rejection of this method. Christian theology had been stretched to the breaking point and had finally suffered interpretational collapse. Luther regained the essence of early biblical Christianity, guided by a much superior approach to interpretation.

CHAPTER 8

FORREST GUMP AND THE USE OF SIMILES AND METAPHORS

LANGUAGE, WRITTEN OR SPOKEN, can cause misery, frustration, and disappointment. Language can be misleading, intentionally or unintentionally. Why is it that so many words can mean many different things? Why can't we develop a language where each word or symbol has one meaning and only one meaning? Would not that be an advancement for humankind?

There have been attempts to develop a language which could eliminate ambiguity and confusion in communications. Gottfried Leibniz, the seventeenth-century philosopher and mathematician, proposed a universal language with the goal of creating an alphabet of human thought, a universal symbolic language for science, mathematics, and metaphysics. Leibniz stated,

> And although learned men have long since thought of some kind of language or universal characteristic by which all concepts and things can be put into beautiful order, and with whose help different nations might

communicate their thoughts and each read in his own language what another has written in his, yet no one has attempted a language or characteristic which includes at once both the arts of discovery and judgment, that is, one whose signs and characters serve the same purpose that arithmetical signs serve for numbers, and algebraic signs for qualities taken abstractly. Yet it does seem that since God has bestowed these two sciences in mankind, he has sought to notify us that a far greater secret lies hidden in our understanding, of which these are but the shadows.[1]

One of the purposes of his universal language was to help spread the Christian faith. In *Initia et specimina scientiae generalis,* Liebniz describes this possible use of the universal language by saying,

Where this language can be introduced by missionaries, the true religion, which is in complete agreement with reason, will be established, and apostasy will no more be feared in the future than would an apostasy of men from the arithmetic or geometry which they have once learned. So I repeat what I have often said: that no man who is not a prophet or a prince can ever undertake anything good to mankind or more fitting for the divine glory.[2]

1   Gottfried Leibniz, *Zur allegemeinen Charakteristik,* translation from Leroy Loemker, *Leibniz: Philosophical Papers and Letters* (Dordrecht: D. Reidel), 222.
2   Gottfried Liebniz, *Leibniz: Philosophical Essays,* translated by

However, Leibniz never developed this *characteristica uni-versalis* (universal language). Many philosophers and linguists have considered it an absurd fantasy. G. H. R. Parkinson put it this way:

> Leibniz's views about the systematic character of all knowledge are linked with his plans for a universal symbolism, a *Characteristica Universalis*. This was to be a calculus which would cover all thought, and replace controversy by calculation. The idea now seems absurdly optimistic...[3]

In reality, our fallen, terrestrial languages will never be completely emancipated from the Tower of Babel.

Liebniz was not the first to want to revamp language to improve communication and eliminate much of the misery caused by miscommunication. Many before and after him have tried. Of course, we should always try for improvements, but there never will be, in this world, a universal language which will usher in a utopia of understanding. Some have said that wars are caused because nations do not understand each other. However, many wars are caused because we understand each other perfectly well.

Language can be frustrating. Anyone with teenagers knows that to be true. One summer morning before I left for work, I left a note to my twelve-year old son telling him to take out the garbage before he went skateboarding. I

Daniel Garber & Roger Ariew (Indianapolis: Hackett Publishing Company, 2015), 9.

3   G. H. R. Parkinson & Mary Morris, *Leibniz: Philosophical Writings* (London: J. M. Dent, 1973), ix.

had heard him the night before discussing skating with his friends. When I arrived home after work the garbage was still where it was when I left. I asked him if he had read my note and his response was, "Yes, but you said to take out the garbage before we went skating. We didn't go skating, we went fishing." Yes, he was technically correct—a glaring case of literalism or textualism. But the real problem was not a case of language's ambiguity, but a case of immature willfulness—he saw a technical interpretive loophole which he thought could mask his irresponsibility when he knew what I actually meant. Again, insincerity is the enemy of sensible language.

But we also revel in the playful uses of language's ambiguities. Without language's ambiguities and elasticities there would be no poetry or puns, no similes or parables, no metaphors or overstatements. Many jokes, especially double-meaning jokes, would not exist. (I'm feeling quite confident about that job interview. The interviewer said they want somebody responsible. "Oh, I'm totally your man," I told her, "whatever problem came up at my last job, they always said I was responsible!") Why do we climb linguistic mountains? Because they are there—and because we can. It would be a dry, didactic linguistic landscape strewn with utilitarian facts and endless logic—a landscape more suited for the Vulcan, Spock, than for man as he is. It would be a language more suited for computers. A computer program cannot function properly if one symbol is assigned two or more meanings, yet normal human language manages that every day.

> I digress: In the early 1970s, a retired Russian general was looking out the window of his dacha and said to his wife, "It's starting to rain." She said it was snow. "No, dear, it is rain," he retorted. Again, she said, "Rudolph, it is snow." Perturbed, he exclaims, "Rudolph, the Red, knows rain, dear!"

To ask for the complete eradication of figurative language and other less literal forms of speech would be asking for less, not more. It would be a language more on Forrest Gump's level. His IQ, being 75, did not allow him the ability to utilize language at the level most people can. His mother did attempt to introduce him to higher orders of language—figurative language—such as similes. Similes are the simplest and the least abstract of all figures of speech. It is the level at which children are introduced to second-order references. She knew that metaphors, such as "Life is a box of chocolates," were too abstract for him. She told him "Life is *like* a box of chocolates," the *like* making the analogy a simile. Also, she included the interpretation, "You never know what you're going to get," because she doubted he could make the connection himself. Each time he repeated the simile, he always repeated the interpretation, thinking it was a natural part of the discourse. A person with a normal IQ would use the simile version or the metaphor version of the statement and never feel compelled to include an interpretation.

Forrest could not process slang. When in Vietnam, he said that he and his company "were always looking for this guy named Charlie." A normal person can quickly recognize and use slang with little or no explanation. For Forrest to understand that "Charlie" was slang for the Viet Cong, Lieutenant Dan would have to look him straight in the eye and say, "Look, you imbecile, Charlie is not a person. Charlie is a modified abbreviation of Viet Cong. Viet Cong was simplified to VC, which in the NATO phonic alphabet is pronounced 'Victor-Charlie,' which gave rise to the further shortened 'Charlie' designation. Get it, you moron!"

When Lieutenant Dan maliciously asked Forrest if he had found Jesus, a puzzled Forrest said, "I didn't know I was supposed to be looking for Him." Forrest's capacity for experiencing the joys and full range of human language was attenuated by his low IQ. We can acknowledge and enjoy the flexibility and playfulness of words and speech without the fear of undermining the objective principles of language and genre. The belief in these objective principles does not require us to reject figurative language. We can confidently and naturally make assertions such as "Queen Victoria was made of steel." Forrest could not.

CHAPTER 9

THE VOCABULARY OF INTERPRETATION: KEY TERMS IN HERMENEUTICS DISCUSSION

THAT WHICH REMAINS UNNAMED remains unseen. That which remains vaguely defined remains vaguely understood. To define (definite) a word is to fix the limits of its meaning. An undefined word's meaning is infinite.

There is a "common" vocabulary shared by a language community which makes it possible for members of that community to communicate. Whether a plumber, doctor, roofer, philosopher, teacher, truck driver, politician, or preacher, that common vocabulary facilitates communication among them all. However, within a language community there are sub-communities with their own "special" vocabularies. Plumbers communicate with other plumbers and use specialized vocabularies that will be difficult for non-plumbers to understand. The same is true for many of the other sub-communities. Having spent over forty years as a furniture and antique restorer, I can quickly evaluate a customer's understanding of woodworking and furniture by their use of woodworking terms. The use, or misuse, of those terms can be very revealing.

The list below contains many terms that are essential to understanding the issues of interpretation. This list does not include many terms which are beyond the scope of the intent of this book. This book is only an introduction to the general principles of interpretation of ordinary language and of sacred and legal interpretation.

The definitions here are based on the theory that universally valid principles of writing and reading, and speaking and hearing, do exist. They are in line with the method of interpretation known as grammatical-historical hermeneutics. I am prescribing these definitions as being their proper description. Our ideological opponents, that is, those who reject universally valid interpretive principles, such as the French philosopher Jacques Derrida and his disciples, would define these terms more in line with their subjective theories.

If we successfully converse with one another, it will be only after we have defined our terms. It is important to have a clear understanding of the terms used in promoting and defending the objective principles of reading and writing.

1. TEXT: A TEXT IS ANY DISCOURSE FIXED IN WRITING.

A text is some type of physical object such as paper, clay, computer screen, papyrus, stone, parchment, etc., which has some type of discourse fixed onto it. Discourses which are only spoken are limited to a particular time, place, and audience. By fixing a discourse onto some physical object the discourse is emancipated from the here and now. The text then shelters the discourse from evaporation into the ether—as a proverb says, "What is written remains, what is spoken vanishes into air." Unlike the author who spoke or wrote the discourse, the text can travel through time and space, and can reach audiences never imagined by the author. The text serves as a surrogate for the author. As Isidore wrote in *Etymologies*, "Letters have the power to convey to us silently the sayings of those who are absent."[1] A text can live on long after the author has died. A text does not fulfill its ultimate purpose until the death of the author. The text is the basis for communication through distance.

The text "divides the act of writing and the act of reading into two sides, between which there is no communication. The reader is absent from the act of writing; the writer is absent from the act of reading,"[2] wrote Paul Ricoeur in *Hermeneutics and the Human Sciences*.

2. READING: READING IS THE RECOVERY OF MEANING.

To read is to recover meaning which was placed into the text by its author. Reading is the attempt to grasp the soul of the author. It allows us to render near what was afar. Our ideological opponents believe reading should be an

---

1   Isidoro de Sevilla, *Libri sententiae*, III, 13: 9, quoted in *Etimologias*, ed. Manuel C. Diaz (Madrid, 1982-1983).
2   Paul Ricoeur, *Hermeneutics and the Human Sciences*, trans. John B. Thompson (Cambridge: Press Syndicate of the University of Cambridge, 1981), 146-147.

activity where the reader's role is to actively produce and construct meaning.

3. AUTHOR: THE AUTHOR IS THE CREATOR OF THE TEXT.

The author is the creator and determiner of the meaning which he placed into the text. The author is the master of the text, not the reader. This assumption is the only compelling normative principle which could provide validity to an interpretation.

4. WRITING: WRITING IS THE FIXATION OF KNOWLEDGE.

Writing is the ability to fix knowledge onto some type of medium. That ability is the basis for one of the major classifications of civilizations. A prehistoric civilization is one which left no written records. Our knowledge of prehistoric civilizations is obtained mainly through archaeology. A historic civilization is one which did leave written records. The texts they left communicate to us much of their history, although archaeology can add to our knowledge of their history. Writing is fixed speech or fixed thought. Writing preserves discourse. It makes it an archive for collective and individual memory. In the thirteenth century, Richard de Bury, Bishop of Durham, alludes to this archival aspect of writing when he said, "All the glory of the world would be buried in oblivion, unless God had provided mortals with the remedy of books."[3]

---

3   Richard de Bury, *The Philobiblon*, trans. Anthony Fleming West (New York: Dover Publication, 2019).

5. HERMENEUTICS: THE SCIENCE OF INTERPRETATION.

Hermeneutics is the investigation of the universally valid principles of writing and reading. It discovers the rules that involve the properties of language and genre, which, in turn, can inform careful reading. Of course, there is also an art to interpretation and not all aspects of interpretation are limited to "rule following." However, our ideological opponents have continually attempted to undermine the objectivity of universal principles of all the human sciences, including hermeneutics. Much of the motivation for this is their desire to circumvent the restrictions which documents of ultimate authority have imposed on their moral and political agendas.

6. EXEGESIS: EXEGESIS IS THE READING OF MEANING FROM THE TEXT.

To perform exegesis is to allow the author to speak to the reader through the text. It is the refusal to give in to the temptation to impose the reader's opinions onto the text. Exegesis is the process of reconstructing all the various contexts in which the text originally occurred. Those contexts influenced the author's choice of tone, vocabulary, and subjects. Many hermeneuticists divide hermeneutics into two major categories: exegesis (what was the text's meaning to its original audience) and hermeneutics (what is the text's meaning for us). The first question should always be "what was the text's original meaning to the original audience?" not "what is its meaning to us?" Though "what is the text's meaning to us?" is usually the most important thing we want answered, it should not be our first question. What the text meant to them then serves to impose limits on what the text can mean for us now.

7. EISEGESIS: EISEGESIS IS THE READING OF MEANING INTO THE TEXT.

To perform eisegesis is not allowing the author to speak to the reader through the text. It is giving in to the temptation to impose the reader's opinions onto the text. Eisegesis begins with asking what the text means to the reader without considering its original contexts. There are two major reasons a reader engages in eisegesis. First, the reader unintentionally misrepresents the text because they are not informed enough regarding the proper means of interpretation. Second, the reader intentionally misrepresents the texts because the text says something that does not suit the reader's agenda or policy preferences. The reader understands the proper means of interpretation, yet ignores them for personal gain or ambition.

Here is a mathematical example of unintentional eisegesis: If a person was born in 10 B.C. and dies in A.D. 10, how old is that person when he dies? If you, like most people, answer twenty years old, then you have just committed an act of eisegesis. That person would be nineteen years old, not twenty. Most people attempt to answer the question using a wrong number line. They use our current understanding of a number line which has a zero as the starting point, with positive numbers to the right of the zero and negative numbers to the left. However, when the dating system using B.C. and A.D. was developed, the number zero was not yet included in their mathematics. As Charles Seife stated in *Zero: The Biography of a Dangerous Idea,* "To Bede, also ignorant of the number zero, the year that came before 1 AD was 1 BC. There was no year zero. After all, to Bede, zero didn't exist."[4] The eisegesis occurred because the wrong number line was employed in the attempt to answer the question.

8. CONTEXT: THE TEXT'S COORDINATES.

Most texts depend on circumstances outside of themselves to be adequately understood. Some do not. "Water is composed of two hydrogen atoms and one oxygen atom" can be understood with little or no context. However, a statement such as "my mother loves climbing vines" has several possible meanings. The correct meaning of these types of statements cannot be determined until some information external to the text is woven to it. If the reader has no access to the context for "my mother loves climbing vines," then the reader can only list the possible meanings and cannot specify the particular meaning intended by its author. Fortunately, the vast majority of statements which have the possibility for multiple interpretations come to us with, implicitly or explicitly, the prerequisite information that allows us to determine the correct meaning from the list of possible meanings. If you know that "Boy," Tarzan and Jane's adopted son, made the statement, then it is very

---

4   Charles Seife, *Zero: The Biography of a Dangerous Idea* (New York: Penguin Group, 2000), 56.

likely that he meant that his mother loved climbing vines in the same way his father did. On the other hand, if you find out that the statement was made by a seventy-year-old friend, then you can most certainly determine that the statement means that she loves landscaping vines such as Arctic Kiwi, Autumn Clematis, Climbing Hydrangea, etc.

That prerequisite information serves as a type of textual GPS system, whose coordinates inform where the text is located. Those coordinates can inform the reader as to whether the text is in the domain of fiction or nonfiction, poetry or didactic, etc. The determination of the text's domain is a fundamental part of context construction.

9. INTERPRETATION: INTERPRETATION IS THE ADDITION OF CONTENT TO SYMBOLS.

To interpret is to take a symbol whose meaning is unknown to someone and placing in that symbol the appropriate content. At that point, the symbol becomes interpreted for that person. The more appropriate content is placed into that symbol, the more interpreted it becomes. As I was writing the definition of this term, my wife interrupted me with her "Word for the Day." The word was "Apiary," which I did not know the meaning of. It means a place where bees are kept; a collection of beehives. A word which was an abstraction to me became interpreted.

A + B = C is a mathematical abstraction. When content, such as 2, 3, and 5 are placed into that abstraction, it becomes the interpreted mathematical equation 2 + 3 = 5.

When we add more content, 2 apples + 3 apples = 5 apples, it becomes even more interpreted.

10. ABSTRACTION: ABSTRACTION IS THE REMOVAL OF CONTENT FROM SYMBOLS.

When the meaning of a symbol is unknown, that symbol is an abstraction. That symbol may be a word or a modern hieroglyphic. During the 1970s, with the increase of international travel, a set of symbols was developed by the American Institute of Graphic Arts, along with the United States Department of Transportation, for use in airports and other travel facilities. These hieroglyphics were to aid travelers without a command of English. These symbols were, for the most part, self-interpreting—pictures of a fork and knife replacing the English word "Restaurant," pictures of a taxi replacing the word "Taxi," pictures of a suitcase replacing the word "Luggage," etc. Most of these travel hieroglyphs were obvious, although a few were slightly abstract and required some interpretation.

If 2 apples + 3 apples = 5 apples is reduced to 2 + 3 = 5, then one layer of interpretation has been removed and the expression becomes abstracted. When the numbers are removed, it becomes the further abstracted expression A + B = C. Abstraction is the opposite of interpretation. They have an inverse relationship.

11. DISTANCIATION: CASES OF DISTANCIATION ARE SITUATIONS WHICH CAUSE ABSTRACTION.

Distanciation simply means distances which separate the reader from a spontaneous understanding of a text being read. There are different types of distances. Historical distance is a temporal obstacle which has the potential of attenuating the understanding of a text. The greater the historical distance usually means the greater the potential of misunderstanding. Geographical distance is a spatial obstacle. Cultural distance is the distance between the culture in which the text was written and the culture in which the text is being read. Linguistic distance is the distance between the language in which the text was written and in the language in which it is being read. A text which was written in Greek, then translated into Latin, and then translated into English has a high degree of linguistic distance.

Someone in Orlando, Florida, reading a personal letter from a friend in Atlanta, Georgia, encounters much less distanciation than if that person were trying to read the engravings at the Egyptian "House of Books," in Edfu, written circa 2000 B.C. These engravings contain a catalogue of books: *The Book of the Domains, The Book of the Stations of the Sun and the Moon, The List of All Writings Engraved in Wood, The Book of What is Found in the Temple, The Book of Places and What is Found in Them,* to name a few. It is incredible that we can understand so much of these, even though we encounter a very high degree of distanciation: 4,000 years of historical distance, 6,700 miles of geographical distance, an extinct ancient Egyptian culture vs.

THE VOCABULARY OF INTERPRETATION

an American culture, and a linguistic distance caused by translating from Egyptian hieroglyphics to English.

Both we and our ideological opponents acknowledge that distanciation can attenuate the ability to understand texts. The major difference is that we believe these various distances can, in the vast majority of cases, be successfully bridged. They do not. To them, the distances are unbridgeable. It is a major argument of this book that their problem is not that the distances cannot be bridged, but that the real motivation is they do not like what they find after bridging those distances. Once bridged, they discover that these "unbridgeable" distances render interpretations which would impede their policy preferences. Justice William Brennan claimed these types of distances were obstacles which were too great to overcome in constitutional interpretation. In a speech at Georgetown University, October 12, 1985, he declared,

> in truth [fidelity to the intention of the Framers] is little more than arrogance cloaked in humility. It is arrogant to pretend that from our vantage we can gauge accurately the intent of the Framers on application of principles to specific, contemporary questions. Apart from the problematic nature of the source, our distance of two centuries cannot but work as a prism refracting all we perceive.[5]

---

5   William Brennen, Speech at Georgetown University, October 12, 1985. Reprinted in *The New York Times* (October 13, 1985), 36. Copyright 1985 by the New York Times Company.

If Brennan is correct that two centuries is too long ago for an accurate interpretation of what the Framers wrote, then what would he think about interpreting the hieroglyphic texts at Edfu (2000 B.C.), or the Code of Hammurubi (1750 B.C.), or interpreting the writings of Aristotle (350 B.C.), or the Apostle Paul (A.D. 60), or the Magna Carta (A.D. 1215)? Based on Brennan's rate at which textual meaning decays, then these other documents should be relegated to the interpretive trash heap. If 200 years is too much, how about 100 years, or 75, or 50? At what point can we have confidence that a text has not decayed too far for an accurate interpretation? At the time of this writing, it has been 36 years since Brennan's speech at Georgetown. Am I cloaking arrogance in humility to claim that 36 years ago he intended to say our distance of 200 years is too much elapsed time to avoid the prism-like refraction of all we think the Framers meant?

12. LINGUISTIC NIHILISM (OBSCURASISTS): THEY SEE IN LANGUAGE A DEARTH OF MEANING.

Nihilism (Latin, *nihil*, "nothing") literally means nothingness. It is the philosophical position that denies any objective ground or state of truth. It is the theory that nothing is knowable and all claims of knowledge are illusionary, insignificant, and relative. It has several manifestations: moral nihilism, metaphysical nihilism, political nihilism, epistemological nihilism, and linguistic nihilism (or semantic nihilism).

In *What is Deconstruction?* Christopher Norris and Andrew Benjamin confidently tell us we can have no confidence in objectivity. They say,

> We should therefore reject this whole bad legacy—whether Kantian, Hegelian, Marxist, or whatever—and acknowledge that there is no ultimate truth, no final 'meta-narrative' or standpoint of absolute reason from which to adjudicate the issue.... With their demise we can see what should always have been obvious, were it not for the hold of certain stubborn preconceptions about language, meaning and reality. That is to say, there is no truth, either inward or outward, that could validate one set of codes and conventions above another, or serve as the ultimate reference-point for a history of the novel—or of any other genre— conceived in terms of some grand teleology. All we have are the various narratives, language-games or fictive devices that in the end refer to nothing beyond their own transient power to make sense of an otherwise unknowable reality.[6]

"Skeptical subjectivism" is the term Wilhelm Dilthey uses in reference to linguistic nihilism. He states, "The ultimate goal of hermeneutics is to establish theoretically, against the constant intrusion of romantic whim and skeptical subjectivism into the domain of history, the universal

---

6   Christopher Norris and Andrew Benjamin, *What is Deconstruction?*, (London: Academy Editions, 1988), 29.

validity of interpretation, upon which all certitude in history rest."[7] Linguistic nihilism is a direct assault on the belief in universally valid principles of interpretation.

13. LINGUISTIC ROMANTICISM (PLITORISTS): THEY SEE IN LANGUAGE A PLENITUDE OF MEANING.

While the nihilists reject interpretation's universally valid principles because they claim there is nothing in language, the linguistic romanticists reject them because they claim there is too much in language. They believe the attempt to objectify interpretation by the development of a hermeneutical "science" puts too many limits on the interpreter. To them, there is a never-ending plenitude of meaning which can be mined by those who are imaginative enough. Dilthey referred to this approach as "romantic whim." Any attempt to objectify interpretation was, to them, putting language into a straitjacket. The nihilists don't see enough; the romanticists see too much. And that is what this book is about: defending the text from its hostile enemies and from its over-zealous admirers.

Examples of linguistic romanticism is found in Jewish and Christian allegorism, medieval four-fold exegesis, gematria, letterism and numerology of the Cabbalists and, in modern times, the Living Constitution and *The Bible Code* by Michael Drosnin. These approaches to interpretation

---

7   Paul Ricoeur, *Hermeneutics and the Human Sciences*, trans. John B. Thompson (Cambridge: Press Syndicate of the University of Cambridge, 1981), 51.

assume there exists an interpretive key which can unlock meaning which is hidden behind the words of the text.

14. MAGISTERIUM: A MAGISTERIUM IS THE AUTHORITATIVE CONTROLLER OF INTERPRETATION.

An interpretive community orbits around a document of ultimate authority which defines that community. That document emits the gravity which tugs at the members of that community. That document makes some kind of demand on the behavior and/or beliefs of the members. Those communities need some type of authority over the interpretation of its document and that role is provided by a magisterium.

For the Roman Catholic Church, the magisterium is the pope and the bishops. They have the authority to interpret the Bible for their members. For Protestants, they claim the Bible *is* their magisterium. That was one of the defining aspects of the Protestant Reformation. On a more practical level, the various denominations establish "statements of faith" which they believe align with the Bible. Applicants are required to assent to these statements of faith if they desire to become members of that denomination. In that way, these denominations, with their statements of faith which they affirm are based on the Bible, serve as the magisterium for that particular interpretive community.

The US Constitution is the document of ultimate authority regarding the federal aspects of American government. For good or bad, the US Supreme Court is the magisterium of the Constitution.

15. ORIGINAL INTENT: THE AUTHOR'S PURPOSE FOR WRITING IS KNOWN AS ORIGINAL INTENT.

The term means the author's intention for writing—what did the author intend to communicate to his audience? It is also the name of a theory of interpretation which applies to both sacred and legal interpretation. It is one of the theories in the originalist family. It has some affinities to other theories such as original meaning, strict constructionism, and textualism. It is opposed to the theory known as Living Constitutionalism.

16. *SOLA SCRIPTURA* (LATIN: BY SCRIPTURE ALONE): *SOLA SCRIPTURA* IS THE FORMAL PRINCIPLE OF THE PROTESTANT REFORMATION.

The formal principle of the Protestant Reformation is *sola scriptura*; the material principle is *sola fide* (Latin: faith alone). *Sola scriptura* is the method by which *sola fide* was excavated from under fifteen centuries of obscuring layers of papal bulls, commentaries, ecumenical councils, and interpretive mischief. It is the belief that the Bible is the sole infallible source of authority for Christian belief and behavior. It was a theological rejection of what Protestants believed was the excessive reliance of the Catholic Church on tradition.

17. *NUDA SCRIPTURA* (LATIN: SCRIPTURE UNCLOTHED): *NUDA SCRIPTURA* IS A CARICATURE OF WHAT IS BELIEVED TO BE THE EXCESSES OF *SOLA SCRIPTURA*.

Many Catholics believe their view of the role of Scripture and tradition has been misunderstood by the advocates of *sola scriptura*. They claim that *sola scriptura* has denuded the Scriptures of their churchly context. As stated in the article "Your Word is Truth,"

> we affirm that Scripture is the divinely inspired and uniquely authoritative written revelation of God; as such it is normative for the teaching and life of the Church. We also affirm that tradition, rightly understood as the proper reflection of biblical teaching, is the faithful transmission of the truth of the gospel from generation to generation through the power of the Holy Spirit...we affirm together the coinherence of Scripture and tradition: tradition is not a second source of revelation alongside the Bible but must ever be corrected and informed by it, and Scripture itself is not understood in a vacuum apart from the historical existence and life of the community of faith.[8]

There is much in this which Protestants can agree with. However, in the sixteenth century, Martin Luther was dealing with a radically different Catholic Church, one

---

8   The Editors, "Your Word is Truth," *First Things*, no. 125 (August/September 2002):40.

desperately in need of reformation. There have been misunderstandings and abuses of *sola scriptura*, but Protestants' accusation that the Catholic Church had lost its biblical way were certainly valid in the sixteenth century.

18. INTERPRETATIVE COMMUNITY: A GROUP OF PEOPLE WHOSE BELIEFS AND/OR BEHAVIORS ARE TO BE INFLUENCED BY A DOCUMENT OF ULTIMATE AUTHORITY.

All of Christianity (Catholic, Orthodox, Protestant) forms an interpretive community. Each of these also form a sub-community. What each community has in common is that their beliefs and behaviors are in some way dictated or influenced by the interpretation of a document which codifies their religious lives. The members of a community may strongly disagree with each other, but the disagreement is over a common document.

All Americans form an interpretive community with the US Constitution as its document of ultimate authority in regards to federal issues. Even though conservatives and liberals disagree over the Constitution's meaning, the disagreement does not nullify the fact that they are a community. Floridians form another interpretive community whose common document is the Constitution of the State of Florida.

The teams who play Major League Baseball, along with the referees and league officials, compose an interpretive community. Their authoritative document is the Official Baseball Rules book. This document defines the game and sets the rules which govern the league. Disputes are settled by referring to that document. Chaos would prevail in the game without the availability of an objective document.

Florida drivers, traffic law enforcement, and the government of Florida constitute another interpretive community. The Florida Department of Motor Vehicles (Florida Driver's Manual) is the document of authority for those using Florida's highway system. Driving tickets are issued based on driving situations which violate that document.

> I digress: My wife's interpretation of a Stop sign differs from most. She claims that slowing down and stopping is the same thing. I've warned her that her Stop sign interpretation could cost her a ticket. Sure enough, recently she was pulled over by a highway patrolman. He told her she didn't come to a compete stop at the last Stop sign. She said she slowed down a lot and that is the same thing as stopping. They argued for twenty minutes until the patrolman, tired of the matter, took out his billy club and began repeatedly striking her in the head and asked, "Mrs. Richardson, do you want me to slow down or do you want me to stop?"

Membership in some interpretive communities is voluntary, like religious affiliation and participation in Major League Baseball. In these, members can voluntarily leave and are no longer under the jurisdiction of that community's authority. Others are not voluntary. Living in the US obligates a person to be governed by the US Constitution.

THE JOY OF INTERPRETATION

The sovereign citizen movement claims they are answerable to no government statutes or proceedings. They view all government as illegitimate and are answerable only to their interpretations of common law. However, if they violate US law, they are prosecuted according to the dictates of those laws. They are not allowed to live in the US and remain autonomous.

CHAPTER 10

THE ROLE OF INTELLECTUAL VIRTUES IN INTERPRETATION

OUR RELATIONSHIP TO TRUTH

Do I really want truth? Do we really want truth? I'm not talking about any particular truth, but truth in and of itself—truthness. What if it turns out that the truth costs more than we are willing to pay? At times, the truth is uncomfortable, demanding changes to our behavior or some cherished belief. It is much easier to "say" we love the truth than to "faithfully" love the truth. If asked if we like a food which we have never tasted, then there is nothing defective about our moral or intellectual faculties to answer, "I can't know if I will like that food until I taste it." Yet, our relationship to truth can't be like that. Truth is not something we can have a "wait and see" attitude towards. Our attitude regarding how we will respond to truth is one of the first primary presuppositions we grapple with, consciously or not, as we begin the sprouting of our moral and intellectual lives, as we cultivate our metaphysical dream of the world.

Thou shalt not lie. Why? Because to lie is to negate the truth. To lie is to value something more than truth. Lying disorders the hierarchy of our moral and intellectual allegiances. At the root of the vast majority of lies is selfishness—the vicious pursuit of disordered allegiances as opposed to the virtuous pursuit of ordered allegiances.

I think I love truth. I hope I love truth. But I would not be the first to have thought so, only to discover I had just not yet found the limits of my self-congratulatory virtue inventory. Do I embrace what I believe to be truth because I faithfully believe it to be truth, or because it benefits me financially, or brings me the acceptance I desire, or is just the path of least resistance in my cultural settings?

Am I just like the rich young man in Matthew 19, who was naively overconfident in his own appraisal of his commitment to truth? He was religious, he knew there were such things as "good things," that good things "must be done," and that "eternal life" existed. He did not mind "not murdering," "not committing adultery," "not stealing," or "honoring his father and mother." None of those issues taxed his commitment to truth. But when he asked Jesus, "What do I still lack?" one gets the feeling that he thought Jesus was going to say something like, "Not much, you are ready for eternal life." Jesus, knowing the limits of his commitment to truth, said, "If you want to be perfect, go, sell your possessions and give to the poor, and you will have treasure in heaven. Then, come and follow me" (Matt. 19:21). Now, Jesus did not tell every rich person to sell their possessions, nor did he tell everyone to physically follow him (the man in Mark 5 who had been demon-possessed begged Jesus to let him follow Him, but Jesus did not let him). However, Jesus knew that this young man's great wealth was his spiritual Achilles' heel. The rich young man left sad. What is my Achilles' heel? Not being aware that we *could* "leave sad" increases the likelihood that we *will* "leave sad." That awareness assists us in our pursuit of the moral and intellectual virtues, virtues which can guard us from over-confidence and self-deception.

WHERE THERE'S A WILL, THERE'S A WAY

The adage "Where there's a will, there's a way" is normally used in a positive sense. We say it to encourage someone when we know they are facing a difficult task that requires focus and determination. In this context, "will" is a virtue. However, the adage has a negative sense. "Where there's a will, there's a way" can also refer to "willfulness"—the stubborn drive to achieve one's agenda, even if it requires dishonesty and unethical behavior. In this context "will" is a vice.

In theology, some in the church have willfully twisted Scripture to support a Health and Wealth doctrine from a motivation to enrich themselves at the expense of gullible parishioners. Their willfulness and love of money caused them to "create" a theology that is not hermeneutically legitimate. Their vices blind them to what is legitimately there and causes them to see things that are not there. *Quod volumus, facile credimus*—what suits our wishes, is forwardly believed.

In US government, the political willfulness of liberals and the Left has done much damage to the federal style of government prescribed in the US Constitution. Of course, the Right at times has embraced political goals at odds with the Constitution, but nothing like the liberals' and the Left's perennial assaults on constitutional governance. The massive amount of textual violence they have perpetrated against the Constitution is necessary because their political agendas are so obviously contrary to the Constitution. For example, President Roosevelt's New Deal adviser, Rexford Tugwell, admitted that many of FDR's policies "were tortured interpretations of a document [the Constitution] intended to prevent them."[1] It's not that the liberals and the Left can't understand the Constitution; it's that they don't like what it says. They will never stop trying to dismantle the constitutional barriers erected by the Founding Fathers, barriers which impede their political willfulness.

THE INTELLECTUAL VIRTUES

When we speak of virtues, what usually comes to mind are moral virtues: temperance, fortitude, generosity, rectitude, patience, courage, empathy, fairness, loyalty, and dependability. These play a large role in a well-ordered life and contribute to the type of persons we are. Yet there is another set of virtues which have received less attention—the intellectual virtues. These are the virtues which make us good "knowers." To be a good knower is to foster the habits of mind which aid us in our pursuit of truth and in our maintaining of truth. Some of these virtues are prudence,

---

1   Rexford G. Tugwell, "A Center Report: Rewriting the
     Constitution," *Center Magazine*, March 1968, 20.

inquisitiveness, rigor, teachability, understanding, studiousness, humility, truthfulness, prudence, and wisdom. Intellectual virtues help promote our success in becoming good knowers—they train our epistemic faculties. They also protect us from intellectual vices: gullibility, pride, stubbornness, indiscretion, laziness of thought, folly, and inattentiveness. It is a protection we need to acquire and diligently maintain. We should consider the monk in Fyodor Dostoyevsky's *The Brothers Karamazov*. Father Zossima narrates the story of his conversation with his fellow monks. He had been a debonair officer in his early career with all the "polish and courtesy of worldly manners." In the city where he was stationed, he was received into its upper class and became attracted to one of its young ladies. Certainly, he assumed, she had to be infatuated with him.

> Then suddenly I happened to be ordered
> to another district for two months. I came
> back two months later and suddenly
> discovered that the girl had already married
> a local landowner.... I was so struck by this
> unexpected event that my mind even became
> clouded. And the chief thing was, as I learned
> only then, that this young landowner had long
> been her fiancé, and that I myself had met him
> many times in their house but had noticed
> nothing, being blinded by my merits. And that
> was what offended me most of all: how was
> it possible that almost everyone knew, and I
> alone knew nothing?[2]

---

2   Fyodor Dostoyevsky, *The Brothers Karamazov*, trans. Richard

"Father Zossima's mind didn't suddenly become clouded, of course; it has been clouded all along by his arrogance. His pride so impaired his cognitive faculties that he had remained ignorant of what was obvious to everyone else,"[3] states Jay W. Wood in *Epistemology*.

One general way of viewing these virtues is as follows: the moral virtues produce benefits for our fellow citizens. The intellectual virtues make us good knowers—that is, they benefit the epistemic good for ourselves.

EPISTEMOLOGY AND THE INTELLECTUAL VIRTUES

Epistemology is one of the three main areas which philosophy is uniquely qualified to investigate (the others being ontology and ethics). It investigates the following types of questions: how do I know what I believe to be true is true? What is knowledge and how is it obtained? How is it justified? Is justification internal or external to our own minds? Do we, as thinking beings, possess the cognitive faculties to be rational? Is it possible for knowers to be unbiased?

Many of us are unaware that every day we make epistemological decisions. We encounter truth claims constantly: You must sell all your stocks, the market is going to crash. Light cannot escape from black holes. This is the best vehicle to protect you and your loved ones. Fermat's Last Theorem has been solved. Vote for me and all your dreams will come true. Water is composed of two hydrogen

Pevear and Larissa Volokhonsky (New York: Vintage, 1990), 296.

3   W. Jay Wood, *Epistemology: Becoming Intellectually Virtuous* (Illinois: InterVarsity Press, 1998), 18.

atoms and one oxygen atom. A sighting of Bigfoot has been confirmed.

As knowers analyze the constant barrage of truth claims thrown at them, as they embrace or reject these claims, they are engaging in epistemic activities. Yet, if we ignore the intellectual virtues, we will not successfully navigate through this barrage. Our unexamined "loves" and "hates" will maim our ability to know.

In some ways, societies are aware of our epistemic limitations. For good reasons, we do not allow the father of a basketball player to referee his son's game. For good reasons, the National Baseball League does not allow its coaches to gamble on the outcomes of their games. For good reasons, we do not allow the mother of a defendant to sit on the jury which will determine her son's guilt or innocence. We know that, in all probability, her "love" would be too powerful a force to qualify her to be an unbiased juror. On the other hand, we know that the mother of the victim could not be an unbiased juror because her "hate" would cripple her epistemic faculties. The process of jury selection is to try to obtain unbiased jurors—good knowers. But the demands of truth scream to us that we are all in a never-ending "jury selection," from our age of accountability until our death bed.

LOCKE'S UNFLATTERING ACCOUNT OF OUR EPISTEMIC SOUND-NESS

A little over three hundred years ago, the philosopher John Locke gave an unflattering account of our epistemic soundness.

> All men are liable to error, and most men are in many points, by passion and interest, under temptation to it. If we could but see the secret motives that influenced the men of name and learning in the world, and the leaders of parties, we should not always find that it was the embracing of truth for its own sake, that made them espouse the doctrines they owned and maintained.

> Let ever so much probability hang on one side of a covetous man's reasoning, and money on the other; it is easy to foresee which will outweigh. Earthly minds, like mud walls, resist the strongest batteries: and though, perhaps, sometimes the force of a clear argument may make some impression, yet they nevertheless stand firm, and keep out the enemy, truth, that would captivate or disturb them. . . .*Quod volumus, facile credimus;* what suits our wishes, is forwardly believed.[4]

---

4   John Locke, *An Essay Concerning Human Understanding*, (Oxford: Oxford University Press, 1979), 12.

Wood summarizes Locke's account:

> Vice plays a powerful role in any account
> of the way we acquire and sustain belief. In
> particular, we observe how passions and
> self-interest of various sorts prevent us from
> being intellectually honest with ourselves (in
> the form of self-deception) and with others
> (in the form of various kinds of lies and
> misrepresentation).... We ignore, inflate,
> discount or subtly shade the meaning of
> information unfavorable to our cherished
> opinions. We refuse to follow an argument
> wherever it leads because we see that its
> conclusion is unpalatable to beliefs we hold
> dear.[5]

WYCLIF'S EPISTEMIC ORDERING

Which epistemic faculty is preeminent in the ordering of
faculties as we endeavor to be successful knowers? In the
traditional medieval ordering of faculties, the intellect was
placed before the will. The thirteenth century Oxford professor and theologian, John Wyclif, advocated that will
was preeminent over intellect. He is now considered an
important predecessor to Protestantism, and in his time,
he was an influential dissident within the Roman Catholic priesthood. His inversion of the will-intellect ordering was irritating to established academic fashion. They

---

5   W. Jay Wood, *Epistemology: Becoming Intellectually Virtuous*
     (Downers Grove: Intervarsity Press, 1998), 61—62.

also disapproved of his insistence that less attention should be given to non-canonical authorities (including Aristotle) which had been substituted for legitimate exegetical study of the text of Scripture. He saw that the text of Scripture was becoming a peripheral concern in the formation of theological curriculum and initiated efforts to return it to its proper role at the center.

Wyclif was becoming intensely distressed by a rising trend of conflicts in interpretation. Though the Reformation was still over one hundred years from erupting, the Church was already experiencing the consequences of interpretational collapse. Wyclif was beginning to see the effects of the hermeneutical tortures which were being inflicted on the text of Scripture. He was beginning to see faintly what Luther eventually came to see clearly—specious interpretive methods producing specious theology.

Wyclif was deeply concerned with the will of the reader. Does the reader really want to know what Scripture is saying? Was the reader willing to efface himself sufficiently enough to let the text make its case? What was the reader's true motivation when approaching the text? Is the reader humble enough to let the text speak, to let the Author say what the Author wants the reader to know? He knew, of course, that it was easy for the reader to answer in the affirmative, but his biblical understanding of the reader's fallenness informed him that becoming a faithful reader took prudence and moral perseverance. Wyclif knew the reader would, at times, be tempted to evade or slight an evident truth of the text.

In the following devotional, Wyclif connects the success of the interpreter with the practice of the virtues:

> Let each do his duty, not thrusting himself forward, but modestly, according to the measure meted out to him, in praise of God, the giver. One works in the school, another in the church, one in the world, another in the cloister of virtues, one praying, deep in contemplation, with Mary, another ministering to the people with Martha. Let us go forward as pilgrims, without discord, seeking not our private advancement, but the unity and perfection of Christ's mystical body, until we ourselves come to perfection, are taught all truth, have full knowledge of Scripture, *and read unfailingly in the book of life, in proportion to our meritorious acts and habits.*[6] (emphasis added)

Intellect is indispensable for human survival, but Wyclif rightly chided the disordered allegiance given to it by so many. It is difficult to resist the temptation to equate a high IQ with inevitable success in moral development. Mental dexterity does not assure moral dexterity, yet the haunting inclination to think so is difficult to resist.

The psychologist Howard Gardner has advanced the theory of multiple intelligences—that there is not one type of intelligence, but several. In *Multiple Intelligences*, he proposes that there are about eight intelligences:

---

6   Johannes Wyclif, *Principium "Wyclif's Postilla"*, trans. Beryl Smalley, 276.

logical/mathematical, musical, visual-spatial, verbal-linguistic, interpersonal, bodily-kinesthetic, intrapersonal, and naturalistic. Later on, he become open to the concepts of moral intelligence and spiritual intelligence. But Robert Cole proposed several others, which he called "immoral intelligence," "mischievous intelligence," and "wicked intelligence."

Cole argued that Nazi intellectuals, though some of the world's most highly educated individuals, used their mental power in service to one of history's most barbaric programs. It should be remembered that Germany was the most literate country in Europe in the 1940s. Regarding a conversation he had with the poet William Carlos Williams, Cole says,

> As Williams once reminded me about the Nazi Joseph Goebbels and William's own friend Ezra Pound: "Look at the two of them, one a Ph.D. and smart as they come, and the other, one of the twentieth century's most original poets, also as brilliant as they come in certain ways—and they both end up peddling hate, front men for the worst scum the world has ever seen".[7]

A high IQ is a tool like any other. A hammer can be used by a craftsman to build with or by a thief to smash a window. A truck can deliver Meals on Wheels or victims of sex trafficking. The IQ has no more innate tendency toward

---

7   Robert Coles, *The Call of Stories* (Boston: Houghton Mifflin, 1989), 195.

constructive use than the hammer or the truck. The virtuous and proper use of our tools, abilities, and resources, and the avoidance of their vicious use, is achieved through training informed by Scripture and philosophy. One of many injunctions found in Scripture is Hebrews 5:14, "But solid food is for the mature, who by constant use have trained themselves to distinguish good from evil."

G. K. Chesterton once said, "The word 'good' has many meanings. For example, if a man were to shoot his grandmother at a range of five hundred yards, I should call him a good shot, but not necessarily a good man."[8] Skill, IQ, and personal charisma only make a person efficient and effective in their vicious plans, if isolated from Scripture, reason, experience, and the virtues. Quoting Chesterton again, "Thinking in isolation and with pride ends in being an idiot. Every man who will not have softening of the heart must at last have softening of the brain."[9]

If we are to be good knowers, if we are going to be good interpreters, if we are going to be successful in acquiring truth and avoiding error, then we must pursue the moral and intellectual virtues. We must avoid the temptation to place too much unexamined confidence in mental prowess while forgetting the maintenance of our will. Wood warns us,

---

8   As cited by Connie Robertson, editor, *The Wordsworth Dictionary of Quotations* (Ware: Wordsworth Editions, 1998), 82.

9   G. K. Chesterton, *Orthodoxy: The Romance of Faith* (New York: Doubleday, 1959), 42.

our ability to lay hold of the truth about important matters turns on more than our IQ or the caliber of school we attended; it also depends on whether we have fostered within ourselves virtuous habits of mind. Our careers as cognitive agents, as persons concerned to lay hold of truth and pursue other important intellectual goals, will in large measure succeed or fail as we cultivate our intellectual virtues.[10]

Good interpreters can do no less.

---

10 W. Jay Wood, *Epistemology: Becoming Intellectual Virtuous* (Downers Grove; Inter Varsity Press, 1998), 16.

CHAPTER 11

THE ROLE OF ORTHODOXY AND HERESY IN INTERPRETATION

MAINTAINING ORTHODOXY AND AVOIDING HERESY

Two of the goals of interpretation are maintaining orthodoxy and avoiding heresy. If interpretive communities are not vigilant, the orthodoxy archived in their documents of ultimate authority (DUA) could morph into distortions unfaithful and harmful to the original body of doctrine. Those communities troubled themselves enough to compose those documents to objectify certain doctrines, contracts, theories, pledges, or agreements which were advantageous to their wellbeing in some way. In most cases, regnant in the minds of the documents' composers was the awareness that distorting pressures would eventually attempt to supplant their intentions. For example, St. Paul in 1 Timothy 4:16 reminded us to "Watch your life [orthopraxy] and doctrine [orthodoxy]," and Jefferson warned against "trying what meaning may be squeezed out of the text, or invented against it."[1]

WHAT IS ORTHODOXY AND HERESY?

Orthodoxy means "straight teaching" or "true teaching." It is from the Greek word *orthodoxos*, "having the right opinion" (*orthos*, "right, true, straight" + *doxa*, "opinion"). It is related to the word orthodontics, which means "straight teeth," and orthopedics meaning "straight children." Orthopraxy, in contrast with orthodoxy, emphasizes conduct, and means "straight behavior."

Not everything which goes by the name "orthodoxy" is actually true, but if the body of beliefs or agreements are in line with the textual contents of the DUA, then that body is orthodoxy for that interpretive community. Islamic teaching is orthodox if it truly represents the Koran, and Jewish teaching is orthodox if it truly represents the Torah. Those two "orthodoxies" may contradict each other, but if they actually represent the DUAs of those respective communities, then they are orthodox to them.

Heresy is also known as heterodoxy, which in Greek is *heterodoxos* (*heteros*, "other" + *doxa*, "opinion"). Heterodoxy means "not in accordance with established doctrines or opinions." Though orthodoxy and heresy are usually used in referring to theological issues, they also can apply to other fields. Eight balls and two strikes are heresy to the

---

1   Thomas Jefferson, June 12, 1823, in a letter to Justice William Johnson. Thomas Jefferson, *Jefferson Writings*, Merrill D. Peterson, ed. (NY: Literary Classics of the United States, Inc., 1984).

Major League Baseball Official Baseball Rules book, while four balls and three strikes is orthodox.

Buddhism is not a Christian heresy. It is wholly other than. However, Arianism is a Christian heresy. It was an influential heresy that denied the divinity of Christ. Arius (c. 250-c. 336) was an Alexandrian priest who claimed that Jesus, the Son of God, was created by the Father, making Him neither coeternal nor consubstantial with the Father. Hilaire Belloc, in *The Great Heresies*, defines heresy as follows:

> The denial of a scheme wholesale is not heresy, and has not the creative power of heresy. It is of the essence of heresy that it leaves standing a great part of the structure it attacks. On this account it can appeal to believers.... Wherefore, it is said of heresies that 'they survive by the truths they retain' ... heresy originates a new life of its own and vitally affects the society it attacks. The reason that men combat heresy is not only, or principally, conservative ... it is much more a perception that the heresy, in so far as it gains ground, will produce a way of living and a social character at issue with, irritating, and perhaps mortal to, the way of living and the social character produced by the old orthodox scheme.[2]

---

2   H. Belloc, *The Great Heresies* (Manassas: Trinity Communications, 1987), 10.

WHEN HERESY BECOMES SO PERVASIVE

"Heresy sometimes becomes so pervasive that it becomes the new orthodoxy," admonished Judge Bork.[3] Much of what was promoted as Christian orthodoxy during the Middle Ages turned out to be heresy, a result of errors which accumulated over fifteen centuries. Much of what is promoted as constitutional orthodoxy today is heresy, a result of errors which have accumulated over two centuries. "The received wisdom on America's recent constitutional history is, unfortunately, almost entirely wrong. That is why a sweeping reassessment, one that lays bare exactly who killed the Constitution that the Founding Fathers bequeathed us, is necessary,"[4] declared Thomas E. Woods, Jr. and Kevin R. C. Gutzman.

Having been in the furniture and antique restoration business for fifty-four years, I have encountered times when customers thought their piece of furniture was a period piece when it was actually a reproduction or fake. By *period*, it is meant that the piece, for example a Queen Ann chair, is not only in the Queen Ann style, but also that it was made in the Queen Ann period (1720s-1760s). By *reproduction*, it is meant that the chair was in the Queen Ann style, but was made after the Queen Ann period. Reproductions have a long and respectable place in furniture

---

3   Robert Bork, *The Tempting of America: The Political Seduction of the Law* (New York: The Free Press, 1990), 7.

4   Thomas E. Woods, Jr. and Kevin R. C. Gutzman, *Who Killed the Constitution: The Fate of American Liberty from World War I to George W. Bush* (New York: Crown Publishing Group, 2008), 2.

manufacturing, so long as the manufacturers market them as "reproductions."

On the other hand, fakes are the illegitimate products of charlatans who prey on unsuspecting customers who are not experienced in discerning period pieces and reproductions from fakes. Fakers invest a lot of time to intentionally distress their pieces to look antique. One method is to "rasp" worn-looking indentions into chair stretchers to replicate decades of normal, everyday wear and tear, in order to make them appear "authentic." My furniture experience makes it harder for fakers to victimize me. Likewise, my hermeneutical experience makes it harder for interpretive fakers to victimize me. My hope is that the experience of reading this book will, in some way, make it harder for interpretive fakers to victimize you. Interpretive fakers, either through willful intention or interpretive incompetence, torture orthodoxies and nourish heresies. Fakers can "rasp" the texts of sacred and legal DUAs to make them appear to be "authentic." The ability to distinguish between orthodoxy and heresy can both free us from sin and tyranny—it can save both our souls and our republic.

PART TWO
REGARDING BIBLICAL
INTERPRETATION

CHAPTER 12

A HISTORY OF BIBLICAL INTERPRETATION

A SHORT SURVEY OF BIBLICAL interpretation will show how believers before us interpreted biblical texts. The church at times maintained good interpretive principles and at other times made mistakes. By observing history, we can see some of the mistakes they made and see the faulty interpretive methods they employed. As observed by Henry A. Virkler, in *Hermeneutics*, "Many great Christians (e.g., Origen, Augustine, Luther) understood and prescribed better hermeneutical principles than they practiced. We may thus be reminded that knowing a principle needs also to be accompanied by applying it to our own study of the word."[1]

Various methods have been employed for the study of scripture in both the Old and New Testaments. Some of these methods were adopted from surrounding cultures. Some were entirely new methods. Ultimately, the goal of surveying the history of interpretation is to prepare us in

---

1   Henry A. Virkler, *Hermeneutics: Principles and Processes of Biblical Interpretation* (Grand Rapids: Baker Books, 1981), 48.

our attempt to reexamine these methods and to test them anew.

This is a very compressed history. For a more extensive treatment of this subject, the reader is encouraged to refer to *A Short History of the Interpretation of the Bible* by Robert M. Grant and David Tracy, and to an excellent chapter in *Protestant Biblical Interpretation* by Bernard Ramm.

Before addressing the Church's history of interpretation, I would like to address my own. A common temptation among young, zealous Christian believers is to think that they are the first person, or the first group, in the two-thousand-year history of the church who sincerely desire to know the Word of God. I and the band of brothers who composed our small Jesus People church in the early 1970s were guilty of harboring such an idea. At best, the idea is immature—at worst, it can spin off into a cultish obsession. When this immature, and potentially arrogant, attitude is fused to a misguided version of *sola scriptura*, cultish behavior is not far away. *Sola scriptura* is a sound interpretive principle, but only when it is in tandem with the moral and intellectual virtues which can assist the interpreter in a biblical quest for the Word. Arrogance, pride, and willfulness can quickly turn genuine *sola scriptura* into its counterfeit—*nuda scriptura*.

We are guilty of *nuda scriptura* when we attempt to utilize *sola scriptura* in a naïve way. When we assume that every interpreter is a *tabula rosa* (blank slate), that we approach Scripture with no partiality or willfulness, when we do not take our fallenness seriously enough, we are in danger of failing in our pursuit of the truth of Scripture. In

Luke 1:38 Mary said, "be it unto me according to thy word" (KJV). New, zealous converts enthusiastically agree with Mary's submissive attitude, but some things are easier said than done. It is through extended discipleship that "be it unto me according to thy word" actually becomes applied to our lives.

Sola scriptura was a reaction against institutionalized interpretation. However, done the wrong way, it can lead to the other extreme of hyper-privatization of interpretation. We need the help of our fellow church members, our Sunday school teachers, our pastors, and our denominations to get to "Scripture only." We need people around us to ask "Are you stupid or something?" when we stray into strange interpretive territory. C. E. M. Joad, in *Decadence*, said, "Criticism prunes a man's work, keeps him from straying too far from the middle of the road and opens his ears to the still small voice that in the middle of the night whispers, 'Fiddlesticks.'"[2]

In my fifty years as a Christian, I have eaten a lot of theological crow. In fact, it seems like I have dined on the entire avian buffet. I have not changed my views on the fundamentals of Protestant biblical faith, but I have had to realign my faith many times regarding many of the more peripheral issues of biblical Christianity and church life. Therefore, I want to remind myself that I should not, in most cases, harshly judge those in the past who have made interpretive mistakes. I need to remember that I too have at times embraced and advocated some silly interpretations

---

2   C. E. M. Joad, *Decadence: A Philosophical Inquiry* (London: Faber and Faber Limited, 1948), 90.

and interpretive methods. If I do not want to be labelled a heretic every time I make a mistake, then I should extend that courtesy to others. Not every mistake rises to the level of heresy.

The following is a list of some of the interpretive issues I have dealt with. Some are minor mistakes while others are more serious.

1. The allegorizing of the Parable of the Good Samaritan.

   It is a mistake to allegorize this parable. Many years ago, I did teach it as an allegory.

2. The Prosperity Gospel, also known as the Health and Wealth Doctrine.

   This is one interpretive error I never participated in. There are some shysters who have used the doctrine to prey on naïve believers, but I have also known some wonderful Christian people who embrace the teaching. They were simply in error on this subject.

3. Biblical numerology.

   There are some significant numbers in the Bible. We find a few of these repeated in Scripture. However, much of Bible numerology is nothing more than a product of an interpreter with an unbridled imagination. I have never embraced Bible numerology.

4. The "eye of the needle" being a low gate in Jerusalem.

   I have taught that the eye of the needle (Matthew 19:24) was a low gate in Jerusalem. That interpretation is wrong. There is no archaeological evidence for the claim and we find no mention of such an "interpretation" until the eleventh century. A Greek churchman, Theophylact, made the unfounded claim in a commentary.

5. The Seven Churches in Revelation being seven church ages.

I used to enthusiastically believe and teach this. I now believe it is the product of unprincipled speculation.

6. The Bible Code.

I have a two-word critique of *The Bible Code* by Michael Drosnin—unmitigated nonsense.

7. The hyper-allegorizing of Song of Songs.

This is something I once believed and taught. There may be a legitimate allegorical approach to interpreting Song of Songs, but hyper-allegorism is not legitimate. To allegorize "Your two breasts" (4:5) as representing the Old Testament and the New Testament is definitely going too far.

8. Baptizing in the name of the Father, Son, and Holy Spirit or in the name of Jesus only.

I was originally baptized in the name of the Father, Son, and Holy Spirit. Later, we came across the teaching that claimed it should have been in the name of Jesus, so we all went out and were rebaptized. I now believe either way is biblically acceptable.

OLD TESTAMENT EXEGESIS

When the Babylonian captivity ended in 538 B.C., the Jews returned to their homeland a changed people. A good change was their permanent rejection of idolatry. The post-captivity Jews had finally emancipated themselves from that perennial vice. On the other hand, the seventy years had stripped them of much of their culture, traditions, and language. Several generations had been without the temple ministry, corporate worship, and reading and instruction from the Book of the Law.

In Nehemiah 8, the Israelites "came together as one in the square before the Water Gate. They told Ezra the teacher of the Law to bring out the Book of the Law of Moses, which the LORD had commanded for Israel" (verse 1). Ezra, standing on a high wooden platform, read from daybreak until noon. Then, the Levites "instructed the people in the Law while the people were standing there. They read from the Book of the Law of God, making it clear and giving the meaning so the people could understand what was being read" (7-8). This chapter emphasizes both the reading of the Law and interpretation of that Law.

There is much regarding reading, interpreting, and writing in the several chapters connected to Nehemiah 8. In chapter 7, Nehemiah demonstrates the importance and objectivity of writing and reading by saying, "I found the genealogical record of those who had been the first to return. This is what I found written there:..." In that same chapter he said, "but they could not show that their families were descended from Israel... These searched for their family records, but they could not find them and so were excluded from the priesthood as unclean" (61, 64). In chapter 9, the Israelites "show" their understanding of the Law by their fasting, wearing of sackcloth, putting dust on their heads, and corporate repentance. In chapter 10, they make "a binding agreement, putting it in writing, and our leaders, our Levites and our priests are affixing their seals to it" (9:38). These chapters demonstrate that the Israelites strongly believed in the discipline of writing and reading, along with the necessary presuppositions which make possible the discipline's objectivity.

The method of interpreting exhibited here strongly appears to be one which uses language in the normal way that people communicate. There is no indication that Ezra and the Levites employed esoteric, coded language games. The closest example of figurative language was in 9:11 where it says, "[God] hurled their pursuers into the depths, like a stone into mighty waters." This scripture is not literally accurate. The Egyptians pursuing the Israelites were enclosed by the sea, not thrown into the sea. This use of figurative language may have been part of the "making it clear and giving the meaning so they could understand" which the Levites conducted. Their use of this simile reveals they were not prisoners to the idea that all communication had to be literal. Figurative language, such as metaphors, similes, overstatements, hyperbole, and parables are well within the domain of normal language use.

The Levites, scribes, and teachers had a high view of Scripture, and that view was expressed by their dedication to carefully preserving the texts for their transmission across the centuries. However, can a person have too high a view of Scripture? Perhaps the question should be stated this way: can a person embrace a misguided view of Scripture, out of an over-zealous enthusiasm, so that they claim forms of "divine inspiration" which the Author

113

never intended? As stated earlier, defending and promoting the universally valid principles of writing and reading is an attempt to defend against, not only their enemies, but also their over-zealous, misguided supporters. Eventually, rabbis began interpreting Scripture in ways other than those which communication is normally interpreted. An example is "letterism." This was a method which placed interpretive significance upon the very shapes of the letters. This misguided method displaced the author's intended meaning and replaced it with unprincipled speculation.

Later, gematria was grafted into the interpretive methods of some rabbis. It is the assigning of numeric value to letters (aleph = 1, bet = 2, gimel = 3, etc.), and then, through some algorithm, the word is transformed into a numeric value which can be equated to some interpretive significance. Gematria was believed to reveal secret, coded truths in the Torah. One famous example is an interpretation of Genesis 14:14, which goes as follows: the verse mentions that the household of Abraham consisted of 318 men. The numerical equivalent of the name of Abraham's servant, Eliezer, was 318. This, supposedly, suggests that it was only Eliezer who came with Abraham, not all 318 men.

In modern times, gematria can be found in *The Bible Code* by Michael Drasin. Also, a gematria calculator can be accessed on the internet. This method is unmitigated nonsense, on par with "hepatoscopy," the "looking in the liver" of a sacrificed animal for divination, which the king of Babylon did, as recorded in Ezekiel 21:21.

Eventually, an elaborate interpretive enterprise developed during the last several centuries leading up to Christ's time. Jewish interpretation was classified into four main types:

1. The literal method (*peshat*) was employed, but quite often was viewed as banal by the more "sophisticated" exegetes.

2. Midrashic interpretation, because it ignored context, tended toward wildly speculative exegesis. Texts which contained similar phrases or words were combined, whether or not the texts referred to the same idea. Gematria was a midrashic method.

3. *Pesher* interpretation put a strong emphasis on eschatology. Advocates of this method believed that the prophets concealed eschatological meanings which were shrouded in mystery.

4. Allegorical interpretation assumed that beneath the literal meaning of the text lay the true meaning intended by the author. Allegorical interpretation is a valid form of interpretation, so long as the text being allegorized was intended by the author to be an allegory. Some modern examples are George Orwell's *Animal Farm* and Edmund Spenser's *The Faerie Queene*. An invalid form is to allegorize a text which was not intended to be allegorized. The Hellenistic culture propagated by the Greeks and Romans influenced the Jews in many ways. Among the Greeks, a tension had developed between their religious traditions and philosophical heritage. Some aspects of their religious traditions were beginning to be embarrassments to developments in their philosophy. To retain both their religious traditions and

philosophical heritage, they synthesized the two through a hermeneutical ploy—allegorization. This allowed them to retain texts, heroes, and cherished myths which were integral to their cultural identities, while embracing what were considered advances in their philosophy—a case of the proverbial "having your cake and eating it too."

The "icons" were preserved, but their meaning was eviscerated and substituted with content more palatable to current sympathies.

Some examples of Greek allegories: Chronos swallowing its own children becomes time creating things and then them withering away. Athena coming out of her father's head becomes the emergence of wisdom. References to Ares represent anger and the Erymanthian Boar the rejection of the basest impulses of our nature.

As Greek Platonic thinking began infiltrating Jewish theology, allegorization was seen as a way of reinterpreting the Old Testament to the Jews who wanted to remain faithful to the Mosaic tradition yet adopt Greek Platonic philosophy. Philo of Alexandria was a Hellenistic Jewish philosopher (c. 20 B.C.-c. A.D. 50) who advocated allegory to harmonize the Torah with Greek philosophy. Bernard Ramm cites this example from Philo and his contemporaries:

Abraham's trek to Palestine is *really* the story of a Stoic philosopher who leaves Chaldea (sensual understanding) and stops at Haran, which means 'holes', and signifies the emptiness of knowing things by the holes, that is the senses. When he becomes Abraham he becomes a truly enlightened philosopher. To marry Sarah is to marry abstract wisdom.[3]

In summary, Jewish interpretation in Christ's time was a mix of conservative approaches to interpretation, midrashic exegesis, mild allegorizing, and extreme forms of allegorical exegetical methods. Much of the interpretive error which Jesus encountered was the interference with the Word of God from the "traditions of the elders." Jesus excavated the Word from under the accumulated layers of interpretive errors and invalid theological inferences.

THE INTERPRETATION OF THE OLD TESTAMENT IN THE NEW TESTAMENT

A large portion of the New Testament consists of quotations, allusions, and paraphrases of the Old Testament. By observing how these New Testament interpreters used this significant body of Old Testament texts, several conclusions can be drawn about methods which they shunned and those which they embraced.

HOW JESUS AND THE APOSTLES DID NOT USE THE OLD TESTAMENT

The "letterism" employed by some Jewish rabbis is not found in the interpretive methods of those expounding on Old Testament texts. Neither Jesus nor any of the Apostles

---

3   Bernard Ramm, *Protestant Biblical Interpretation* (Grand Rapids: Baker, 1970), 28.

attempted to "discover" hidden meanings in the shapes of the letters or in the speculative rearranging of the letters. The gematria employed by some Jewish rabbis was not used by Jesus or the Apostles. They were able to avoid the philosophical and theological intimidation which came from the pressures to adapt Jewish theology to Hellenistic Platonic thinking. There are no instances in their exposition of the Old Testament of such things as transforming Abraham's "318 servants" into "Eliezer."

The allegorization as practiced by Philo was not used. They did not succumb to the pressures to disparage the literal treatment of Old Testament texts. Again, much of the impetus to allegorize came from the attempt to synthesize Jewish theology with Platonic philosophy.

The "tradition of the elders" method as employed by the Pharisees and teachers of the Law was not accepted by them. Jesus and the Apostles promoted a type of *sola scriptura* which focused theology back on the Word of God. That Word had become buried under centuries of interpretive mistakes, specious inferences drawn from speculative conjectures, and many of the other exegetical pathologies which come to afflict most interpretive communities. From time to time, an interpretive community has to drydock its theological ship to scrape off the accumulation of interpretive barnacles. Jesus found a vast amount of theological dust which had to be swept away to re-reveal the Word.

HOW JESUS AND THE APOSTLES USED THE OLD TESTAMENT

Jesus and the Apostles esteemed the literal sense of the Old Testament. The literal sense represented the meaning of the author, and it was from that sense that theological meaning was drawn. They did not view the literal sense as immature or carnal. They did build theology on the literal texts, but did not do so by disparaging the literal or by being intimidated by alien philosophical or theological systems. Their theological applications were drawn from the normal meaning of texts.

They were consistent in treating the historical texts as unequivocal facts. When they referenced Abraham, they meant the historical Abraham. They did not mean a fictional character that serving as a fount from which a plethora of speculative meaning could pour.

Jesus and the Apostles did use many forms of language to communicate their message: overstatement, irony, riddles, literal recountings of events, parables, proverbs, puns, a fortiori, poetry, questions, metaphors, hyperbole, and types. On occasion, they used allegory. The occasional use of allegory is one thing—the unlimited and indiscriminate use of allegorizing is quite another.

When Jesus taught using the Parable of the Sower (Matthew 13:3-23), He intended it to be allegorized. An allegory is a chain of metaphors. The various elements of the parable—seed, path, types of soil, sun, thorns, birds—are a series of metaphors, which, taken together, illustrates a truth about spiritual reality. However, when Jesus used the Parable of the Good Samaritan (Luke 10:25-37), He did not intend for it to be allegorized. The various elements of that parable—Jerusalem, Jericho, robbers, half-dead, Samaritan, donkey, etc.—did not each contain hidden meanings which demanded interpretation. To allegorize this parable is to undermine the point Jesus was trying to communicate.

When Paul writes concerning Abraham and his two sons (Galatians 4:21-31), he states, "Which things are an allegory" (KJV). This statement in the ESV is "Now this may be interpreted allegorically," in the NKJV it is "which things are symbolic," and in the HCSB it is "These things are being taken figuratively." Paul's use of allegory will be dealt with in more detail in a coming chapter (Parables). For now, though, it will have to suffice to say that when approaching allegory, it is better to practice interpretive restraint, rather than interpretive activism, especially in light of the doctrinal damage which has been inflicted on the church by the perennial abuse of interpretive options.

INTERPRETATION IN THE PATRISTIC ERA

Like the Jewish theologians in the Old Testament period, the theologians in the Patristic Era were motivated by the proper belief that Scripture was given by God. While many of these interpreters got it right, too many influential ones did not. The employment of illegitimate interpretive methods crept into their hermeneutics. Many slowly relaxed their grip on the correct assumption that the author's intended meaning should be the governing principle which regulated exegesis. That governing principle was largely displaced by an interpretive error pattern known as allegorization.

CLEMENT OF ALEXANDRIA (A.D. 155-215)

Clement was a Christian theologian and philosopher. He was born in Athens and later became a teacher at the Catechetical School of Alexandria. Though he was a convert to Christianity, he had been well-educated in classical Greek philosophy. Clement was greatly influenced by Hellenistic philosophy, in particular Plato and the Stoics. This influence contributed to his embracing the allegorical method of the Jewish theologian, Philo of Alexandria. Philo attempted to synthesize Greek philosophy with Old Testament Scripture. Clement attempted the same with Christian scripture.

He believed Scripture contained multiple layers of meaning which could be appropriated by a two-fold exegesis—corresponding to the dual nature of humans, the body being the literal and the soul, the spiritual. Genesis 22:1-5, when Abraham took Isaac to be sacrificed on Moriah, is an example of Clement's synthesized exegesis:

> Abraham, when he came to the place God told him of on the third day, looked up, saw the place afar off. For the first day is that which constituted by the sight of good things; and the second is the soul's best desire; on the third the mind perceives spiritual things, the eyes of the understanding being opened by the Teacher who rose on the third day. The three days may be the mystery of the seal (baptism) in which God is really believed. It is, consequently, afar off that he perceives the place. For the reign of God is hard to attain, which Plato calls the

reign of ideas, having all things universally. But it is seen by Abraham afar off, rightly, because of his being in the realms of generation, and he is therefore initiated by the angel. Thence says the apostle, "Now we see through a glass, but then face to face," by those sole pure and incorporeal applications of the intellect.[4]

ORIGEN (A.D. 185-254)

Origen was an early church father who was associated with the School of Alexandria and its use of the allegorical interpretation. He was a student of Clement. Based on 1 Thessalonians 5:23, he taught that Scripture had a three-fold sense—a literal sense (body), a moral sense (soul), and a doctrinal sense (spirit). He devalued the literal sense, while clearly advocating for the moral and spiritual, whose meaning was accessible through allegorizing.

JOHN CHRYSOSTOM (A.D. 354-407)

John was a well-known figure of the Antiochian School of interpretation. His preaching ability earned him the name *Chrysostomos*, meaning "golden mouth." His preaching was guided by his adherence to the Antiochian principles of biblical exegesis. Those principles, in contrast to Alexandrian principles, stressed the literal and historical meaning of Scripture, known today as grammatical-historical hermeneutics.

---

4   Milton S. Terry, *Biblical Hermeneutics* (Grand Rapids: Zondervan, 1974), 639.

JEROME (A.D. 347-420)

Jerome is best known for his Latin translation of the Bible, known as the Vulgate. The school of Antioch influenced his approach to interpretation, though he never completely rejected allegorization.

AUGUSTINE OF HIPPO (A.D. 354-430)

Augustine was by far the most influential Christian theologian and apologist of his time. The four-fold exegesis he advocated became the dominate interpretive system for Catholic biblical interpretation from his time in the fourth century until the Reformation in the sixteenth century. The four different meanings of Scripture were: literal, moral, allegorical, and anagogical (prophetic).

In his book, *On Christian Doctrine,* he stated a number of interpretive rules, many of which remain in use today, and some of which contradict much of his own exegetical behavior. Here are few of his rules, rules which he seems to forget or ignore in later works: the task of the expositor is to understand the meaning of the author, not to bring his own meaning to the text. A verse should be studied in its context, not in isolation from the verses around it. The literal and historical meaning of Scripture should be held in high regard.

Augustine abandoned many of these principles and employed a high degree of allegory in his teaching. One of the most famous of his misguided allegorical interpretations is his version of the Parable of the Good Samaritan.

THE ANTIOCHIAN SCHOOL OF INTERPRETATION

On the ideological spectrum of interpretive theory, the Antiochian School is at the opposite end from the Alexandrian School. They rejected allegorical interpretation and adamantly defended what is now called grammatical-historical interpretation. For them, Scripture's authentic meaning should be determined by taking seriously the rules of grammar and the facts of history.

For example, Virkler says, "according to the allegorists, Abraham's departure from Haran signifies his rejection of knowing things by the senses; to the Antiochians, Abraham's departure from Haran represented an act of faith and trust as he followed God's call to go from the historical city of Haran to the land of Canaan."[5] If the Antiochian School's exegesis had prevailed the Church could have prevented, or minimized, much of the doctrinal drift which quickly ensued.

INTERPRETATION DURING THE MIDDLE AGES

The dominant method of biblical interpretation during the Middle Ages was Augustine's four-fold exegesis. For memorization, the four senses were set to verse:

> The letter shows us what God and our fathers did;
>
> The allegory shows us where our faith is hid;
>
> The moral meaning gives us rules of daily life;

5   Henry A. Virkler, *Hermeneutics: Principles and Processes of Biblical Interpretation* (Grand Rapids: Baker, 1981), 62.

The anagogy shows us where we end our strife.[6]

Also, the role of tradition was elevated to an authoritative level as institutional interpretation congealed. As the Catholic Church developed a monopoly over biblical teaching, doctrines which did not align with their views were suppressed and persecuted.

As occurs with most interpretive communities, the authentic meaning of their documents of ultimate authority eventually becomes damaged by the cumulative effect of torturous methods of exegesis, interpretational drift, political intrigue, and the willfulness of some members of that community whose agendas are hampered by fidelity to original meaning. The effects of the damage can become so obvious and the interpretational drift so massive that the documents can experience interpretive collapse. In the case of biblical interpretation towards the end of the Middle Ages, the egregious doctrinal pathologies in Church dogma could no longer be sustained.

There had been significant attempts at reforming the Catholic Church before Martin Luther. The reforms were absolutely necessary. Yet, Constance and Basel-Ferrara-Florence-Rome failed in correcting problems the church had to face: simony (buying church offices), ambition, pluralism (the buying of many offices), greed, poor clerical training, and worldliness. Earlier critics such as Geert Groote, Jan Hus, Peter Waldo, Thomas à Kempis,

---

6   Robert Grant, *A Short History of the Interpretation of the Bible* (New York: Macmillan, 1963), 119.

Nicolas of Lyra, and John Wyclif advocated for reform. Their work softened the ground in which Luther's reformational seeds sprouted.

INTERPRETATION DURING THE REFORMATION

Biblical illiteracy in the late Middle Ages was widespread. Even among the clergy, ignorance of the content of Scripture was so prevalent that many doctors of divinity had never read the entire Bible. Martin Luther observed that one of his colleagues, Andreas Bodenstein von Karlstadt, held a doctorate of theology eight years before reading the Bible, and that this was typical. At that time, the Bible had not been widely published in the common vernacular languages. This helped the Catholic Church to maintain their monopoly on theological dogma.

MARTIN LUTHER (1483-1546)

During his teaching career at the University of Wittenberg, Luther began to see exegetically how the Roman Catholic Church had departed from the faith of the early church. In his lectures on Romans, from November 3, 1515, to September 7, 1516, he was still employing the four-fold exegesis, the typical method of Scholasticism. He found that the method often left his students confused and he considered it the "chopped-up method." However, when he gave his lectures on Galatians, from October 27, 1516, to March 10, 1517, the four-fold method had been discarded. The four senses were displaced by an emphasis on the literal and spiritual. He was convinced that neither the Fathers nor the Apostle Paul used any other method. Exegesis in his classroom was governed by the principles of the grammatical-historical method.

As happens in any interpretive community, when the documents of ultimate authority are subjected to a change of interpretive method, there will be an inevitable change in the content. The four-fold method had enslaved Scripture's meaning—the grammatical-historical method freed it. Luther used the tools of the grammatical-historical method to excavate "*sola fide*" from beneath the stratigraphy of fifteen centuries of exegetical mischief. *Sola fide* is *what* he discovered—*sola scriptura* is *how* he discovered it. The Reformation was now underway. "The Bible once more became Christo-centric, and Luther's lectures breathed the atmosphere of first-century Christianity," says E. G. Schwiebert.[7]

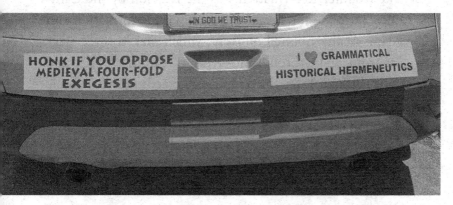

If bumper stickers had existed in Luther's day, these could have been on his back of his carriage.

---

7   E. G. Schwiebert, *Luther and His Times: The Reformation from a New Perspective* (Saint Louis: Concordia, 1950), 289.

JEAN CALVIN (1509-1564)

Calvin was the leading French Protestant reformer who broke with the Roman Catholic Church around 1530. He was one the Reformation's greatest exegetes. Like Luther, he rejected allegorical interpretation, regarding it as a contrivance of Satan. He built on Luther's interpretive method. He stated that "it is the first business of an interpreter to let the author say what he does say, instead of attributing to him what we think he ought to say."[8]

INTERPRETATION DURING THE POST-REFORMATION ERA (1540-1800)

CONFESSIONALISM

The Counter-Reformation was the reaction by the Catholic Church to the rise of the Protestant Reformation and Islam. At the Council of Trent, which met in three stages, from 1545 through 1547, 1551 through 1552, and 1562 through 1563, the dogma and creeds of the Catholic Church were set forth. The Protestants responded by developing creeds in an attempt to clarify their biblical doctrines. During this era, doctrinal purity and creeds were the major focus of the Protestants. However, the Reformers' great confidence in the perspicuity of Scripture—the claim that the Bible is a clear book—began to seem rather misplaced. Attention to sound hermeneutical methods was diminished. Many important cities had their own

---

8   F. W. Farrar, *History of Interpretation* (1885; reprint ed., Grand Rapids: Baker, 1961) 347.

creeds, and these did not always agree. Controversies ensued, and, as Farrar states, theologians began reading "the Bible by the unnatural glare of theological hatred."[9]

PIETISM

Confessionalism was followed by a movement which claimed that the church had developed an unbalanced emphasis on doctrine and creeds. Pietism emerged in the seventeenth century among German Lutherans but quickly spread throughout Europe, England, and America. The movement called for an emphasis on personal faith, holiness, devotion, and religious renewal. In the Pietists' view, religion had been divorced from personal experience and was failing in its responsibility to provide spiritual nourishment.

Many ministers had become distressed by the degeneracy and lack of Christian piety. Some of the figures in the Pietistic and related movements were John Bunyan, Richard Baxter, William Ames, Phillip Jakob Spener, August Hermann Francke, Henry Melchior Muhlenberg, and John Wesley. They sought to replace a dead orthodoxy which had reduced church members to the mere adherence of church order and formal theology. For them, the Bible is the guide to holy living.

Many Pietists discarded sound hermeneutical methods, favoring instead spiritual guidance from an experience referred to as "inner light," "inward light," or "an unction from the Holy One." However, this method proved to be

---

9   F. W. Farrar, *History of Interpretation* (1885; reprint ed., Grand Rapids: Baker, 1961), 363—364.

very subjective and produced conflicting interpretations which ignored contexts and the author's intent.

INTERPRETATION DURING THE LATE MODERN ERA (1800-PRESENT)

LIBERALISM

Interpretation before the Modern Era was motivated by two presuppositions: 1) God had written an important letter to man. 2) Man had better read it right. Hermeneutics was primarily viewed as the proper methods by which that letter could be understood. However, the trajectory of the development of hermeneutics was affected by the shift from ecclesiastical centers to "secular" universities. Also, the rise of rationalism and empiricism, with their rejection of revelation, morphed biblical studies from a quest for prescriptive religious inspiration to a quest for descriptive anthropological information.

From the influence of Hegel and Darwin, many Bible scholars came to value it as a source of information regarding ancient cultures, languages, religious practices, and historical events, while considering it no more divinely inspired than the Rosetta Stone or the Egyptian *Book of the Dead*. Their goal was academic, not devotional. The philosophical demands of rational empiricism dismissed all claims of miracles and the supernatural. These developments laid the foundation for liberalism in theology.

THE "NEW HERMENEUTICS" MOVEMENT

New hermeneutics sought to accommodate the Bible to the philosophical demands of the modern worldview. One of its strongest proponents was the German theologian Rudolf Bultmann (1884-1976). By "demythologizing" the Bible, Bultmann believed that the gospel message could be promoted among those with "scientific" mindsets with less resistance. According to him, the Bible was written during periods which embraced mythological ideas. By separating the clutter of myth, the authentic gospel proclamation (*kerygma*) can be preached to moderns.

By approaching biblical interpretation from an existential standpoint, Scripture's historical claims were considered unnecessary to the "meaning" of the crucifixion, death, resurrection, and ascension of Christ. Duncan Ferguson describes Bultmann's method thusly:

> The real issue for faith is not what happened *then* but what happens *now* in the moment of existential decision.... The meaning of the *kerygma* is not to be sought in uncovering the historical Jesus, which is impossible anyway, but in the awareness of one's responsibility before God. Brute facts, uncovered by disinterested and objective history, are unimportant for faith.[10] (Emphasis original)

---

10   Duncan Ferguson, *Biblical Hermeneutics: An Introduction* (Atlanta: John Knox Press, 1986), 171, 53.

POSTMODERN HERMENEUTICS

Postmodernism is a movement which questions key assumptions of Western thought. Perhaps postmodern philosophy could be better comprehended by referring to it as "post-truth" philosophy. The *Oxford Dictionary* selected "post-truth" as its 2016 Word of the Year and defined it as "relating to or denoting circumstances in which objective facts are less influential in shaping public opinion than appeals to emotion and personal beliefs." Starting in the late twentieth century, it began "deconstructing" truth claims in all areas of human interest: philosophy, theology, hermeneutics, mathematics, historiography, morals, science, etc. Whereas modernism made a demi-god of certainty, post-modernism made a demi-god of doubt.

It is best to place postmodernism in a historical setting to better understand its significance. Scholars divide the history of Western thought into three eras: premodern, modern, and postmodern. In the premodern era, the belief that God existed and that the Bible was God's Word were commonly held positions. Truth was a theological presupposition, and that truth came from above, was knowable, and was objective. Based on those presuppositions, pre-moderns developed their hermeneutics with objective principles for discovering God's Word in biblical texts.

In the modern era, the rise of reason in philosophy and religion began undermining belief in God and that the Bible was His revelation to man. The belief in truth as actually existing and discoverable was retained, but the belief that truth came from above was replaced by the belief that it was only discoverable in this physical world. Truth was to be found through rational and empirical means. These assumptions affected hermeneutics by explaining away references to the supernatural while asserting that the meaning of texts was attainable. "While modern historical critics may not view the authors of the Bible as inspired, the original meaning remains the object of interpretation for them as well," says Kevin Vanhoozer.[11]

In the postmodern era, all claims to universal principles and categories are rejected. For them, there are no unconditional "true" presuppositions that are binding on all persons, places, and times, no metanarratives or immutable essence. Language and hermeneutics have been a major focus of the postmodernists. Their chief literary theory is known as deconstruction, which insists that language and texts are irreducibly complex and unstable, and any claims to truth regarding them are illusionary. They also reject the idea that readers can be objective in their "reading"; that is, readers can never be able to adequately emancipate themselves from the whole host of biases which they bring to texts. These biases thwart any program which thinks it can discover the intent of the author.

Jacques Derrida (1930-2004) is one of the major figures who promoted postmodern philosophy and deconstruction. His views are reflected by Norris and Benjamin as they say,

> For any such argument would have to
> be premissed [sic] on a certain lingering

---

11 Kevin Vanhoozer, *"Is There a Meaning in This Text?" The Bible, the Reader, and the Morality of Literary Knowledge* (Grand Rapids: Zondervan, 1998), 47.

'enlightenment' ethos, a conviction not only that truth can be attained, but that the best way to reach it is by criticizing those false beliefs, ideologies or pseudo-truths that have so far delayed its advent. We should therefore reject this whole bad legacy — whether Kantian, Hegelian, Marxist, or whatever — and acknowledge that there is no ultimate truth, no final 'metanarrative' or standpoint of absolute reason from which to adjudicate the issue.[12]

Regarding postmodernism's influence in historiography, Keith Windschuttle, in *The Killing of History*, wrote:

Almost every week, the book review pages of the newspapers and magazines in most of the world's large English-speaking cities repeat a message that is rapidly becoming one of the intellectual axioms of our age: there is no longer a clear distinction between works of fiction and non-fiction. Hence, academics are only deluding themselves if they think that when they undertake research and write about society they are engaged in the pursuit of truth and knowledge.[13]

History is under a radical assault from the Left by their attempts to undermine the concepts of objectivity and

12 Christopher Norris and Andrew Benjamin, *What is Deconstruction?* (London: Academy Editions, 1988), 29.
13 Keith Windschuttle, *The Killing of History: How Literary Critics and Social Theorists are Murdering Our Past* (New York: The Free Press, 1996), 7.

certain knowledge, while claiming that different intellectual and political movements create their own forms of "knowledge." Postmodernism's assaults on texts and language is an anti-historical, anti-biblical, and anti-constitutional activity.

CONTEMPORARY EVANGELICAL HERMENEUTICS

Contemporary Evangelical churches and their seminaries generally embrace and promote the type of hermeneutics which was practiced in the New Testament and the very early church. Their interpretive affinities would align more with the Antiochian School than with the Alexandrian School. Grammatical-historical hermeneutics is their preferred exegetical method. They believe the correct interpretive task is to attain the intended meaning of the author. Their exegesis is governed by seeking to understand what the Scriptural revelation meant to its original recipients. For the most part, they have developed mature and balanced versions of the Protestant formal principle of *sola scriptura*.

Evangelical churches and their seminaries reject from their interpretive programs most of the exegetical pathologies which have distracted the church throughout some of its history. They are not embracing letterism, gematria, Scholastic four-fold exegesis, numerology, inner light, "New Hermeneutics," or Bultmann's existential exegesis. These bewildering approaches to interpretation pretend to offer erudite "keys" which unlock meanings unattainable by the normal use of language, texts, and genre.

Evangelical apologists must firmly stand for the objective, universally valid principles of the grammatical-historical method. They must defend proper methods against its "enemies," forces such as relativism, deconstruction, and religious pluralism. Also, they must defend proper methods against the over-zealous "friends" who "see" in Scripture a never-ending plethora of meanings. In the future, the church will continue to be tempted to acquiesce to pressures from nihilistic interpretive pessimists and from naïve interpretive optimists.

CHAPTER 13

HOW TO INTERPRET

THIS CHAPTER CONTAINS PRINCIPLES which pertain to any texts, but specifically the interpretation of the Bible. Much of what is said is relevant to the interpretation of the US Constitution, but its interpretation will be addressed later.

It was about 2005 that I developed an outline of a course which I have used in teaching hermeneutics in churches and prison ministries, titled "Introduction to Biblical Interpretation." My goal was to introduce my audience to the basic ideas of interpretation, in hopes that they would pursue the subject by reading scholarly treatments such as *How to Read the Bible for All its Worth* by Gordon Fee and Douglas Stewart, *Principles and Processes of Biblical Interpretation* by Henry A. Virkler, *A Basic Guide to Interpreting the Bible* by Robert H. Stein, and *People of the Book* by David Lyle Jeffery. The section of this book treating biblical interpretation, in reality, is only an "introduction" to the introduction of biblical interpretation. Unlike Fee, Virkler, Stein, and Jeffery, I'm not offering a hermeneutical buffet, but more of a hermeneutical sampler platter. If I encourage the uninitiated to further hermeneutical studies, then I will have accomplished my goal.

A large body of works regarding hermeneutics has been produced over the last two thousand years by Christian apologists. Not one of those books covered all subjects within the domain of biblical hermeneutics. Each of these authors chose to address subjects which were of interest to them, or were chosen because of the particular philosophical and theological challenges of their times. The Antiochian apologists (fourth century) had to address challenges coming from Hellenism, Augustine (fourth century) those coming from Pelagianism and Manichaeism, and Matthias Flacius Illyricus (sixteenth century) from Catholic Church authority and tradition. Closer to our times, Christian apologists have been forced to deal with Marxism, scientific materialism, religious pluralism, philosophical naturalism, existentialism, and deconstruction. And as the winds of fashionable intellectual theories come and go, future Christian apologists will be required to treat new challenges which are certain to arise.

TWO CATEGORIES OF HERMENEUTICS

The following chapters prescribe how interpretation should be conducted and an apologetic for those prescriptions. They will also contain criticism of alternative modes of interpretation and describe various error patterns in interpretation. First, I will prescribe principles regarding general hermeneutics—principles which apply to the interpretation of *any* text (poetry, lawnmower manual, Scripture, Stop sign, history, Constitution, menu, newspaper, etc.). Next, I will address the principles regarding special hermeneutics—principles pertaining to particular types of texts and genres (historical narratives, parables, law, metaphors, prophecy, poetry, hyperbole, epistles, etc.). My focus will be on the interpretation of sacred Scripture, the Bible, then on secular scripture, the US Constitution.

But first, where do these principles come from? Who determines the rules? Are these principles and rules discovered or created?

These principles and rules are not arbitrary human fabrications. They are discovered in the domain of knowledge found in the immaterial region of reality. It should be remembered, contrary to much contemporary thought, that reality is not exhausted by the physical stuff of the universe. There is much to be found in the immaterial world, and this immaterial stuff acts as a type of software on which the hardware of the universe is programmed to function. It is the domain from which the truths of logic and mathematics come from. It is also the domain from which the principles and rules of hermeneutics emanate. These interpretive conventions "are" because of the way reality is constituted. Edmund Burke (eighteenth century) mentions the conventions of the immaterial domain when he said, "It is ordained in the eternal constitution of things...."[1]

Concerning the immaterial domain, Jeffery says,

> Even the science of numbers, yet another convention, is part of what is required in a

---

1   Edmund Burke, "A Letter to a Member of the National Assembly," in *The Works of the Right Honorable Edmund Burke* (Boston: Little, Brown, and Company, 1871), 51-52.

THE JOY OF INTERPRETATION

reader, and certainly the science of logic, notably 'the truth of valid inference,' is essential to good reading. These examples from mathematics and logic show that not all conventions are a result of human invention; some are a result of human observation of systemizations preexisting in the creation itself, 'perpetually instituted by God in the reasonable order of things. Thus, the person who narrates the order of events in time does not compose that *ordo* himself.[2]

The task of the hermeneuticist is to study and systematize the science of interpretation into a defensible theory which elaborates its conventions. This legitimizes the program, similar to how chemistry is defensible and alchemy is not, and in the way astronomy is defensible and astrology is not.

GENERAL HERMENEUTICS

It is important to understand the basic issues surrounding general hermeneutics before proceeding to special hermeneutics. It will help bring into focus what it is that writers and readers are trying to accomplish, and the strengths and weaknesses of this form of communication. The principles of general hermeneutics are the primary presuppositions which underpin the hermeneutical program. The following principles apply to any text, no matter the genre.

---

2   David Lyle Jeffery, *People of the Book: Christian Identity and Literary Culture* (Grand Rapids: Eerdmans, 1996), 86.

1. The role of the author: It would be difficult to over-
   emphasize the importance of the role of the author
   in a theoretically sound hermeneutic. The author
   is the creator and the determiner of the text and its
   meaning. However, this principle is at the center of
   controversy in the interpretational wars we witness
   these days (i.e., Supreme Court appointments). Theories of authorial irrelevance seek to dislodge the
   author and his intent from its proper position in the
   hermeneutical program. However, if the author does
   not have a privileged position in determining a text's
   meaning, then there remains no objective principle
   for determining its meaning. Without that normative rule, there can be no validity in interpretation.

   A text means what its author intended it to mean.
   This self-evident, common sense assumption does
   not need a prodigious defense; what does need a
   prodigious defense is the absurd polemic against it.
   As Hirsch has said, "It is a task for [interpreters] to
   explain why there has been in the past four decades
   a heavy and largely victorious assault on the sensible
   belief that a text means what its author meant."[3] The
   assault is being waged predominantly by those hostile to the patently obvious meaning of DUA which
   wield some type of controlling demands unfavorable
   over the assailants' beliefs or behavior. It is not that
   the assailants do not understand the strictures, it is
   that they do not like them. The adage "Insincerity

3   E. D. Hirsch, Jr., *Validity in Interpretation* (New Haven: Yale
   University Press, 1967), 1.

is the enemy of sensible language" applies to these assailants. Because they are a part of an interpretive community unwilling to blatantly dispose of the DUA, the assailants advocate a mode of interpretation which can dislodge the author's privileged role, thereby removing the only normative principle that can render the actual meaning of the DUA. Liberals don't mind if the images and icons remain, just so long as they are allowed to eviscerate them of their meanings (the Left, not so much). Assaulting the role of the author is their foremost path to achieving their objectives.

It would be a mistake to attribute insincere motives to all who do not privilege the author when trying to determine a text's meaning. Many of those are disciples of philosophical and theological movements whose primary presuppositions led them down a path that renders that sincere, though decadent, conclusion. In biblical hermeneutics, some Bultmannian disciples, probably sincere, advance the idea that Scripture is a new revelation to each succeeding generation. In law, some judges, for pragmatic reasons, advocate that the meaning of a law is what contemporary judges say it means. In philosophy, some existentialists embrace a philosophy which rejects all truth-claims and the legitimacy of all methodologies professing to objectively render those claims. Their philosophy erodes our confidence in all fields: law, mathematics, science, the arts, morals, theology, and hermeneutics, to name a few. Doubt is their product—intellectual helpless-ness their method. Chesterton describes them when he said:

> We are on the road to producing a race of men who are too mentally modest to believe in the multiplication table. We're in danger of seeing philosophers who doubt the law of gravity as being a mere fancy of their own. Scoffers of old time were too proud to be convinced; but these are too humble to be convinced. The meek do inherit the earth; but the modern sceptics are too meek to even claim their inheritance. It is exactly this intellectual helplessness which is our problem.[4]

They reject the privileged position of the author be-cause they reject all normative principles.

2. The role of the text: A text is any discourse fixed in writing. It transmits information through space and time. As Ricoeur said, "The text is, *par excellence*, the basis for communication in and through distance."[5] Texts come to us in many forms: menus, stop signs, lawnmower manuals, recordings, math books, novels, computer screens, newspapers, le-gal instruments, mortgages, smoke signals, etc. All these are physical objects which have been encoded

---

4   G. K. Chesterton, *Orthodoxy: The Romance of Faith* (New York: Doubleday, 1959), 32.
5   Paul Ricoeur, *Hermeneutics and the Human Sciences* (Cambridge: Press Syndicate, 1981), 111.

in some fashion with the intent of conveying information of some kind to an audience.

The text is what the author and reader have in common—though the reader is not present during the writing, nor the author present during the reading (the author may not be alive). The text is the personal representative of the author, asking the reader to set aside their prejudices long enough for the author to be heard. It is that which guarantees the persistence of the author's speech or thoughts.

A dialogue makes possible an exchange of questions and answers. A text does not allow for this. A text enacts a type of monologue, where the text speaks and the reader listens.

> The [text] divides the act of writing and the act of reading into two sides, between which there is no communication. The reader is absent from the act of writing; the writer is absent from the act of reading. The text thus produces a double eclipse of the reader and the writer. It thereby replaces the relation of dialogue, which directly connects the voice of one to the hearing of the other.[6]

As I'm writing this, it is a tremendously beautiful fall afternoon. Instead of walking along our neighborhood waterfront and over its graceful drawbridge, I'm stuck at home writing. Why not just talk to

---

6   Ibid., 146-147.

people about all this? Yes, I know a book can reach a much broader audience, and for that I'm writing. But for this text, any text, my text, to ultimately become what texts are, I must die. As long as I'm living a reader can ask me what this chapter means, or what I intended in a particular paragraph. With my death, though, the reader is left with only the text— my death brings about the fulfillment of the text's life. I can no longer respond. You may only read my text.

3. The role of the audience: No writer writes without having an audience in mind. An audience acts as a control over the writer. The perceived audience dictates to the author his style, vocabulary, subject matter, organization, and tone. For example, if you were called to substitute a Sunday class, it would matter a great deal if the class was an adult class or a children's class. The determining of which class will greatly impact your teaching session. If it's a children's class, you more than likely would not teach from the book of Revelation or from the more violent biblical narratives. You would not teach on marriage or the Reformation. Nor would you use a vocabulary which included soteriology, theodicy, prevenient grace, pneumatology, or plenary inspiration.

Yet, an author could not possibly tailor his text to anticipate every audience that could eventually come in contact with it. Neither Isaiah, St. Paul, Thomas Aquinas, Thomas Jefferson, nor any other writer could so shape their discourses to accommodate audiences separated from them by thousands of miles, by hundreds of years, and by layers of cultural differences. This is a reality with which authors labor.

4. The role of distance: A variety of distances (scholars refer to it as distanciation) have the potential to interfere with a fruitful, spontaneous understanding of a text. These distances exert an abstracting effect on the message intended by the author. A letter received from your mother has no, or very little, distanciation. Under normal circumstances, you and your mother speak the same language, which eliminates the need for a translation. The two of you are living during the same time. Therefore, temporal distance is not an issue. You two are probably not separated by much distance. Of course, you could be in Orlando, Florida and she could live in Townsville, Australia, a distance of 9,340 miles. But in most cases, mothers and adult children, if separated, are a couple of cities or states apart. You and your mother most likely share the same basic religious tradition, so there would be little or no religious distance to span. The same applies to culture, familial customs, and philosophy.

Understanding a letter from your mother makes a spontaneous reading effortless. But what if you came home and found on your doorstep that FedEx had delivered the Rosetta Stone to you? The Rosetta Stone was discovered in Egypt in July 1799 during Napoleon Bonaparte's Egyptian campaign. Would your understanding of that text be spontaneous? Of course, because of the internet, translations and interpretations of it are just a click away. But without that, you would face an overwhelming amount of exegetical work ahead of you. To begin with, you would have to learn Greek, so that the other two Egyptian scripts could be translated. You would need to learn much about Egyptian religion, government, and history once you get past the language distance. Unlike your mother's letter, between you and the Rosetta Stone there is a vast language distance, twenty-two centuries of historical distance, and a massive cultural distance, not to mention all the philosophical and religious distances.

Fortunately, most people seldom, if ever, need to interpret texts with such massive amounts of distances, and with such intense degrees of distance, as those surrounding the Rosetta Stone. Yet, we do come in contact with texts which have greater distances than we might at first assume. We sometimes commit interpretive mistakes because distances come to us stealthily, flying under our exegetical radar. That is part of our hermeneutical program, to be aware that distanciation exists and to train ourselves to detect and mitigate their consequences to our epistemic faculties.

Whether sincere or not, interpretive pessimists advocate that the consequences of distanciation are too great for any objective hermeneutical program to succeed. For them, the distances are too broad—the distances cannot be spanned. On the other hand, interpretive optimists advocate that it is possible to span those distances. For them, an objective, defensible hermeneutical theory can elaborate how to span the distances, so that interpreters can "grasp the soul of the author." Distances do not render hermeneutists impotent, any more than it does archaeologists or crime scene investigators.

5. The role of exegesis and eisegesis: In a nutshell, the goal of the hermeneutical program is to enable readers to do exegesis and avoid eisegesis. When exegesis is properly done, a reader reads meaning out of the text. The reader will have taken the proper steps which, in the end, will allow the text to do its job—it will successfully be the representative of the author who is absent. First, the reader will have taken the prudent steps to bridle his prejudices and preconceptions—he will resist the temptation to be a willful reader. Next, he will identify the genre which is under investigation. If the reader proceeds to interpret without determining the genre, he will not know which language game is being played and, therefore, will not know the rules by which the game is to be played. Next, he will have done the proper work to place the text into all the relevant contexts. He will define and use the words in the manner in which the author originally meant for them to be used. Next, he will determine what type of distances exist between him and the text being read, and then take the careful steps needed to bridge them. These are some

of the exegetical procedures which must be followed if the reader is to avoid the various error patterns which commonly derail proper interpretation.

Eisegesis is the opposite, causing the reader to read meaning into the text—meaning which is alien to the author's intent. Eisegetical meaning is the product of the reader's imagination, or wrong assumptions and information, or invalid inferences. In these cases, the reader may think they have "grasped the soul of the author," when they have actually grasped anything but that.

All interpreters commit eisegetical mistakes. The realistic goal is to minimize the frequency and degree of those mistakes. Though proper exegesis may be our goal, it is unlikely that any of us have fully attained that goal. Harbored somewhere in the body of "knowledge" obtained during our interpretive pursuits are instances of eisegesis. Being a competent exegete means to employ proper interpretive skills to the new texts we encounter, but also to employ them in the re-examining of prior texts. Becoming a competent exegete requires that we develop a taste for eating interpretive "crow." Though some eisegetical mistakes rise to the level of heresy, most are small mistakes with minimal long-term impact on orthodoxy.

6. The role of context: When we refer to context, we are seeking the text's coordinates. That is, we are trying to find where the text resides—where it is in time, space, and genre. Most texts depend on

circumstances outside of themselves to be adequately understood. Some do not. "Water is composed of two hydrogen atoms and one oxygen atom" can be understood with little or no context. These types of propositions are not highly context-dependent. However, a statement such as "my mother loves climbing vines" has several possible meanings. The correct meaning of these types of statements cannot be determined until some information external to the text is woven to it. If the reader has no access to the context for "my mother loves climbing vines," then the reader can only list the possible meanings and cannot specify the particular meaning intended by its author. Fortunately, the vast majority of statements which have the possibility for multiple interpretations come to us with, implicitly or explicitly, the prerequisite information that allows us to discriminate the correct meaning from the list of possible meanings.

That prerequisite information serves as a type of textual GPS system, whose coordinates inform the reader where the text is located. Those coordinates can inform the reader as to whether the text is in the domain of fiction or nonfiction, poetry or didactic, etc. The determination of the text's domain is a fundamental part of context construction.

7. The role of the reader: The reader's role is to recover the author's meaning from the text. An author does not demand a reader to unconditionally assent to what he said in his text, but he does demand

unconditionally that the reader first allow the author's intent to be heard. Writing is no easy task, and the labor and sacrifice authors submit to in order to smith a text should not be flippantly misrepresented by a careless or willful reader.

Of course, there are exceptions to all of this. One author, T. S. Eliot, embraced a type of semantic autonomy, where he refused to comment on the meaning of his texts. His refusal reflected his view that one reading was a valid as another, since there were no universally valid principles to govern interpretation. Consistent with his theory, Eliot did not complain that he was misrepresented or that his texts were misinterpreted.

Not all authors are successful in writing a text which is comprehensible and whose meaning is accessible. Sometimes authors fail. However, in most cases authors do succeed. But the reader's right to agree or disagree with the author only begins after the author has been accurately heard.

The "reading" war raging today between interpretive optimists and interpretive pessimists is fought on many different grounds, but one of the major grounds is the role of the reader. The optimists insist that the reader approach the text with the assumption that it was written with the intention of transmitting a specific, precise message. The reader is to assume a passive role of taking in the meaning fixed in the text. The optimists empower the writer. The writer is the master of the text.

"Modern social science is guided by general rules of method that direct the conduct of research. Its most orthodox practitioners assume that there is but a single method, self-correcting scientific method that is universal in its application across disciplines," says Pauline Marie Rosenau.[7]

On the other hand, the pessimists insist that the reader approach the text with the assumption that the reader is the empowered one, not the writer. This reader-oriented approach grants to the reader the privilege to create, construct, and produce meaning at will, since there are no universally valid principles which could throttle such activity. The pessimists claim there are no rules, no methods of investigation to which they must conform. They are the party of anti-rules. With this "anything goes" hermeneutic, the reader is the master of the text.

It is difficult to exaggerate the corrosive effects these pessimistic theories have on the discipline of writing and reading, and on the activities which rely on its objectivity. Those theories are anti-literature, anti-theological, anti-constitutional, and anti-science activities.

8. The distinction between exegesis and hermeneutics: The discipline of hermeneutics is divided into two major categories. The first is exegesis, the study of a text with the explicit purpose of discovering the

---

7   Pauline Marie Rosenau, *Post-Modernism and the Social Sciences: Insights, Inroads, and Intrusions* (New Jersey: Princeton, 1992), 116.

author's originally intended meaning. The other category is the more narrowly defined use of the word, "hermeneutics." In this narrower sense it refers to the activity of determining the relevance of ancient texts to contemporary audiences.

Few novice interpreters can resist the temptation to first ask what a biblical text means to them. Though that is what the ultimate objective should be, *it must never be the first question.* The first question must always be to know what the author of the text originally meant to his original audience.

Learning to do exegesis involves two main things. The first is to develop good reading skills. The ability to read carefully is indispensable to the intelligent study of sacred Scriptures. Mortimer J. Adler's *How to Read a Book* is one resource for improving reading skills. Second is learning to ask exegetical questions: what type of literary genre is this text? What is the context in which the text originally occurs? When did this text appear in history? What did the words of the text's content mean to the intended hearers? These are some exegetical questions which must first guide the laying of a solid foundation on which the hermeneutical "relevance" is to be built. If the exegetical foundation is wrong, the hermeneutical "relevance" built on it will most certainly be wrong. Exegesis serves as a control and governor on interpretation; it sets hermeneutical parameters. Without it, speculative "relevancy" claims can run rampant.

It is only after exegesis is done that the interpreter's next task is to begin—the task of hermeneutics. In this task the interpreter begins to build relevancy. The interpreters—the students of sacred Scripture— are ultimately concerned with how the ancient texts are to inform and impact their beliefs and behaviors. These interpreters have different goals than the students of antiquarianism. They are not just interested in history for its own sake. The study of Ancient Near East cuneiform and the Rosetta Stone are worthy studies, yet these do not have the same spiritual and eternal relevance which the Scriptures have.

A major hermeneutical principle is that no Scripture can mean to us in the "here and now" something which it never meant to them "then and there." For example, 1 Corinthians 14 encourages believers to seek spiritual gifts. Some denominations teach that these spiritual gifts are no longer part of present church life. The disregarding of these gifts is, according to them, based on an interpretation of 1 Corinthians 13:10 which says, "but when that which is perfect is come, then that which is in part shall be done away." They interpret this to mean that spiritual gifts ceased when the New Testament (that which is perfect) was completed. Proper exegesis disqualifies this because neither Paul nor his readers could not have known that a "New Testament" would develop as it has. This interpretation would have seemed baffling to them.

An interpreter who approaches a text—any text—without grasping the distinction between exegesis and hermeneutics is going to have a difficult time, especially with being consistent in the interpretation of the Epistles.

SPECIAL HERMENEUTICS AND THE BIBLE

Authors participate in many different language games in order to communicate their messages. Man has been given the capacity to play these games with great success—but not always. Sometimes confusion in communication occurs when the reader misses, for various reasons, which game the author intended to play. It is easy to see what confusion would occur if a basketball game was refereed using a baseball rule book.

CONCERNING FIRST ORDER AND SECOND ORDER REFERENCES

In a "literal" game, the author *means what he says*, but in other "non-literal" games (similes, parables, hyperbole, etc.), the author *means what he means*. Because the Bible consists of so many types of genres, it is imperative that readers understand the difference between games which are literal and non-literal. A first order reference is literal language. It is the language of science, history, engineering, law—any straightforward didactic discourse. On the other hand, second order references are figurative language—any un-straightforward discourse. It is language which has some form of abstraction, either thinly or thickly, applied to it. Some second order references are parables,

hyperbole, overstatements, allegories, similes, and metaphors, to name a few. For example:

Literal   John is very intelligent.
Simile   John is like a fox.
Metaphor   John is a fox.
Overstatement   John is the smartest man in the
                 world.
Hyperbole   John is smarter than everybody in
                 the world put together.

Much emphasis, and rightly so, has been placed on *what*
Jesus taught. Also of great importance, though, is *how* He
said what He said. Jesus was a master teacher, and He employed nearly the full range of modes of speech in His
teaching. He used parables, overstatement, poetry, hyperbole, the use of questions, puns, irony, similes, *a fortiori*,
metaphors, riddles, and proverbs. His teaching methodology caused His message to stick in the spirits and brains of
those who heard Him.

Jesus knew there was a need, at times, for straightforward, didactic teaching. He also knew that method had its
limits. He wanted to change peoples' minds, but also wanted to change their wills. Eighteen centuries later, Søren Kierkegaard, the great parabolic teacher who wrote hundreds
of parables, said, "All communication of knowledge is direct communication. All communication of [will-chang-
ing] is indirect communication."[8] In a similar vein, the
poet, William Carlos Williams, declared, "It is difficult / to
get the news from poems / yet men die miserably every day

---

8   Soren Kierkegaard, *Parables of Kierkegaard* (New Jersey:
     Princeton, 1978), xv.

/ for lack / of what is found there."[9] Furthermore, Chesterton said, "Every healthy person at some time must feed on fiction as well as fact."[10] Facts are important, but man does not live by facts alone.

This overview of special hermeneutics will show some of the differences in the various language games found in Scripture and the guidelines which govern their interpretation. However, this overview contains only *brief* descriptions of these genres. They are longer than those found in James D. Hernando's *Dictionary of Hermeneutics*, but much less comprehensive than Virkler's *Hermeneutics*, Klein/Blomberg/Hubbards' *Introduction to Biblical Interpretation*, Stein's *The Method and Message of Jesus' Teaching* and *A Basic Guide to Interpreting the Bible*, and (my all-time favorite) Fee/Stewart's *How to Read the Bible for All Its Worth*. My overview is a sampler platter; theirs is an all-you-can-eat buffet. *Bon appetit!*

PROVERBS—THE WISDOM GAME

WHAT IS A PROVERB?

The following are some brief descriptions which define a biblical proverb:

- A short pithy saying, frequently using metaphorical language, which expresses a wise, general truth concerning life from a divine perspective.

---

9   William Carlos Williams, *Asphodel, That Greeny Flower and Other Love Poems* (New York: New Directions, 1938).

10   G. K. Chesterton, *The Spice of Life and Other Essays*, ed. by Dorothy Collins (Beaconsfield: Darwen Finlayson, 1964), 10.

- A concise, memorable statement of truth learned over extended human experience.
- A pithy advisory statement.
- A terse pithy saying that contains in a striking manner a memorable statement, is characterized by its succinctness, an ethical maxim.
- A pithy wisdom saying, which often uses figurative language to express a general truth about life, a maxim, an adage, an aphorism.
- A saying that is terse, brief, has a little kick to it, and a little bit of salt as well, a nice slogan, a good motto.

A proverb is a wisdom Tweet, at least in their briefness and economy of language. It is obvious from these descriptions that a proverb is playing a completely different language game than the one played by historical narratives, such as the lengthy narratives found in Joshua, Judges, and Ezra.

THE USES OF A PROVERB

Proverbs, whether biblical ("Lazy people are soon poor" [Prov. 10:4 NLT]) or non-biblical ("A stitch in time saves nine"), are useful in educating both children and adults. However, it should be noted that there is a strong emphasis in the Book of Proverbs that its proverbs, generally, are directed toward pedagogy—the art and science of teaching children. Of course, they are useful in andragogy—the art and science of teaching adults. Yet, so much of what is taught in them is so obvious, so fundamental, so self-evident, that addressing them to adults is a bit odd. If a forty-year-old person does not already know that "Lazy people are soon poor," then attempting to instill that instruction at that age seems a little futile ("A fool at forty is a fool indeed"). Perhaps the proverb "Better late than never" could be true here, but to not know that at that age reveals that they suffer from a serious moral or intellectual malady. This has not been said to discourage adults from reading Proverbs, but to point out the interpretive perspective that they are, generally, directed to the instruction of the young. The phrases "my son," "my sons," and "a wise son" are repeated many times throughout Proverbs, as is "Listen to your father's instruction" and "Do not forsake your mother's teaching."

DIVINELY-SANCTIONED PROVERBS AND NATURAL REVELATION PROVERBS

Biblical proverbs are divinely-sanctioned wisdom sayings. They carry an endorsement and authority which non-biblical proverbs do not. "A stitch in time saves nine" is just as true as "Lazy people are soon poor," but is not "divinely sanctioned." Biblical proverbs are not divinely "revealed"; they are divinely "endorsed." Divine revelation is knowledge we do not obtain through reason or experience, but by an act of God. When Peter declared to Jesus, in Matthew 16:16, "You are the Messiah, the Son of the living God," Jesus replied, "Blessed are you, Simon son of Jonah, for this was not revealed to you by flesh and blood, but by my Father in heaven." Peter had received knowledge by divine revelation.

On the other hand, "Being lazy will make you poor" is knowledge obtained by "natural" revelation—man drawing true conclusions by observing extended human experience. There is much man has to depend on divine revelation to know, but "Being lazy will make you poor" is not one of them. It is not an obscure, esoteric knowledge which can be understood only by a small group of people with specialized interests. A person does not have to attend a Sunday school class, a seminary, or take a hermeneutics course to know the truth of this proverb.

> I digress: *A priori* is Latin for "from what is before," that is, before the senses. *A priori* knowledge is obtained through reason, such as the associative property of mathematics. *A posteriori* knowledge is obtained through empirical observation and experience, like "robins' eggs are blue." These are the two traditional epistemological categories embraced by Western Civilization. However, I have never resolved how divine revelation fits into these two. What category should Peter's knowledge regarding Christ be placed in? I think a third category is necessary—*a revelatio.*

PETER'S USE OF BIBLICAL AND NON-BIBLICAL PROVERBS

There is an intriguing exegetical event in 2 Peter 2:22 when Peter states, "Of them the proverbs are true: 'A dog returns to its vomit,' and, 'A sow that is washed returns to her wallowing in the mud.'" The first proverb regarding the dog is a biblical proverb found in Proverbs 26:11, but the second one is not. It probably comes from a common collection used in the rabbinical tradition, who may have gotten it from the story of Ahikar, a fifth century B.C. Syrian wisdom teacher. It is claimed that he said in a letter, "My son, thou hast behaved like the swine, which went to the bath with people of quality, and, when he came out, saw a stinking drain, and went and rolled himself in it." The dog/swine rhetorical coupling Peter used was also used earlier by Jesus when He declared, "Don't give that which is holy to the dogs, neither throw your pearls before the pigs" (Matt. 7:6 WEB).

Why would Peter treat the non-biblical proverb in the same manner as the biblical proverb? Already in this chapter on proverbs, I have explicitly discriminated between biblical and non-biblical proverbs, but Peter saw no need to do so. Well, for one reason he was not teaching a hermeneutics class, he was ministering the Word. Another reason is the very nature of proverbs. We are all so saturated in proverbial teaching that much of it goes unnoticed, and, in fact, their use is inescapable. Whether we are a school teacher, a minister, a parent, a plumber, or a president, proverbs roll from our lips continuously. There are, and always have been, hundreds of proverbs available for use in human discourse. Listed below are just a few, some of which we are aware are proverbs, but some can surprise us once pointed out:

- Birds of a feather flock together.
- A picture is worth a thousand words.
- There's no place like home.
- The early bird catches the worm.

- Keep your friends close and your enemies closer.
- A bird in the hand is worth two in the bush.
- Strike while the iron is hot.
- Rome wasn't built in a day.
- Curiosity killed the cat.
- You can't make an omelet without breaking a few eggs.
- Blood is thicker than water.
- All that glitters is not gold.
- Don't bite the hand that feeds you.
- A fool and his money are soon parted.
- A fool and his money are soon partying.
- A chain is only as strong as its weakest link.
- First things first.
- It's the tip of the iceberg.
- The pen is mightier than the sword.
- Don't count your chickens before they hatch.
- Love is blind.

Hundreds more could easily be added here. What pastor has not used one of these "non-biblical" proverbs without including the disclaimer, "I'm about to make a point here, but I'm going to use a non-biblical proverb to make it." Pastors, like all of us, successfully utilize this language game.

Proverbs are a strange genre. At the same time, they are both the easiest and the hardest to interpret. They are easy in that we know, abstractly, what they mean. But in application, they depend heavily on interpretation. Sure, "Lazy people are soon poor" and "Strike when the iron is hot" communicate a concept that is undeniable, but will "not being lazy" guarantee a person will not ever become poor? And, is it always wise to jump into the stock market when it is "hot"? Knowing when a proverb applies is the interpretationally difficult thing. Ask Job's comforters.

Job's suffering was not because he was an unrighteous man. Yet, his comforters confronted him with proverbs which they claimed proved his suffering was the result of his sin. They quoted proverbs found in their wisdom tradition, and, while not biblically-endorsed proverbs, these make assertions much like those found in biblical proverbs:

- "Consider now: Who, being innocent, has ever perished? Where were the upright ever destroyed? As I have observed, those who plow evil and those who sow trouble reap it." (Job 4:7-8)
- "He saves the needy from the sword in their mouth; he saves them from the clutches of the powerful." (Job 5:15)

God rebuked Job's comforters, not because their proverbs were faulty, but because they did not apply to Job. Stein explains, "Their error is that they assume that these proverbs are absolute laws without exceptions."[11] Peter had correctly applied his dog/swine proverbs to false teachers, and stated, "*Of them* the proverbs are true. . ." (emphasis added).

PROVERBS ARE NOT PROMISES

To assume that proverbs are making universal truth-claims is to misunderstand their purpose. Many incorrectly

---

11 Robert H. Stein, *A Basic Guide to Interpreting the Bible: Playing by the Rules* (Grand Rapids: Baker, 1994), 86.

approach proverbs as though they were promises. If that were the case, the book should be titled Promises. This interpretive error has caused much unnecessary misery and guilt to parents whose children are prodigal. In Proverbs 22:6, it says, "Train up a child in the way he should go: and when he is old, he will not depart from it" (KJV). Many parents have blamed themselves for the waywardness of their prodigal children. Some of them may have contributed to some of that, but this proverb is not a promise to be fulfilled in every case. There are cases of great parents having prodigal children, and of foolish and debauched parents having well-adjusted and upright children. But the proverb is true when correctly understood as what a proverb actually is. Proverbs 22:6 is saying that parents contribute much to the development of their children, and great care should be taken in their training. In most cases, such training pays great dividends, but not always. When encountering this language game, it is important to remember that there are always exceptions, and that proverbs are not absolute laws like the laws of thermodynamics.

Proverbs, of course, can be found in the book of Proverbs, but also in parts of Job, Ecclesiastes, and James. Jesus used proverbs in His teaching. In Matthew 26:52, we are told, "Then said Jesus unto him, Put up again thy sword into his place: for all they that take the sword shall perish with the sword" (KJV).

STRENGTHS AND WEAKNESSES OF PROVERBS

A proverb's short pithiness has its strengths, but also contributes to some weaknesses. A major strength of a proverb is that its highly condensed form lends itself to easy memorization. In Hebrew, many of the biblical proverbs had some type of sound repetition or rhythm designed to aid in learning. An English example of this is the non-biblical proverb, "An apple a day keeps the doctor away." The rhyme is catchy, and its briefness is easier to retain than the more lengthy, though more accurate, version, "A proper and balanced diet consisting of the five major food groups, fruit and vegetables, starchy food, dairy, protein, and fat, if consumed on a daily basis, will lessen your chances that you will be in need of medical care."

A major weakness of proverbial teaching in Scripture is the tendency for believers to interpret them as absolute truth. Many believe that if they follow the prescriptions found in a proverb, then they have a divine guarantee that positive results will follow. Proverbs 3:9-10 is such a proverb, claimed by many to assure success: "Honor the LORD with your wealth, with the firstfruits of all your crops; then your barns will be filled to overflowing, and your vats will brim over with new wine." But the proverb is stating a general truth, one that is probably going to be successful. It is saying that honoring the Lord is the best chance of success in most cases. However, there is always a possibility of failure. It should be remembered that business failure is not the same thing as moral failure. Many God-fearing people have experienced bankruptcies, droughts, economic recessions, and errant business choices.

TYPES OF PROVERBS

There are various types of proverbs. Prescriptive proverbs prescribe a course of action that the hearer should follow. Proverbs 3:5-6 is an example: "Trust in the LORD with all your heart and lean not to your own understanding; in all your ways submit to him, and he will make your paths straight." Descriptive proverbs simply describe an observation of human experience. One can be found in Proverbs 14:17: "A quick-tempered person does foolish things, and the one who devises evil schemes is hated."

Antithetical proverbs are the most common form of proverbs. There is a large concentration of them found in Proverbs 10-15. They consist of a positive statement followed by a negative statement, or vice versa. The shocking contrast is to spur the hearer to choose a wise course and to reject a foolish course. Proverbs 10:20 is an antithetical proverb: "The tongue of the righteous is choice silver, but the heart of the wicked is of little value."

Another type is numerical proverbs, which follow the formula x / x + 1 in the introductory line, as in Proverbs 30:18-19:

There are three things that are too amazing for me,
four that I do not understand:
the way of an eagle in the sky,
the way of a snake on a rock,
the way of a ship on the high seas,
and the way of a man with a young woman.

CONCLUSION

The goal of this section is to cultivate in the reader a greater understanding of the type of language game played by proverbial instruction, and prescribe some of the rules by which this game is played. The interpretive principles offered here should foster better understanding of proverbs and increase the reader's ability to recognize and avoid erroneous interpretive methods.

PARABLES—THE COMPARISON GAME

This section deals with parables—the language game of comparison. Parables are second order references, and are figurative in nature. They are embedded in a layer of abstraction designed to challenge the will and mind of the hearer. The next three chapters will deal with metaphors, allegories, and similes, which are also games of comparison. The theory of comparison, which I will now advance, applies to all three.

THE THEORY OF COMPARISON

The theory of comparison states that for two different things to be compared, the two must have some points in common, but not too many. To be a "good" comparison two things must have a balanced degree of commonality. An imbalanced commonality will err by having too many points in common, which results in an uninstructive tautology, or not enough in common, resulting in a contradiction.

If someone did not know what an apple was, and was told that an apple is like an apple, then they have been told nothing to help further their understanding. Of course, an apple is like an apple, but this description introduces nothing new. The comparison has too many (all) points in common to be helpful. It's a tautology—saying the same thing more than once, sometimes in different words. Gertrude Stein's "A rose is a rose is a rose," for example. The reason "an apple is like an apple" is not a "good" comparison is that the two have all points in common.

On the other hand, if they were told that an apple is like Elvis Presley, then they have been given a comparison with very few common points—almost a contradiction. An apple and Elvis do have some common, but trivial, points. Both are carbon-based life forms, both have been sighted in Mississippi, and both could be sat on a motorcycle. Yet, this comparison has not advanced, in any significant way, the understanding of what an apple is.

Comparing an apple to a cucumber is a much better comparison. Obviously, the two have many more points in common than the Elvis comparison. But using an orange is even better, and better than that, using a pear is the best of all these options (assuming the person knows what a pear is). The more common points in a comparison, the better, yet a comparison collapses when all points are common.

A good understanding of the theory of comparison is important when approaching the use and interpretation of parables. Similes, metaphors, and allegories are other language games used for comparing, though the rules governing their interpretation vary somewhat. All four of these are used to intensify the impact of a message, to improve communication of information, and to enhance its memorability—shocking the hearers' minds with images.

FIRST, DE-DOMESTICATE THE PARABLES

It is customary to begin an exposition of a subject, like parables, by defining them technically. Though that is important and will be done, it is being postponed so attention can be focused on the *most urgent* need in our times regarding the "interpretation" of parables (particularly the Good Samaritan)—the need to de-domesticate them.

The shockingly brutal impact Jesus intended for the Good Samaritan has been lost through its domestication into a polite, amiable bedtime story. To de-domesticate it, let's start by renaming it. The way something is named influences how it is perceived (fetus vs. unborn child). *That which remains misnamed remains misunderstood.* The name "Good Samaritan" bends our initial perception of it in a direction other than that intended by Jesus. The parable would be more accurately named "The Despised Samaritan."

A TEN-YEAR OLD'S REVEALING WORD GAME

To test the claim that the parable had become domesticated, Stein asked his ten-year old daughter to play a word game with him.[12] She agreed to immediately say the terms which came into her mind when he said a word.

---

12   Robert H. Stein, *A Basic Guide to Interpreting the Bible: Playing by the Rules* (Grand Rapids: Baker, 1994), 143-144.

He said, "Samaritan," to which she responded with terms like "good," "loving," "Christian." On saying "priest," she responded with somewhat negative terms. And, as Stein goes on to say, probably most people would have similar responses, at least to the term "Samaritan." Herein is the exegetical problem—her choice of terms are the exact opposite of the terms that would have been used by Jesus' intended audience.

TRUE PARABLES

Two categories of parables are true parables and semi-allegorical parables. A true parable is one which does not call for interpreting the particulars of the story part. In this type, the particulars serve as props to support the parable's "point." In the Good Samaritan, it really made no difference whether the innkeeper had been given two denarii or six, or whether the man was going down to Jericho or up to Jerusalem. In a true parable these particulars do not have individual meanings. In a semi-allegorical parable, they do.

When Jesus told the Parable of the Good Samaritan, found in Luke 10:25-37, He intended for it to elicit a particular reaction. Of course, He ultimately wanted His audience to repent and obey the Word, but to get there often required Him to shock, offend, bewilder, exasperate, or anger them. Jesus' parables were not asking for platonic, mental assent—He tried and usually succeeded in getting "under their skin." Yet, our ability to "grasp" that intended reaction has been thwarted by a cacophony of well-meaning, though distracting, interpretive "insights." Jesus' intention was not to teach us to be nice to needy people. He did not intend to inform us that oil and wine were used for medicinal purposes in His time. He did not intend to give us a geography lesson when he said the man was going "down" from Jerusalem to Jericho, though Jerusalem is 3,300 feet lower in elevation than Jericho. He was not trying to inform us that donkeys were a mode of transportation, nor that silver coins were used as currency at that time. All these particulars are true, but undue focus on them will "muddy the water" of Jesus' intention.

This was Jesus' intention: to "catch" the expert in the law in a spiritual and moral dilemma, one he was unaware he was guilty of. Verse 29 says, "But he wanted to justify himself, so he asked Jesus, 'And who is my neighbor?'" It is then that Jesus exposes the lawyer's thin and petty self-justifying allegiance to God's Word. The lawyer thought his technical compliance with the love commandments was a justifiable loophole which God would condone. He was wrong.

If it were possible to go back and play Stein's word game with the lawyer, his immediate responses would have been the opposite of Stein's daughter's. For "Samaritan" he would have said, "despised," "hated," or maybe "loathed." For almost a thousand years there had been great animosity between the Jews and Samaritans. The Jewish attitude towards the Samaritans is shown in John 8:48: "The Jews answered him, 'Aren't we right in saying that you are a Samaritan and demon-possessed?'" But our domestication of this parable submerged this detrimentally important fact under many layers of misguided niceties. Likewise, the lawyer's

terms for "priest" and "Levite" would have been positive, opposite of her negative terms. This complete reversal
of terms *is* what eventually occurs in all interpretive communities (sacred or legal), and *is* why attention to sound
interpretive principles is necessary. It is the very purpose
of this book.

THE LOGICAL SHAPE OF A TRUE PARABLE

Figure 1 is the attempt to illustrate the logical shape of a
true parable. Parabolas and parables share a common logical form. They each have a side with a corresponding,
symmetrical, counter side. A parabola has an x-intercept
side with a mirror-image y-intercept side, while a parable
has a picture side with a mirror-image meaning side.

Figure 1.

THE PARABLE OF
THE GOOD SAMARITAN

JESUS'S STORY

THE TRUTH IT UNVEILED

PICTURE SIDE
COMMISSIVE LANGUAGE

MEANING SIDE
REFERENTIAL LANGUAGE

- A GRAPH OF A <u>TRUE</u> PARABLE
- A COMPARISON OF TWO SIMILAR THINGS
- A COMPARISON OF A <u>PARABOLA</u> AND A <u>PARABLE</u>
- WHAT A PARABLE LOOKS LIKE IN LOGICAL SPACE

RETELLING THE PARABLE FOR OUR CULTURE

One way of de-domesticating the parables is to retell the story by interjecting our cultural particulars into those of Jesus' time. If done properly, present-day hearers can better experience what the original hearers "heard." This was done by Fee and Stewart,[13] and assumes a typical, well-dressed, middle-American Protestant congregation:

> A family of disheveled, unkempt individuals was stranded by the side of a major road on a Sunday morning. They were obviously in distress. The mother was sitting on a tattered suitcase, hair uncombed, clothes in disarray, with a glazed look in her eyes, holding a smelly, poorly clad, crying baby. The father was unshaved, dressed in coveralls, the look of despair as he tried to corral two other youngsters. Beside them was a run-down old car that had obviously just given up the ghost.
>
> Down the road came a car driven by the local bishop; he was on his way to church. And though the father of the family waved frantically, the bishop could not hold up his parishioners, so he acted as if he didn't see them.
>
> Soon came another car, and again the father waved furiously. But the car was driven by the president of the Kiwanis Club, and he was late for a statewide meeting of Kiwanis presidents in a nearby city. He too acted as if he did not see them, and kept his eyes straight on the road ahead of him.

---

13 Gordon D. Fee and Douglas Stuart, *How to Read the Bible for All Its Worth: A Guide to Understanding the Bible* (Grand Rapids: Zondervan, 1982), 133.

The next car that came by was driven by an outspoken local atheist, who had never been to church in his life. When he saw the family's distress, he took them into his car. After inquiring as to their need, he took them to a local motel, where he paid for a week's lodging while the father found work. He also paid for the father to rent a car so that he could look for work and gave the mother cash for food and clothes.

One of the authors (Fee or Stewart, they did not say which) tried this once, and from the startled and angered response of the congregation, witnessed that that was the first time they really "heard" the parable in their lives. The congregation, like the lawyer, were not surprised that religious orders other than their own were indifferent to suffering. But surely one from their order would be the chosen virtuous exemplar. Yet, one from their order was not chosen, and, to make matters worse, one was chosen from "the last group on earth" they thought could have been chosen. As Yoda would say, "Caught they were!"

ALLEGORIZATION—A WOLF IN SHEEP'S CLOTHING

I declared earlier that the most urgent need regarding the "interpretation" of the parables is to de-domesticate them. I believe it to be true for our time. However, throughout church history, a different interpretive error has contributed to torturous abuses of parabolic teaching. It is the perennial interpretive error pattern known as allegorization—interpreting language games allegorically when they are not allegories. The Bible does contain allegories (Judges 9:7-20; Ezekiel 16:1-5, 17:2-20; Mark 4:3-9, 13-20, 12:1-11). Interpreting allegories allegorically is legitimate. Interpreting true parables, or hyperbole, or historical narratives allegorically is illegitimate. Hyperbole should be interpreted hyperbolically, parables parabolically, and metaphors metaphorically. Problems arise when a reader mistakes one language game with another, and applies rules to one intended for another.

Again, we return to the Good Samaritan to illustrate this point. While all parables have suffered from allegorization, this parable has suffered the most. The famous fourth-century scholar, Augustine, was part of the Alexandrian school of biblical interpretation. This school embraced allegorization, not only as a legitimate method, but as the superior method, available to the most spiritually enlightened. This method was rejected by Antiochian school as a misguided approach to biblical exegesis.

Augustine advanced the following as an appropriate interpretation of the Good Samaritan:

- A man went down from Jerusalem to Jericho = Adam
- Jerusalem = City of Heavenly Peace
- Jericho = the moon, which signifies Adam's mortality
- Robbers = Satan and his angels
- Stripped him = took away his immortality
- Beating him = persuading him to sin
- And left him half-dead = he became dead spiritually though still physically alive

- The priest = priesthood of the Old Testament, the Law
- The Levite = the ministry of the Old Testament, the prophets
- The Samaritan = Jesus Christ
- Bandaged his wounds = restraining his sin
- Oil = comfort and hope
- Wine = exhortation to labor with fervent spirit
- Donkey = body of Christ
- Inn = the church
- The morrow = after the Resurrection
- Two denarii = the promise of this life and the life to come
- Innkeeper = Paul

This may be interesting, and its esoteric nature may be tempting, yet it is certainly not what Jesus intended. It should be acknowledged that there is nothing inaccurate with the theology of the "interpretation." The theology is sound, and the two sides of this proposal do share a common logical form. But just because two things share a common logical form does not exegetically justify such an interpretation. One should appeal to the clear biblical references to establish this theology, not base it on a specious method. The embracing of this error pattern appears at first to be a small error, but error invites error, and can lead to compoundingly greater errors when extended through time. At the time, the ultimate consequences of the "small" interpretive error were not obvious to the Alexandrian school.

The error was embraced by church fathers, seminaries, universities, and other church institutions. It was a significant element of their exegetical approach to biblical interpretation. Many unwittingly harbored the error without knowing from where it came. Only when the repugnant conclusions to which this reasoning carried the church became obvious was it impelled to retrace its exegetical steps and find where it went wrong. Retracing those steps was the task taken up eleven centuries later by the Protestant Reformation in general and Martin Luther in particular. Luther wrote, "It was very difficult for me to break away from my habitual zeal for allegory. And yet I was aware that allegories were empty speculations and the froth, as it were, of the Holy Scriptures. It is the historical sense alone which supplies the true and sound doctrine."[14] It was after this that the error which first appeared innocent was revealed as the culprit—an allegorical wolf in sheep's exegetical clothing.

"GOT IT"—NO NEED FOR INTERPRETATION

There was absolutely no need for "interpreting" the Good Samaritan parable to Jesus' audience. They knew the cultural particulars needed for immediate, spontaneous understanding. The lawyer "got it." The people present "got it." The disciples "got it." It is us, those separate from that time and place, who must make the effort to "get it." Yet, in one way, we can never get it the way they got it. That way

---

14   Luther, Martin, *Luther's Works Volume 1: Lectures on Genesis Chapter 1-5*, ed. Jaroslav Pelikan (St. Louis: Concordia Publishing House, 1958), 233.

is similar to the way a joke works. A joke works if laughter follows it, or it has failed in its task. If a joke has to be explained, then it has fundamentally failed. Either it was a flawed joke, or, more likely, a good joke told to a person without the prerequisite information.

My daughter and son experienced this on our trip to Townville, Australia in 2004. With some Australian friends they met at church, they attended the movie, Shrek II. In it, the fairy godmother is making a love potion, and one potential ingredient was Ex-Lax, to which my children responded with laughter. However, no one else in the theater laughed. After the movie, they asked the Australians why they didn't laugh. They answered that they didn't know what Ex-Lax was. This is very much like what can occur with the parables.

SEMI-ALLEGORICAL PARABLES

A different type of parable probably contributed to later church fathers' use of the allegorical method, though it should not have been taken as a license to do so. The Parable of the Sower is a semi-allegorical parable, unlike the Good Samaritan, which is a true parable. This parable appears in Matthew 13:1-23, Mark 4:1-20, and Luke 8:4-15. Jesus did not intend for individual meanings to be assigned to the particulars in the Good Samaritan. This was not the case with the Sower. This was one of the parables whose meaning was not immediately understood by Jesus' audience, nor by His disciples.

When asked for an interpretation, He revealed that the seed was the Word of God, the four soils were types of human hearts, the birds were the devil, and the thorns were worries, riches, and pleasures. This was a parable which could legitimately be semi-allegorized. The later church fathers mistook this as an endorsement of full-blown, unbridled, endless allegorization. Of them the proverb is true: give people an inch and they will take a mile.

THE LOGICAL SHAPE OF A SEMI-ALLEGORICAL PARABLE

Figure 2 is the attempt to illustrate the logical shape of a semi-allegorical parable. Many of the individual elements in the picture side have corresponding individual elements in the meaning side.

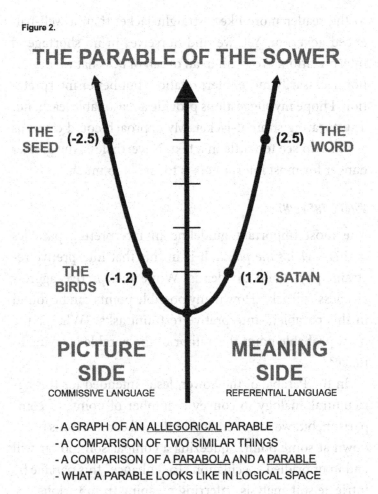

Figure 2.

THE PARABLE OF THE SOWER

THE SEED (-2.5) (2.5) THE WORD

THE BIRDS (-1.2) (1.2) SATAN

PICTURE SIDE
COMMISSIVE LANGUAGE

MEANING SIDE
REFERENTIAL LANGUAGE

- A GRAPH OF AN <u>ALLEGORICAL</u> PARABLE
- A COMPARISON OF TWO SIMILAR THINGS
- A COMPARISON OF A <u>PARABOLA</u> AND A <u>PARABLE</u>
- WHAT A PARABLE LOOKS LIKE IN LOGICAL SPACE

A REASONABLE LEASH OR A STRAIGHT-JACKET

I must confess my natural tendency when it comes to the interpretation of Scripture, or any other texts, which is to favor interpretive restraint, rather than interpretive aggressiveness. I'm aware that my natural tendency could be too restrictive at times, and though well-meaning, may feel

181

to the reader more like a straight-jacket than a well-balanced governor. Yet, we find ourselves in no shortage of interpretation. We swim in an ocean of it. What we need is not necessarily more interpretation, but better interpretation. I hope my suggestions provide a reasonable leash, not a suffocating straight-jacket. My approach could cause us at times to see too little in a text. Nevertheless, the greater danger for most interpreters is to "see" too much.

WHAT'S THE POINT!

The most important guideline in interpreting parables is this—*what's the point?* It is in this that interpretive restraint pays good dividends. While interpretive aggressiveness will ask, "How many possible points can be found in this parable?," interpretive restraint asks, "What is the most probable point the author of the parable is trying to make?"

In the Parable of the Sower, Jesus intended for this agricultural analogy to convey a number of points of comparison, but we must remember that all comparisons break down at some point. Squeezing a comparison too far will end in unbridled speculation. To "enhance" this parable by intricate soil analysis, inferring meaning from various potential bird species that were in Israel, or attempting esoteric insights into sowing methods, all go beyond the objective guidelines which govern the use of parables. Don't allow distractions to erode this important guideline—*what's the point!*

ASKING THE RIGHT QUESTIONS

Examining the questions readers ask about parables can reveal if they correctly understand the language game they are playing. To ask what Nathan's intention was concerning the parable he told King David in 2 Samuel 12 is an appropriate question. What town the rich man and poor man lived in is not. How many children the poor man had is not. Nor would asking how many sheep and cattle the rich man owned be a proper question for this genre. These can be legitimate questions, though, for historical narratives.

Authors record historical narratives with an intention in mind, and the facts of culture, geography, politics, time, and religion dictate and feed that intention. The particulars in historical narratives are non-malleable facts which the author works with and through. The reverse is true for a parable. The particulars in a parable are malleable fictions created by the author to serve his intention. In the first, the intention is the slave to the facts; in the latter, the fictions are slave to the intention.

HYPERBOLE—THE EXAGGERATION GAME

Hyperbole is one of the second order references employed by Jesus in His teaching. He deliberately used extreme exaggeration to stress a point. The effects of this type of figure of speech usually produced outrageous images or shocked the emotions of His hearers—effects not easily forgotten. Jesus knew that relying too heavily on literal pedagogy can be counterproductive, given the way the human mind, heart, and will function. Exaggeration increased the "stickability" of His message for His audience. Exaggeration is not exact. It is not precise. But it is not lying. Lying is intending to conceal—exaggeration is intending to reveal what cannot be conveyed through technically accurate language. Exaggeration "works" when both parties, the speaker and the audience, understand that a language game is being played. Lying is a language game which "works" when only one party, the speaker, knows it is being played.

Hyperbole is a type of commissive language. Commissive language is the language of coaches, poets, artists, and lovers. It sacrifices technical precision on the altar of emotion and passion. Conversely, referential language is the language of scientists, engineers, mathematicians, economists, and physicists. It sacrifices emotion and passion on the altar of precision.

Try to imagine building a space rocket from plans written in commissive language—"Tighten the tank bolts on the five million pounds of highly explosive rocket fuel until the cows come home!" Few astronauts could be persuaded to sit on top of a space rocket built in that manner.

Try to imagine a man expressing love to his lady using literal referential language—"My love, when I think of you, my blood pressure, normally 120 mm Hg systolic and 80 mm Hg diastolic, goes to levels above 140 mm Hg systolic and 90 mm Hg diastolic, almost an 18% increase." No, a lady wants such things expressed with less technically precise commissive language—"My heart is going to explode from all my love for you!"

One category of hyperbole is exaggeration which is "possible" to do, and is known as overstatement. When using overstatement, the author does not intend for his audience to actually do the stated action, even though it would be possible. It should be remembered that second order references do not *say* what they mean, they *mean* what they mean.

In Matthew 5:29-30, Jesus shocked His audience by saying, "If your right eye causes you to stumble, gouge it out and throw it away. It is better for you to lose one part of your body than for your whole body to be thrown into hell. And if your right hand causes you to stumble, cut it off and throw it away. It is better for you to lose one part of your body than for your whole body to go to hell." One of the ways to recognize overstatement is to determine if literal obedience will accomplish what the author intends. Not only is Jewish and Christian theology opposed to self-mutilation, they also know physical mutilation does not produce righteous behavior. A one-eyed person can lust as easily as a two-eyed person, and a one-handed person can continue to steal. Jesus was simply making a true statement in a non-literal, though shocking, way.

The other category, hyperbole, is exaggeration which is "impossible" to do. The Bible, in both the Old and New Testaments, uses these figures of speech to express what literal speech is nearly impotent at expressing. In Psalm 22:14, the psalmist said, "I am poured out like water, and all my bones are out of joint. My heart has turned to wax; it has melted within me." Certainly, these are not literal facts, but are language devices conveying deep emotional and physical distress. In Matthew 23:24, Jesus said, "You blind guides! You strain out a gnat but swallow a camel." This was an effective way of saying that their spiritual priorities were disordered.

One case of hyperbole which is often mistakenly treat- ed as overstatement is the "Eye of the Needle." Jesus said, in Mark 10:24b-25, "Children, how hard it is to enter the kingdom of God! It is easier for a camel to go through the eye of a needle than for someone who is rich to enter the kingdom of God." I have heard, and in years past repeated, the exegetical error which claims that Jesus was referring to a small gate in Jerusalem designed only for pedestrians, which a camel could go through, with great difficulty, if it crawled on its knees. This theology legend, like an urban legend, was probably started with a well-intended, but un- founded, attempt to explain a difficult phenomenon. Once started, these can become part of the culturally assumed backdrop and proliferate through hearsay. This interpre- tive error was printed in *Why Do We Say It? The Stories Be- hind the Words, Expressions and Cliches We Use*.[15]

However, this "exegesis" cannot be found in the theo- logical writings of the early church fathers, and has not been substantiated by archaeological discovery. It appears that it was first proffered by the eleventh-century Greek churchman, Theophylact.

---

15   No author listed, *Why Do We Say It? The Stories Behind the Words, Expressions and Cliches We Use* (New York: Castle Books, 1985), 90.

The following suggestions for detecting statements which are exaggeration in the Bible can be found in Stein's *A Basic Guide to Interpreting the Bible*.[16]

1. The statement is literally impossible.
2. The statement conflicts with what the speaker says elsewhere.
3. The statement conflicts with the actions of the speaker elsewhere.
4. The statement conflicts with the teachings of the Old Testament.
5. The statement conflicts with the teachings of the New Testament.
6. The statement is interpreted by another biblical author in a non-literal way.
7. The statement has not been literally fulfilled.
8. The statement would not achieve its desired goal.
9. The statement uses a literary form prone to exaggeration.

IDIOMS—THE LINGO GAME

A strange phenomenon occurs in the Bible. On the one hand there is a biblical prohibition on hatred, then on another Jesus demanded that we hate our parents. How is this apparent contradiction resolved?

This contradiction only arises when the reader does not understand the nature of the language game being played. It should not be surprising, since idioms are one of the

---

16   Robert H. Stein, *A Basic Guide to Interpreting the Bible: Playing by the Rules* (Grand Rapids: Baker, 1994), 126-133.

most difficult figures of speech to interpret. In 1 John 3:15, we are told, "Everyone who hates his brother is a murderer, and you know that no murderer has eternal life abiding in him" (ESV). Then we are told by Jesus in Luke 14:26, "If anyone comes to me and does not hate his own father and mother and wife and children and brothers and sisters, yes, and even his own life, he cannot be my disciple" (ESV). The tension between these two statements is resolved by understanding how idioms function.

Most idioms have a strong element of exaggeration in them. The "hate" tension here is a case of that. Jesus did not literally mean for His followers to hate. It was His way of shocking His audience. The "hate" idiom was familiar to His audience, it being in the last book of their Bible—"I have loved Jacob, but Esau I have hated" (Mal. 1:2-3).

One of the reasons we know that Jesus did not literally mean for His disciples to hate their parents can be found by comparing the wording of the Luke 14:26 "hate" imperative with the wording of Matthew 10:37. The "hate" imperative is worded by Matthew as "Whoever loves father or mother more than me is not worthy of me, and whoever loves son or daughter more than me is not worthy of me" (ESV, emphasis added). The interpretive difference here is that the Luke version is a case of word-for-word translation, while the Matthew version is a thought-for-thought translation. Luke tells us what Jesus said; Matthew tells us what He meant.

Another way we can tell an idiom has been encountered (given their use of exaggeration) can be seen in five of Stein's suggestions regarding exaggeration:

- Suggestion 2. The statement conflicts with what the speaker says elsewhere.
- Suggestion 3. The statement conflicts with the actions of the speaker elsewhere.
- Suggestion 4. The statement conflicts with the teachings of the New Testament.
- Suggestion 6. The statement is interpreted by another biblical writer in a non-literal way.
- Suggestion 9. The statement uses a literary form prone to exaggeration.

It is helpful to try to comprehend the difficulties which translators face, particularly, the attempt to find an adequate way of translating idioms. To try to translate an idiom in a word-for-word way is almost useless, seeing that the words of an idiom seldom mean anything close to what the idiom *meant* to the original audience. How should the French idiom, "*avoir le cafard,*" be translated into English? If translators use a literal English word-for-word approach, it would read, "I have the cockroach," which does not tell us anything about what the idiom means. A word-for-word translation would be a more literal version, but would leave the English reader with some interpretive work to do. On the other hand, if translated thought-for-thought, it would read, "I am depressed," or "I have the blues." This approach to translation is less literal, but assists the reader in a way which word-for-word does not.

Suppose a baseball fan takes his black chihuahua to a baseball game on a beautiful summer day. During the game the fan says, "Hot dog." How should a translator render that into French? Well, first the translator will need some contextual information to choose which idiom the fan meant, because, given this scenario, there are many possibilities. "Hot dog" could mean:

1. His dog could be experiencing hyperthermia from exposure to direct sunlight.
2. If the fan is hungry, he may be asking a vendor for a frankfurter.
3. He may be declaring that his dog is fashionable.
4. It could mean his dog is one he stole.
5. Perhaps the dog is sexually aroused.
6. The fan's team just hit a grand slam, to which he exclaims, "Hot dog."
7. The dog may be angry.
8. His dog is sick and has a fever.

An American would most certainly choose possibility #6 as the most likely explanation for this idiom. Yet, a French translator may not be culturally and linguistically literate enough with the American context in which this event transpires. One may know everything literally about "hot" and "dog," but that will not help determine what the enthusiastic idiom, "hot dog," means. This is the dilemma which translators face when trying to deal with idioms.

EPISTLES—THE CORRESPONDENCE GAME

The epistles are letters. They are a literary form which facilitates correspondence between an author and their audience. Quite often the author was responding to a letter, one meant to update him on the status of a church and to ask questions regarding theology and church problems.

For example, in 1 Corinthians 1:10-12, Paul says he had been informed by members of Chloe's household. In 5:1 he writes concerning reported information. And in 7:1 Paul states, "Now concerning the things about which you wrote." While the author of a historical narrative does not presume a response, the author of an epistle quite often does. Epistles are more personal than most other literary forms. They are in a sense an authoritative substitute for the personal presence of the author.

Grasping the theology contained in a historical narrative is a more complex task than that contained in epistles. The epistles are more deliberate and directly didactic than other genres. The theology of the epistles lay more closely to the surface than that found in Psalms, prophecies, and the wisdom books. Even without a hermeneutics textbook, armed only with a common-sense hermeneutic, a person can survey Romans and see Paul's teaching concerning God's plan of salvation, from man's sinfulness to justification through Jesus Christ to sanctification by the Holy Spirit.

However, we need to be aware of the problems which arise from the "one-sided conversation" nature of epistles, which can contribute to exegetical (what the text meant to them) problems. Also, we must comprehend the "occasional" nature of epistles and the hermeneutical (what the text means to us) challenges that presents to us.

To say that an epistle is a one-sided conversation means that we are hearing, usually, the answers to questions being asked of the author without the aid of hearing the original questions. It is much like listening to someone on a telephone. Most of us have attempted to determine the content of a phone conversation from listening to the person in our presence, trying to figure out who the caller is and what they are asking or saying. I have experienced this with my wife. From her tone, accent, and vocabulary, I can usually determine if she is talking with a fellow school teacher or with her father in Apalachicola, Florida. Sometimes I can reconstruct topics and occasions they discuss; other times, not so much. Also, it is similar to reading one side of an ongoing text when you were never part of the conversation. In these situations, your exegetical task is reconstruct, as much as possible, the side you don't have from the side you do have.

The "occasional" nature refers to the impetus for many of the original letters sent to New Testament authors regarding questions of theology and advice for dealing with particular church problems. The authors of these New Testament epistles were seldom sending comprehensive works on systematic theology, but writings which addressed particular problems and questions in particular churches in particular locations. Thus, the epistles can come across as piece-meal at times. This "occasional" nature has great hermeneutical relevance to us.

We find in 1 Corinthians 6:1-8 that Paul prohibits Christian brothers from suing each other in the pagan courts of their time. Rather, the disputed matter should be settled by a wise Christian or group of Christians. The hermeneutical question here is whether this applies to me as a Christian in the United States in the twenty-first century. To answer this, we should begin with the exegetical assumption that if all, or most, of the particulars in the New Testament setting match the particulars in my contemporary setting, then the prohibition applies to me.

I have faced a situation where a Christian brother owed me several thousand dollars and did not pay. I felt that the particulars in my case were too similar to those described by Paul in his prohibition. However, there were a few issues which might have given me interpretive wiggle-room for pursuing a lawsuit in court. For one, it was very questionable whether this person was still a Christian. Also, are American courts pagan? Wasn't America founded on Christian principles? American courts are vastly different from the pagan courts of Paul's time.

If this scenario occurred between two Christian brothers in Tibet, the New Testament prohibition would be more binding on them. Tibet, not being Christian, with institutions uninfluenced by Christianity, would share more particulars with the New Testament setting than the two brothers in the United States. It would damage the reputation of a small Christian community for the Tibetans to see these "Christians" fighting among themselves. While the American Christian brothers are bound by the same Christian "non-retaliation" ethic as the Tibetan brothers, it does appear that they could have fewer interpretive restraints.

In 2018, Hurricane Michael, a Category 5 hurricane, terribly damaged the Florida panhandle and destroyed many churches. Our sanctuary was rendered useless. Fortunately, our detached ministry center was able to serve as a temporary meeting place. A roofing company and a remediation company were paid large sums of money, but did not fulfill the terms of their contracts. Our church sued for breach of contract. Were we justified by pursuing the lawsuit or in violation of Pauls' prohibition? It is the interpretive decision of our church, our denomination, and the other American Christian denominations that the particulars are not similar enough to prohibit a lawsuit under these circumstances.

The American Center for Law and Justice (ACLJ) is a Christian organization which represents religious rights in American courts. Some of their clients are Christians who believe their rights have been violated by a government action or by business practices. The ACLJ has received criticism for this activity by those claiming that no Christian should ever sue under any circumstance. They claim that these government agencies or corporations may employ some Christians, therefore placing the ACLJ in violation of Paul' prohibition. Yet, the particulars in Paul's setting are not similar enough to the particulars in this contemporary setting. Still, the justified Christian claimants are morally and spiritually responsible to avoid retaliation as a motive for pursuing lawsuits. Just because a person may be hermeneutically justified does not guarantee that their motives are in compliance with the ethics of Jesus.

There will be times when the lawsuit issue is not black and white. When presented with a gray scenario, reconsider all reasonable options. Attempt to find some way to remedy the problem without a lawsuit. Make certain that the motivation for the lawsuit is not stubbornness, pride, anger, greed, or any other improper motive. Inquire into the possibility that Christian lawyers, mediators, or judges could help resolve the matter outside of the court system.

The main point here is that Paul wants Christians to resolve their differences among themselves, if at all possible.

We find in the epistles much that is cultural. They also contain moral imperatives which are universal, as applicable to us now as they were in the early church. It is our responsibility as disciples to form—and reform—our theology along sound exegetical lines, and differentiate between that which is universally binding and that which is culturally dependent. The occasional nature of the epistles can contribute to some of the confusion between the two.

Lists of inherently immoral behaviors can be found in Romans 1:29-30, 1 Corinthians 6:9-10, and 2 Timothy 3:2-4. These are universally evil and prohibited at all times and in all cultures. It should be noted, though, that Paul does not include in the sin lists issues which are culturally dependent. He does not include eating idol food, women's head-covering, greeting with a holy kiss, long hair on men, women teaching in church, nor does he include his partiality towards celibacy. These cultural issues can cause conflicts for the church in some cultures, but are completely irrelevant in others.

Being born—and born again—in the South, I have grown up in the Bible Belt (under the "buckle" of the Bible Belt, as some repine). Looking back over the last five decades as a Christian, I'm grateful to all those who invested in me spiritually. Yet, some of what these wonderful people imparted as authentically "Christian" turned out to be "cultural." And I in turn did the same thing. Now, through discipleship and study, I can better discriminate one from the other.

195

I became a Christian during the Jesus Movement, which occurred from about 1969 to 1973. During that revival, many hippies came to Christ. At that time our small group was attending a well-established church. Filling the altar of that church were guys with long hair and beards and girls in bell-bottom jeans with tie-dye shirts and flipflops. Things were fine for a while, but when the guys did not cut their hair, shave their beards, and wear suits and ties, and when the girls did not trade the jeans for dresses, tensions arose. We separated from that church and formed our own young people's church and continued ministering to the hippies. The church we left was a good church, and I'm thankful for the good they did do for us, but they made the hermeneutical error of conflating culturally-conditioned requirements with universally biblical requirements.

One of the hermeneutical methods for discriminating between requirements that are cultural and those that are universal is to evaluate if that issue has uniform treatment throughout the New Testament. Women speaking in the church is an example of an issue which is not treated uniformly. First Timothy 2:12 reads, "I do not permit a woman to teach or to have authority over a man; she must be quiet." This passage appears to be a cultural issue, something causing problems in some churches. It is "task" theology designed for a particular problem in particular churches. Women are allowed ministries in other locales. Phoebe is a "deacon" according to Romans 16:1-2. Junia, in Romans 16:7, was a female apostle (Fee/Stewart state that "Junias" is an unknown masculine name). This lack of uniformity demonstrates that 1 Timothy 2:12 is culturally conditioned.

POETRY—THE RHYTHM GAME

The book of Psalms is what usually comes to mind when we speak of biblical poetry, although it can be found throughout the Bible, in both Old and New Testaments. Exodus, Judges, Job, Proverbs, Matthew, Luke, and Colossians are some of the other books where poetry can be found. Poetry is a genre in which the author is much less concerned with technical accuracy. The author is using poetry to reach an audience's emotions and passions. He is attempting to elicit some sort of strong feeling. He intentionally uses imprecise references, sacrificing the "facts" for a wholly other purpose.

Poetry is commissive language. Commissive language is the language of poets, coaches, politicians, people in love, officers leading men into battle, and motivational speakers, to name a few. They use exaggerated, inspiring language games meant to evoke emotional responses in their audiences. They sacrifice precision on the altar of emotion.

On the other hand, there is referential language—the language of computer technicians, contractors, mathematicians, geologists, physicists, plumbers, and dentists. They are concerned with communicating precise information and technically accurate knowledge. It is "Joe Friday" language. "Just the facts, ma'am" was a common catchphrase attributed to him. Sergeant Joe Friday, played by Jack Webb in the 1960s TV series *Dragnet*, was coldly insensitive to the emotional chaos he often encountered as a crime investigator. His express job was to get the facts.

In situations where referential language is needed it can be dangerous to try to communicate using commissive language. The proper amount of anesthetic drugs used for medical patients undergoing an operation should not be relayed by commissive language. There are times we need Shakespeare and times we need Joe Friday. We definitely need to know the difference.

RHYTHM VS RHYME

Though English poetry relies heavily on rhyme, biblical poetry does not. Its poetic feature is mostly rhythm. This rhythm is usually expressed through parallelism, where one line is followed by one or more, related somehow to the first, and approximately the same length. For example, Matthew 7:7-8 states:

Ask and it will be given to you;

seek and you will find;

knock and the door will be opened to you.

Another feature is its terseness. Lines of poetry tend to be shorter than those of prose. They have a much heavier use of figurative language, such as metaphors, similes, hyperbole, and overstatements. We encounter much more literal language in prose.

There are specific forms of the parallelism on which poetry relies:

SYNONYMOUS PARALLELISM

In synonymous parallelism, the lines which form the passage state the same thought in different words. They tend to strengthen or reinforce the first line.

> Proverbs 16:18: Pride goes before destruction,
>
> a haughty spirit before a fall.
>
> Luke 6:27-28: Love your enemies,
>
> do good to those who hate you,
>
> Bless those who curse you,
>
> pray for those who mistreat you.

ANTITHETICAL PARALLELISM

In antithetical parallelism, the lines are composed of a statement followed by a line, or lines, which are in contrast to the first. It is the most common form of parallelism in the Bible.

> Proverbs 10:1: A wise son brings joy to his father,
>
> but a foolish son brings grief to his mother.
>
> Matthew 10:32-33: "Whoever acknowledges me before others, I will also acknowledge before my Father in heaven.
>
> But whoever disowns me before others, I will disown before my Father in heaven."

STEP PARALLELISM

In step parallelism, the line following the first repeats the first, but in a way which steps up its intensity or clarity. This parallelism draws out the implications of the original line.

> Matthew 5:17: Do not think that I have come to abolish the Law or the Prophets;

> I have not come to abolish them but to fulfill them.

> Matthew 10:40: Anyone who welcomes you welcomes me,

> and anyone who welcomes me welcomes the one who sent me.

BIBLICAL POETRY AND PROSE JUXTAPOSED

A fascinating phenomenon occurs twice in the Bible where a historical event is recorded in a prose version (referential language), then in a poetic version (commissive language). These are the explicit juxtaposition of two radically different language games. These two versions conflict with each other, if read literally. Yet, they only appear to conflict to those who are not in possession of the interpretive concepts which inform a correct understanding of the two versions. These are found in Exodus 14 and 15 and again in Judges 4 and 5. Both historical events involve a military conflict recorded in literal prose followed by a poetic account. We will analyze the Judges event.

In Judges 4:14-24, a battle between Israel and Jabin, a Canaanite king, is recorded. Jabin's army is commanded by Sisera. A prophetess, Deborah, said to Barak, the Israelite commander, "Go! This is the day the LORD has given Sisera into your hands. Has not the LORD gone ahead of you?" Barak advances and defeats the enemy, but Sisera escapes to the tent of Jael, the wife of Heber the Kenite. She "welcomes" Sisera, giving him a blanket and milk. Being exhausted, he falls asleep. Then Jael uses a tent peg and hammer to kill Sisera by nailing him to the ground through his temple.

In chapter 5, we are given a poetic version of this military conflict. It begins by stating, "On that day Deborah and Barak son of Abinoam sang this song...." The song (poetry set to music) extends from verse 2 through 31. It praises and glorifies the Lord for the victory. In this song, statements are made which were not in the referential account. Verses 4 and 5 contain claims that "the earth shook, the heavens poured, the clouds poured down water. The mountains quaked...." However, these weather and geological events do not appear in the other account. These events need not to have occurred for these statements to appear in the poetic account. This type of speech is from the common stock of poetic language (also used extensively in prophetic language). A conflict does not occur because these two language games are playing by different rules. We would have a problem if Deborah never existed—we don't if the weather and geology events never did. We do not require the same type of precision in poetry that we require in historical narratives.

This poem includes a taunt, a language game with the intent to anger, wound, or provoke someone. Verses 28 through 30 record the taunt, which was intended to humiliate Sisera and his people. Part of the taunt states that Sisera's mother cried out, "Why is his chariot so long in coming? Why is the clatter of his chariots delayed?" But if some kind of archaeological evidence proved that Sisera's mother had died at his birth and therefore could not have asked these questions, that evidence would not undermine the functioning of this taunt. The particulars of a taunt, or a poem, do not depend on literal accuracy for them to perform their functions. If a taunt angers or provokes its intended audience, then it has done its job.

My daughter was part of a cheering squad in high school. One of those cheers was a taunt aimed at the opposing football team. Part of it referred to Ebro, a nearby small town considered un-cool, and went:

> E-B-R-O, that's where all your girlfriends go,
> to Ebro, to Ebro
>
> U-G-L-Y, you ain't got no alibi, you're ugly,
> you're ugly
>
> D-A-D-D-Y, you don't even know that guy,
> your Daddy, your Daddy

If none of the football players had girlfriends, the taunt would still work its derisive intent. Even if all the players lived with their fathers, the taunt's goal can succeed. In the several years she was a member of the squad, no one ever challenged the "accuracy" of the taunt's "claims." It's all part of the commonly understood poetic license we grant to these forms of speech.

CONCLUSION

From the large quantity of poetry found throughout the Bible, it is evident that the biblical authors intended to do more than appeal to the human mind—they intended to appeal to the human heart and spirit. They used poetry to touch man in a way that straightforward didacticism could not. They wanted to transmit feelings and emotions as well as information and facts. Yet, they never intended for their poetry to be interpreted in the manner of a biblical narrative.

BIBLICAL NARRATIVES—THE STORY GAME

The biblical narratives make up the largest portion of the Bible—roughly 40% of the Old Testament and 60% of the New Testament. Most people first encounter the Bible by way of these stories. For children, these stories inform their moral imaginations and build their metaphysical dream of the world along the contours of a Judeo-Christian worldview. These stories lay a foundation on which the Prophets and Apostles construct more explicit theology. But narratives are certainly not limited to nurturing young minds. They teach young and old alike, by *showing* God's involvement with, and plan for, mankind.

The narrative books are Genesis, Exodus, and the twelve books from Joshua to Esther. Also, sections of Numbers, Deuteronomy, and the Prophets are narratives, as well as the four Gospels and Acts. The Author of the Bible chose narratives for their ability to penetrate the will in ways the more didactic genre could not. "The story does what no theorem can quite do," said C. S. Lewis.[17]

Most scholars refer to these as "narratives" rather than "stories," because "story" can have the connotation of being untrue or mythical. The term *narrative* is less likely to do that. We need to see how the narrative genre and the more explicit theological genres work in tandem with each other. One, the narrative, "shows" us theology; the other "tells" us theology. This tandem approach speaks to the whole person—not just the heart and emotion, but also the mind and spirit.

ARE THE NARRATIVES HISTORY OR MYTH?

Throughout most of biblical history the narratives were treated as history—true stories that occurred in space and time. As we discussed in the chapter regarding the history of biblical interpretation, it appears that the first time they were treated as mythical was during the period referred to as Ancient Jewish Exegesis. In the latter part of this period, some rabbis were influenced by the Hellenistic interpretive impulse to mythologize narratives which embarrassed their philosophical "insights." The Greeks did it to their narratives and the rabbis followed suit. Not wanting to eradicate these ancient texts, they were allegorized. It was the equivalent of "having your exegetical cake and hermeneutically eating it too." The allegorical dragon has

---

17   C. S. Lewis, *On Stories: And Other Essays on Literature* (San Diego: Harcourt, 1982), 15.

as ravenous an appetite for historical narratives as it does for parables.

The next influence which denied the historical authenticity of the biblical narrative came during the Enlightenment period of the seventeenth and eighteenth centuries. It unleashed a skepticism which first targeted pagan myths and later expanded to biblical narratives. This movement sought to undermine any supernatural claims. Again, not wanting to eradicate these narratives entirely, a way had to be found to both discard the supernatural claims while "discovering" the text's philosophical significance. They abandoned the normal method of exegesis—studying the text for the willed meaning of the author—and replaced it with philosophically-friendly speculations.

PRINCIPLES FOR INTERPRETING NARRATIVES

Given the nature of narratives, the theology embedded in them can be challenging to correctly excavate. That is not to say their theology is "hidden," needing some secret interpretive key to unlock an esoteric message, but that the theology is not as explicitly stated as in other genres. Many times, the theology *shown* in them needs to be substantiated by the theology *told* in other parts of the Bible.

The general principles of the interpretive method of grammatical-historical hermeneutics applies to interpreting biblical narratives in much the same way as to the other genres. To avoid mistakes, we are to take the words of the grammar and the facts of history seriously in our attempt to properly interpret them. That, coupled with investigating for the willed intent of the author, is indispensable to sound exegesis. Listed below are a number of other principles needed for correct interpretation and for avoiding mistakes.

1. Narratives record what happened but include many things not theologically endorsed.

2. It must be remembered that narratives are often incomplete accounts but do include all that the author deemed important.

3. Narratives seldom answer all the theological questions of interest to the interpreter. We must limit ourselves to the specific purpose of the author.

4. Narratives can teach explicitly, but in most cases they teach implicitly.

5. Narratives do not always disclose if a behavior is good or bad. It is often necessary to turn to other places in Scripture for answers to that.

6. The heroes and other characters portrayed in these narratives are not perfect and frequently participate in ungodly behavior.

7. While these narratives deal with many actors and heroes, it must be remembered that God is the ultimate hero.

8. It is difficult to determine personal ethics from narratives.

9. Many parts of a narrative do not in and of themselves have meaning. It is essential to include the larger contexts in which the parts play.

These principles and concepts can make the benefits in the narrative accessible to the interpreter, while mitigating much of the interpretive abuse inflicted on this divinely-chosen genre.

> I digress: It is December 29, 2020. I have just finished a long day of writing and am physically aching. My back is strained, stomach is scrunched, and legs are numb. Now I understand Florencio's lament. Scribes of medieval times worked in difficult conditions; many times it was too hot or too cold, to say nothing of the dim lighting. They sometimes scribbled their complaints in the margins of their books. We know nothing about Florencio except his first name and distressing depiction of his craft: "It is a painful task. It extinguishes the light of the eyes, it bends the back, it crushes the viscera and the ribs, it brings forth pain to the kidneys, and weariness to the whole body." The pen is mightier than the sword, and sometimes heavier.

PROPHECY—THE PROCLAMATION AND PREDICTION GAME

Most Bible readers' view of the prophecy books and the prophets has much in common with the great reformer Martin Luther, who said, "They have a queer way of talking, like people who, instead of proceeding in an orderly manner, ramble off from one thing to the next, so that you cannot make head or tail of them or see what they are getting at."[18] And this from someone who strongly ad-

---

18   G. von Rad, *Old Testament Theology, 2* (New York: Harper and

vocated the doctrine of perspicuity—the teaching that the Bible, contrary to the Roman Catholic claim, is not too obscure and difficult for the common people to understand. In Luther's time, the Catholic Church wanted biblical interpretation to be left to church professionals, claiming that the Bible was too complex and obscure for the laity.

Actually, the doctrine of perspicuity promoted by the Reformers and included in the Westminster Confession of Faith says:

> All things in Scripture are not alike plain in themselves, nor alike clear unto all. Yet, those things that are necessary to be known, believed, and observed for salvation are so clearly propounded, and opened in some place of Scripture or another, that not only the learned, but the unlearned, in a due use of the ordinary means, may attain unto a sufficient understanding of them.[19]

I am in complete agreement with this Westminster tenet. Yet, in some aspects, this doctrine has been misrepresented to promote the over-optimistic idea that all Scripture is equally clear. This notion has led to interpretive anxiety for biblical students who approach prophecy unprepared. The initial darkness of this genre can be startling. They need not feel alone. Here are a few comments from hermeneutics scholars:

Row), 1965, 33.

19   Westminster Confession of Faith 1.7.

- The interpretation of prophecy is a highly complex subject ... Henry A. Virkler[20]
- Probably no part of Scripture mystifies and frustrates readers more than the prophets. Klein/Blomberg/Hubbard[21]
- We should note at the outset that the prophetical books are among the most difficult parts of the Bible to interpret or read with understanding. Fee/Stewart[22]
- I was appalled by the vision; it was beyond understanding. The Prophet Daniel (Daniel 8:27)

The good news is that there is a fruitful way to navigate through the quagmire of biblical prophecy. However, it will require more than a casual "devotional" approach.

WHAT IS PROPHECY?

Some dictionaries contribute to the difficulty of understanding what prophecy is by overemphasizing its predictive nature. While predicting future events is part of what prophecy is, most biblical prophecy is proclamation of the revealed will of God. Prophetic books are more "proclamation" than "prediction," more "forthtelling" than "foretelling." The proclamation prophets were more like preachers

20   Henry A. Virkler, *Hermeneutics: Principles and Processes of Biblical Interpretation* (Grand Rapids: Baker, 1981), 190.
21   Dr. William W. Klein, Dr. Craig L. Blomberg and Dr. Robert L. Hubbard, Jr., *Introduction to Biblical Interpretation* (Dallas: Word Publishing, 1993), 302.
22   Gordon D. Fee and Douglas Stuart, *How to Read the Bible for All Its Worth: A Guide to Understanding the Bible* (Grand Rapids: Zondervan, 1982), 149.

or spokesmen. They were covenant enforcement mediators sent when God's people sinned and forgot His covenant with them. They reminded them of that covenant and the consequences of turning from it.

The four major prophets are Isaiah, Jeremiah, Ezekiel, and Daniel. There are twelve minor prophets and their books comprise the last twelve books of the Old Testament. The minor prophets are called minor because of their shorter length, not lesser importance.

ON EXEGETICAL TOOLS

As said earlier, some readers assume that everything in the Bible should be clear and understandable. Based on a radical form of the doctrine of perspicuity and *sola scriptura*, these readers resist the need for study and outside help of any kind. As is the case with "rebellion" theology, an extreme theological issue is rebelled against only to be replaced with its equally erroneous opposite. Too much interpretive dependence on man (the pope and the bishops) degenerated into too little (the Bible and every man for himself). The askance attitude toward outside helps is represented by the seventeenth-century Baptist minister Samuel Howe, who stated that book-learning may

> in its selfe ... be a good thing, and good in
> its proper place, which is for the repayring of
> the decay which came upon man for sin ...
> but bring it once to be a help to understand
> the mind of God in the holy Scriptures, and
> there is detestable filth, drosse and dung in

that respect, and so good for nothing, but [to] destroy, and cause men to erre.

This is from his *The Sufficiencie of the Spirits Teaching without Humane Learning* (London, 1640), C4.[23] Many Puritans shared this view and thought it sinful or quenching the Spirit to use exegetical aids or commentaries in the study of Scripture. For them, the ideal Christian library consists of one book—the Bible.

This *nuda scriptura* attitude, masquerading as *sola scriptura*, is addressed by Samuel Taylor Coleridge:

> The Papacy elevated the Church to the virtual exclusion or suppression of the Scriptures; the modern Church of England, since Chillingworth, has so raised up the Scriptures as to annul the Church: Both alike have quenched the Holy Spirit, as the mesothesis or indifference of the two, and substituted an alien compound for the genuine Preacher, which should be the synthesis of the Scriptures and the Church, and the sensible voice of the Holy Spirit.[24]

Acting in opposition to Howe's incorrect approach, Fee and Stewart strongly encourage the use of at least three exegetical aids in the study of prophecy. Bible dictionaries, commentaries, and Bible handbooks can provide the reader with vast quantities of exegetical material which the

---

23   Quoted in David Lyle Jeffery, *People of the Book: Christian Identity and Literary Culture* (Grand Rapids: Eerdmans, 1996), 273.

24   Quoted in Ibid., 307.

average reader could not, or would not, invest the necessary time to discover on their own. There is no need to reinvent the exegetical wheel. Sometimes, to see far, we need to stand on the scholarly shoulders of giants.

ASSUMPTIONS

When a prophecy was uttered to the original audience, it was generally understood. That is not to say they believed it, but they understood the vocabulary, grammar, and syntax, as well as the relevant contexts. The Prophets and their audiences shared a common set of assumptions and did not need to engage in the interpretive research we must do. One of our tasks is to grasp the assumptions they shared in order to hear the way they heard. These assumptions embody the rules of the language game being played between them.

It was understood by Jonah and his audience that "Forty more days and Nineveh will be destroyed" actually meant "Forty more days and Nineveh will be destroyed *if it does not repent.*" We can tell from the behavior of both Jonah and the Ninevites that they believed it was a conditional prophecy. Jonah, who actually wanted Nineveh to be destroyed, resisted going there because he knew they might repent and be saved. We can tell from the Ninevites' mourning and repentance that they assumed the prophecy was conditional, otherwise they would not have responded in the manner they did.

READING IN ORACLES, NOT PARAGRAPHS

In many types of biblical genre, we are encouraged to read in paragraphs, but in prophecy we have to learn to read and think in oracles. An oracle is a self-contained prophetic message. The passages of Scripture are best interpreted within the context of the oracle in which they are found. This can be difficult, since the beginning and ending of separate oracles is not always apparent. Learning to isolate individual oracles is necessary for understanding the prophetic books.

FORMS OF PROPHETIC ORACLES

Most oracles fall into three categories. Recognizing these forms will aid in comprehending what the prophet is speaking of. As the Bible is composed of various genres, forms, and language games, oracles are variously composed.

Lawsuit oracles follow the pattern of ancient Israel's legal practices. The prophet presents this oracle using the analogy of a trial, where Israel is accused of the crime of breach of covenant. God is portrayed figuratively as the plaintiff, judge, prosecuting attorney, and bailiff, with the defendant being Israel. It follows the court format of summons, a charge, evidence, and a final verdict. The covenant between God and Israel at Mount Sinai (Exodus 24) stipulated punishments for breaking the agreement. Micah 6:1-5 is one example of the lawsuit oracle:

Call to hear   Listen to what the LORD says:

Summons   "Stand up, plead my case before the
          mountains;
          let the hills hear what you have to say.
          Hear, you mountains, the LORD's accusation;
          Listen, you everlasting foundations of the
          earth.

Grounds   For the LORD has a case against his people;
          He is lodging a charge against Israel."

God's   "My people, what have I done to you?
Testimony   How have I burdened you? Answer me.
           I brought you up out of Egypt
           And redeemed you from the land of slavery.
           I sent Moses to lead you, also Aaron and
           Miriam.
           My people, remember what Balak king of
           Moab plotted
           and what Balaam son of Beor answered.
           Remember your journey from Shittim to
           Gilgal,
           That you may know the righteous acts of the
           LORD."

Other examples of the lawsuit oracle are Isaiah 1:2-3, 3:13-15, Hosea 4:1-3, Jeremiah 2:4-13, and Psalm 50.

Woe oracles are another literary form used by the prophets to pronounce disaster or judgment. The Israelites were familiar with the "woe" expression, one used in their ancient funeral laments. These often begin with "Woe to those who...." These oracles detail the evil behaviors which prompted them, and predicted the divine punishments. Micah 2:1-5 is a "woe" oracle:

Pronouncement
of woe   Woe to those who plan iniquity,
           To those who plot evil on their beds!

Offenses   At morning's light they carry it out
           because it is in their power to do it.
           They covet fields and seize them, and houses, and take them.
           They defraud people of their homes,
           they rob them of their inheritance.

Messenger   Therefore, the LORD says:

Prediction of
punishment   "I am planning disaster against this people,
           From which you cannot save yourselves.
           You will no longer walk proudly,
           for it will be a time of calamity.
           In that day people will ridicule you;
           they will taunt you with this mournful song:
           'We are utterly ruined; my people's possession is divided up.
           He takes it from me!
           He assigns our fields to traitors.'

Therefore you will have no one in the assembly of the LORD
To divide the land by lot."

Promise oracles, also called salvation oracles, are another literary form employed in prophecy. These speak of the restoration of God's people. The Prophet Amos proclaimed a promise oracle in Amos 9:11-15:

Future   "In that day

Restorative
Change   I will restore David's fallen tent.
                  I will repair its broken places,
                  restore its ruins,
                  and build it as it used to be,

Blessing   so that they may possess the remnant of
                  Edom
                  and all the nations that bear my name,"
                  declares the Lord,
                  who will do these things.

The reader who begins to think in oracles, instead of the usual paragraph mode, and can differentiate the various oracle forms, will enhance their ability to comprehend the message of God. For them, these prophetic books will be less dark.

THE PROPHETS' USE OF LANGUAGE

Another step in dispelling the darkness which shrouds these great books is grasping prophetic language. The reader must grasp the figurative nature of these books. The reader must be emancipated from thinking too literally, and begin thinking in a referential manner. The language is not scientifically accurate. Much of God's intended message will remain opaque until the figurative nature of prophecy is grasped.

In Isaiah 13:9-11 we find a case of figurative language:

> See, the day of the LORD is coming—a cruel day, with wrath and fierce anger—to make the land desolate and destroy the sinners within it. *The stars of heaven and constellations will not show their light. The rising sun will be darkened and the moon will not give its light.* I will punish the world for its evil, the wicked for their sins. I will put an end to the arrogance of the haughty and will humble the pride of the ruthless. (emphasis added)

Part of the reader's problem is that passages like this do contain literal language with figurative language dispersed throughout it. Progress in understanding these passages is accomplished by learning to discriminate between the two. Some clauses are literal: *a cruel day, punish the world for its evil, put an end to the arrogance of the haughty,* and *will humble the pride of the ruthless.* These are not the clauses which impede most readers' comprehension. It is the figurative clauses, and not knowing that they are figurative, that impede the reader. Once the figurative is grasped, the reader can make interpretive progress. The figurative clauses, *stars of heaven and constellations will not show their light, sun will be darkened, moon will not give light,* can cease to be impediments and take their rightful place in this literary form.

This figurative language is part of the common stock of terminology shared by the Prophets and their audience. It did not serve as an impediment to them. The Prophets wanted to be understood. The cosmic imagery of *darkness* conveyed the spiritual dreadfulness the Prophets intended.

At times, the use of figurative language can lead to some strange implications, that is, if taken too literally. In the New Jerusalem, an odd circumstance occurs. Revelation 21 tells us the city of New Jerusalem will have walls 144 cubits thick (about 200 feet), and will also have gates which never close. Why would a city have both massively thick, impenetrable walls and gates which never close? These are metaphors intended to portray the security and safety of this divine refuge. Remember, figurative language should be taken seriously, but not literally.

READING SMALL SECTIONS

In our study of the Bible, many biblical books can be better understood by being read in one sitting. However, the larger prophetic books were not intended to be read in this manner. These are better digested in small sections. To avoid interpretive indigestion, read individual oracles, a whole chapter, or several chapters. Setting modest goals is advised for these difficult biblical passages. Setting too aggressive goals will lead to unnecessary frustrations. Cut these books into small bits, unlike my three-year-old grandson who will cram an entire sausage into his mouth.

As the reader cultivates his literary competence with the prophetic books, he should learn to find the major points of the text. Too often, the novice reader will fall into the temptation to be overwhelmed by the details.

THE POETRY FACTOR

Since much prophecy uses poetry, the reader already competent in poetry will have an advantage over those who are not. Poetry is to literacy what calculus is to math—for many, its abstractness is too much of an obstacle to bother with. Many who encounter poetry and calculus don't feel smart afterwards, just frustrated. As one lady confessed, "Even as one of the 'smart kids,' I never got it. And sometimes I felt like we were trying too hard to get something. Like maybe there isn't always an intense deeper meaning but we always had to look for it anyway and I didn't often find it." Marianne Moore even begins her poem, *Poetry*, with this line, "I too, dislike it: . . ." These kinds of feelings and attitudes towards poetry, left unexamined, can frustrate our attempt to grasp how prophecy functions. Grasping prophecy will be easier for those who have grasped poetry.

ON PROPHETIC HERMENEUTICS

Once exegesis has provided all the relevant contexts, hermeneutics can begin. As said earlier, exegesis will properly inform and control our hermeneutics, setting interpretive boundaries as to how the Word of God to them becomes the Word of God to us. Both then and now, God's judgment awaits those who hide their greed in religious garb, who defraud the poor, or disregard His moral imperatives.

PROPHECY: A PLAYGROUND FOR MYSTICS

As I have confessed earlier, I much prefer interpretive restraint over interpretive extravagance. I prefer those interpretations which are more objectively verifiable over those whose objectivity is suspect. I believe the goal of seeking the most probable interpretation is superior to seeking a plurality of possible meanings. There is plenty of spiritual nutrition for believers in sound biblical interpretation without the need to try to draw empty calories from interpretations which are squeezed, specious, or novel.

Any reader who has made it this far without collapsing under the weight of the rule-making will have already seen that I enjoy delineating the contours of language and genre. I'm aware this tendency can go too far. My desire to repudiate a "graveyards in heaven" hermeneutic could foster a "straightjacket" hermeneutic. Perhaps a wise middle ground is possible, similar to Paul, who himself was carried up into heaven, but also advised: "Do not despise prophecies, but test everything; hold fast what is good" (1 Thess. 5:20-21 ESV).

Some of the most mystical, outrageous, and implausible interpretations we encounter are those related to prophecy, in particular the book of Revelation. All biblical genres have suffered some degree of torture during church history. The parables have certainly suffered, but the prophesies seem to draw mystical flies like honey. There seems to an international obsession with "breaking the code of the book of Revelation." The obsession has fostered rampant misreading of Scriptures and has produced some bad theology.

I would like to offer readers four suggestions here:

1. We can exercise a high degree of interpretive confidence in most parts of Scripture, but we should exercise interpretive humility towards some of the eschatological books, especially the book of Revelation.

2. Beware of those who promote secret interpretive keys or mystical codes. These approaches are not new—remember that the interpretive errors of letterism, gematria, numerology, and allegorization were of a similar nature.

3. Proverbs 15:22 tells us that there are times when it is safer to take counsel from many advisors. I recommend not straying very far from the major corporate interpretations advocated by the evangelical churches and their scholars.

4. Don't forget that most unique or novel interpretations turn out to be wrong.

PART THREE
REGARDING CONSTITUTIONAL
INTERPRETATION

A HISTORY OF SUPREME COURT INTERPRETATION (REGARDING THE REMOVAL OF PRAYER FROM PUBLIC SCHOOLS)

IN AN EARLIER CHAPTER I dealt with several major issues regarding biblical interpretation through history. This chapter will survey the history of Supreme Court interpretation regarding this issue—*the changing of the Court's behavior through time regarding church/state relations, and how that change led to the removal of prayer from all American public schools.* The goal is to investigate whether this change in the Court's decision-making is hermeneutically justified, or is it the product of "squeezing" or "inventing against the text." Is it a case of sound exegetical reasoning or eisegetical willfulness?

We all know prayer was taken out of public schools. What is not known to the vast majority is the genealogy of the judicial decisions causing it. Nor is it known to the American public whether these judicial decisions can be hermeneutically and constitutionally justified. The change in the Court's behavior over time has affected many other issues of public policy than public school prayer. However, the analysis of this issue will serve as an interpretive test case illustrating what has occurred and how it happened. The same legal hermeneutical methodology which removed prayer from school also affected freedom of speech, freedom of the press, illegal search and seizure, privacy, cruel and unusual punishments, and many others.

To begin, we must first establish the church/state relationship originally established by the Founding Fathers in the United States Constitution. That church/state relationship did not prohibit the states from allowing school prayer. In our present church/state relationship, the federal government now prohibits the states from allowing school prayer. The "Constitution" we now have has changed since it was ratified and is not the same as the one originally ratified. The analysis of the degree of change and the integrity of that change cannot begin without knowing where we started.

PALEO-CONSTITUTIONALISM AND NEO-CONSTITUTIONALISM

We will call the original Constitution and the Bill of Rights the Paleo-Constitution (Paleo-C for short). The "constitutional language we speak" and the governance of Paleo-C has significantly changed into the Neo-Constitution (Neo-C for short) of today. That change, and specifically how it led to the removal of school prayer, is the subject of this history.

TWO METHODS OF AMENDING THE CONSTITUTION

The Constitution can be changed in two ways. First, it can be changed legitimately by the constitutionally-prescribed process defined in Article V. This is the democratic way—the people's prerogative. It was the way the people told the federal government how it was going to be. Second, it can be changed illegitimately by torturous interpretations, produced either by judicial incompetence or malfeasance. This is the anti-democratic way—the Court's usurpation. It is the way the federal government tells the people how it's going to be.

Incorrect judicial decisions which are the results of incompetence we will call "erroneous" interpretations. These could be avoided if judges, like theologians, whose life's work hinges on correct interpretation, will inculcate principles and concepts which are the cause of our learning to understand a text. The remedy for erroneous interpretations is education.

Incorrect judicial decisions which are the results of malfeasance we will call "vicious" interpretations. These are caused by judges who may know proper interpretive principles and concepts, but choose to suppress or ignore them, preferring to implement their political beliefs through their decision-making. Some vice has persuaded them to betray their constitutionally-prescribed role, usurping the authority of the people and the elected branches of government. The remedy for vicious interpretations is force: impeachment.

227

Since it is difficult to determine the legal attitudes and psychological lives of the Court's justices, this history of Supreme Court decision-making will not discriminate between "erroneous" and "vicious" interpretations. We will call both "false" interpretations. It is these false interpretations, *not the legitimate amendments*, which are mostly responsible for the radical change in our constitutional governance. Our allegiance should be to the original Constitution and the legitimate amendments. The illegitimate "amendments" imposed on the States through Court usurpation are not worthy of our allegiance, but are nothing more than false interpretations, which, along with their spurious legal progeny, should be tossed out.

MODELS OF SUPREME COURT DECISION-MAKING

The majority of false interpretations, those inculcating heretical jurisprudence into public policy, come through the "attitudinal" model of Court decision-making. Heretical jurisprudence is that which is the result of Living Constitutionalism and the Doctrine of Incorporation. This model causes the justices to vote based on their attitudes and ideology towards public policy questions. It is contrasted by the "legal" model, which asserts that the justices decide cases by simply examining the facts, dispassionately applying the law to them, and coming to a ruling. The legal model is found among those who advocate some form of originalism: intentionalism, constructivism, strict constructivism, textualism, grammatical-historical hermeneuticism. "Segal and Spaeth allege that some justices' public support of the legal model is simply designed to obfuscate their efforts to write their policy views into the law," writes Drew Noble Lanier.[1]

Because we cannot directly observe the justices' attitudes and ideologies, we have to infer them from the justices' voting behavior. Over time, patterns develop which indicate the model of decision-making followed by Courts (Taft, Stone, Warren, Rehnquist, etc.) and individual justices. It is possible, Glendon Schubert explains, that scholars can validly infer the psychological variables known as attitudes or values which inform their votes on public policy cases.[2]

CHURCH/STATE RELATIONS IN PALEO-CONSTITUTIONALISM

The earlier attempt to form a central government through the Articles of Confederation failed because the central government was not given sufficient powers to function. The nature of this failure demonstrates the degree to which the thirteen original states jealously guarded their independence and sovereignty, and the intensity of their fear of centralized power. The fact that they had not failed because of sharing *too much* power informs us of their mindset and starting point—to err on the side of caution in sharing power.

---

1   Drew Noble Lanier, *Of Time and Judicial Behavior: United States Supreme Court Agenda-Setting and Decision-Making, 1888-1997* (New Jersey: Associated University Presses, 2003), 26.

2   Glendon Schubert, *The Judicial Mind: Attitudes and Ideologies of Supreme Court Justices, 1946-1963* (Evanston: Northwestern University Press, 1965), 27.

Technically, the Federalists were correct that the Bill of Rights was not needed because the States had retained any powers not explicitly given to the federal government in the Constitution. However, the Anti-Federalists demanded a Bill of Rights which did *explicitly enumerate* the powers the federal government did not have, powers the States chose to retain for themselves. Though many believed it a needless redundancy, a Bill of Rights was added.

THE CLAUSES OF THE BILL OF RIGHTS

Of the Ten Amendments listed in the original Bill of Rights, the first eight catalog what Congress and the federal government could not do. Those eight amendments consist of twenty-eight clauses, listing jurisdictions which the States refused to share with Congress and the federal government, and rights they did not want the federal government to deny to their citizens when accused of a federal crime. Each state would decide how these jurisdictions would be managed and the nature of their respective citizens' rights. Here are those clauses:

AMENDMENT I

- 1-a Congress shall make no law respecting an establishment of religion—the Establishment Clause.
- 1-b Congress shall make no law prohibiting the free exercise of religion—the Free Exercise Clause.
- 1-c Congress shall make no law abridging the freedom of speech.
- 1-d Congress shall make no law abridging the freedom of the press.

- 1-e Congress shall make no law abridging the right of the people peaceably to assemble.
- 1-f Congress shall make no law abridging the right of the people to petition the Government for a redress of grievances.

AMENDMENT II

- 2-a Congress shall make no law infringing on the right of the people to keep and bear arms.

AMENDMENT III

- 3-a Congress, in time of peace, shall not quarter Soldiers in any house without the consent of the Owner.
- 3-b Congress, in time of war, shall not quarter Soldiers in any house but in a manner to be prescribed by law.

AMENDMENT IV

- 4-a Congress shall not violate the right of the people to be secure in their persons, houses, papers, and effects, against unreasonable searches and seizures.
- 4-b Congress shall issue no Warrants, but upon probable cause, supported by Oath or affirmation, and particularly describing the place to be searched, and the persons or things to be seized.

AMENDMENT V

- 5-a Congress shall not hold any person to answer for a capital, or otherwise infamous crime, unless on a presentment or indictment of a Grand Jury, except in cases arising in the land or naval forces, or in the Militia, when in actual service in time of War or public danger.
- 5-b Congress shall not subject any person to jeopardy of life or limb twice for the same offense.
- 5-c Congress shall not compel a person in any criminal case to witness against himself.
- 5-d Congress shall not deprive any person of life, liberty, or property, without due process of law.
- 5-e Congress shall not take private property for public use, without just compensation.

AMENDMENT VI

- 6-a Congress shall not deny the accused a speedy trial.
- 6-b Congress shall not deny the accused a public trial.
- 6-c Congress shall not deny the accused an impartial jury of the State and district wherein the crime shall have been committed.
- 6-d Congress shall not deny the accused the right to be informed of the nature and cause of the accusation.
- 6-e Congress shall not deny the accused the right to be confronted with the witnesses against him.

- 6-f Congress shall not deny the accused the right to have compulsory process for obtaining witnesses in his favor.
- 6-g Congress shall not deny the accused the right to have the assistance of counsel for his defense.

AMENDMENT VII

- 7-a Congress shall not deny the accused the right of trial by jury in Suits at common law, where the value in controversy shall exceed twenty dollars.
- 7-b Congress shall not deny to the accused the right that no fact tried by a jury, shall be otherwise re-examined in any Court of the United States, than according to the rules of the common law.

AMENDMENT VIII

- 8-a Congress shall not require excessive bail.
- 8-b Congress shall not require excessive fines.
- 8-c Congress shall not inflict cruel and unusual punishment.

In the era of Paleo-C (1791-1940s), Americans did not look to the US Constitution and Bill of Rights for providing and defining the nature of their religious freedoms. The citizens of the respective states turned to their state constitutions and legislatures for that. I said earlier in this chapter that the shift from Paleo-C to Neo-C significantly changed the constitutional language we speak. Americans during Paleo-C would have thought it strange for someone to say, "The First Amendment does not allow the government to establish a church." During Paleo-C, an American would say, "The First Amendment does not allow the *federal* government to establish a church." They knew the distinction, and that "Congress shall make no law" did not mean "Michigan shall make no law." *Grasping this distinction* between "government" and "federal government" is crucial to comprehending the vast interpretational drift which led us away from Paleo-C to Neo-C. However, since the 1940s, Americans have, naively, come to use "government" and "federal government" as completely synonymous, without the least degree of awareness or caution regarding its implications.

The conflation of government and federal government is evidence that we have lost our understanding of what federalism is, and how to speak the language of "federalism." And we are also losing our grasp on the importance of the way in which words are used in an argument. This loss has led to the sloppy, imprecise use of words, phrases, and slogans, and to the verbal sleight-of-hand jurisprudence which has allowed the authority of the Supreme Court to spread like wildfire into countless areas of personal and economic activity.

An example of the importance of how words are used occurred when James Madison used the word "national" during a debate about the drafting of the First Amendment. One part of a draft read, "infringe the rights of conscience, or establish a *national* religion" (emphasis added). Elbridge Gerry, a Massachusetts representative to the Constitutional Convention, objected to Madison's use of "national," reminding Madison that the government was federal, not national. Madison conceded Gerry's point and withdrew that draft. This is not to say that national was never used, or should never be used, but that in the context that Madison was writing a founding document, federal would have been more precise.

CHURCH/STATE RELATIONS IN NEO-CONSTITUTIONALISM

The Paleo-Constitution and the First Amendment did not provide or protect the religious liberties of Americans. That sounds like constitutional heresy to Americans now, but Neo-Constitutionalism, since the 1940s, has stealthily insinuated into the American political imagination the idea that the First Amendment does—and that is the real heresy. This is not the first time an interpretive community has experienced a heresy becoming so prevalent and uncritically embraced that it becomes the new orthodoxy, causing real orthodoxy to sound heretical. The point, the *federal* point, in the First Amendment is not whether there would, or would not be, religious establishments in America, but who was not allowed to make them. It was not whether there would be, or would not be, freedom of the press, but who was to determine what the contours of that freedom was going to be. It just says that Congress cannot abridge the freedom of the press. Thomas Jefferson's words to Abigail Adams (September 11, 1804) sound heretical to Neo-Constitutional Americans when he declared, "While we deny that Congress have a right to control the freedom of the press, we have ever asserted the right of the

States, and their exclusive right, to do so."[3] One thing is for sure, Thomas Jefferson could not survive a Supreme Court nomination in the era of Neo-Constitutionalism.

Those believing that the First Amendment protects their religious liberties fall into two groups. One believes it has always done that and there have been no changes in its nature or function. The other believes it did not originally protect religious liberties, but now, because of the 14th Amendment, it does.

THE GREAT RICHARDSON-ABBOTT-BISHOP DEBATE

Those believing the First Amendment has always provided and protected religious liberty are misinformed when it comes to its origins and history. That is the case of one writer, Mike Abbott, in an article to the *Panama City News Herald* on August 1, 2008 ("No Justification for National Religion"). Abbott was saying that I was wrong in my July 26, 2008 article ("Court Subverts Meaning of First Amendment") which stated that First Amendment jurisprudence had changed. He asserted that the First Amendment has always protected religious liberty in the manner in which it does today. I doubt the writer is intentionally disseminating incorrect information. Like many others, he is naively repeating what others have incorrectly reported. It is the harmful tendency to cite present-day "authorities" speaking about the Founders, rather than citing the Founders' actual words. These mistakes have resulted in ill-founded

---

3   Letter from Jefferson to Mrs. John Adams, 11 September 1804, *Writings of Jefferson*, 11:51.

constitutional claims which have resulted in the abuses the Founders intended to avoid.

So, how does Abbott treat the fact that it says "Congress shall make no law," instead of "Congress, nor any state, shall make no law"? Also, how does he *interpret* what Chief Justice John Marshall stated in the 1833 *Barron v. City Council of Baltimore* decision, writing for a united court, that the freedoms guaranteed in the Bill of Rights "contains no expression indicating an intention to apply them to the state governments"? How does he *interpret* the 1845 *Permoli v. Municipality No 1 of the City of New Orleans* decision where the Supreme Court said that "[t]he Constitution makes no provision for protecting the citizens of the respective States in their religious liberties; this is left to the state constitutions and laws"? Or Joseph Story, a Supreme Court justice from 1812 to 1845, who declared that the purpose of the First Amendment was to "exclude the national government all power to act upon the subject of religion"? Or when he later said, "the whole power over the subject of religion is left to the state government, to be acted upon according to their own sense of justice, and the state constitutions"? In the light of these facts from the history of the Supreme Court, how could anyone deny that First Amendment jurisprudence has not changed?

The other group is those who acknowledge that First Amendment jurisprudence has changed, but assert that the change is legitimate, the proper result of the 14th Amendment. A person of this group claimed that I and the other writer were both wrong. Nancy Bishop, in her August 18, 2008 article ("Church-State Separation Applies to the

States"), said that she disagreed with him and agreed with me that the change had occurred. What she disagreed with me about was that she believes the 14th Amendment legitimately altered First Amendment jurisprudence. Bishop said,

> What [the] gentlemen failed to mention was that the Constitution has been amended a number of times over the years; and that, in fact, the 14th Amendment, ratified in July 1868, did apply the First Amendment to the states. Therefore, while Mr. Richardson might be correct that the framers only meant "Congress" when they drafted the Bill of Rights, our democracy decided in 1868 to make a formal change to the Constitution and apply those same protections to the states. Our Constitution now prohibits Congress and the states from making any law 'respecting the establishment of religion, or prohibiting the free exercise thereof.' So, I proffer that as of 1868 it has been appropriate for Supreme Court decisions to use language such as 'government shall make no law...' because that is what our Constitution requires.

Bishop's words are a good representation of the interpretive theory that the 14th Amendment does *legitimately* apply the First Amendment to the states. But is the theory correct? I proffer the theory is incorrect. But maybe our disagreement could have been avoided if the 14th Amendment's purpose had been clarified by a Congress near the time of its ratification. Maybe if that Congress still had members who were in the actual Congress which formulated the amendment. Maybe a Congress, with members like that, could have resolved, once and for all, that the 14th Amendment did, or did not, apply the First Amendment to the states. If only a policy entrepreneur had advocated for such a theory, or maybe suggested a constitutional amendment which would have done just that, then perhaps Bishop and I could have never been presented with an occasion to dispute such a theory.

But there was such a Congress. There were such congressional members. There was a policy entrepreneur advocating for such a First Amendment jurisprudence. There was an amendment proposal.

ATTEMPTS TO CHANGE THE CONSTITUTION BY AMENDMENTS

Just seven years after the ratification of the 14th Amendment, Massachusetts Representative James Blaine, believing the 14th Amendment required a reformulation of the First Amendment, proposed legislation which would have incorporated the First Amendment against the states. The proposed constitutional amendment read:

> No state shall make any law respecting an establishment of religion or prohibiting the free exercise thereof; and no money raised by taxation in any State for the support of public schools or derived from any public fund thereof, nor any public lands devoted thereto, shall ever be under the control of any religious sect, nor shall any money so raised or lands so

devoted be divided between religious sects or denominations.[4]

However, Congress rejected Blaine's proposal. Furthermore, twenty-three members of that Congress were in the Congress in which the 14th Amendment was ratified. They knew the 14th Amendment did not intend to apply the First Amendment or any of the Bill of Rights to the states.

Blaine's amendment failed for a number of reasons, one of which was that other attempts even more radical than his had made demands for radically altering church/state relations—Blaine's being moderate by comparison. Neither Congress nor the states wanted to modify the Constitution in a way that would profoundly change the way religion interacted with the states and the federal government. It was feared that the carefully-crafted wording of the First Amendment might suffer not only intended changes, but many unintended consequences which were not in harmony with the church/states relation the Founders intended.

THE DEMANDS OF LIBERALISM

One earlier, very radical, call for change came in 1872 from Francis Ellingwood Abbot, founder and editor of the *Index*. His goal was "to lay the foundations of a great national party of freedom, which shall demand the entire secularization of our municipal, state, and national government."[5] In the "Demands of Liberalism," he specified:

---

4   Congressional Record, 4(1): 205 (H. R., Dec. 14,1875).
5   "The Demands of Liberalism" (April 6, 1872), republished in
     Report of the Centennial Congress of Liberals, 8.

1. We demand that churches and other ecclesiastical property shall no longer be exempt from just taxation.

2. We demand that the employment of chaplains in Congress, in State Legislatures, in the navy and militia, and in prisons, asylums, and all other institutions supported by public money, shall be discontinued.

3. We demand that all public appropriations for sectarian educational and charitable institutions shall cease.

4. We demand that all religious services now sustained by the government shall be abolished; and especially that the use of the Bible in the public schools, whether ostensibly as a text-book or avowedly as a book of religious worship, shall be prohibited.

5. We demand that the appointment, by the President of the United States or by the Governors of the various States, of all religious festivals and fasts shall wholly cease.

6. We demand that the judicial oath in the courts and in all other departments of the government shall be abolished, and that simple affirmation under the pains and penalties of perjury shall be established in its stead.

7. We demand that all laws directly or indirectly enforcing the observance of Sunday as the Sabbath shall be repealed.

8. We demand that all laws looking to the enforcement of "Christian" morality shall be abrogated, and that

all laws shall be conformed to the requirements of natural morality, equal rights, and impartial liberty.

9. We demand that not only in the Constitution of the United States and of the several States, but also in the practical administration of the same, no privilege or advantage shall be conceded to Christianity or any other special religion; that our entire political system shall be founded and administered on a purely secular basis; and that whatever changes shall prove necessary to this end shall be consistently, unflinchingly, and promptly made.[6]

The "whatever changes shall prove necessary to this end shall be consistently, unflinchingly, and promptly made" means to change the Constitution by the amendment process. The Liberals and anti-Christian secularists openly acknowledged that the US Constitution was a barrier to the model of church/state relations they preferred. Therefore, they struggled to establish their model by constitutional amendment. (While I don't admire their goals, I do admire their methods. Those were the days before Living Constitutionalism, when people had the integrity to play by the rules. However, Living Constitutionalism's progeny discovered that they could circumvent the legitimate constitutional procedures for "amending" the Constitution. Its progeny now knows they can simply ask an ignorant or vicious Court to gift to them their policy preferences.)

Beginning on January 1, 1874, the content and spirit of the "Demands of Liberalism" solidified into a proposal for

---

6   Ibid.

a constitutional amendment. This proposal ran every week for two years in the *Index*:

> SECTION 1.—Congress shall make no law respecting an establishment of religion, or favoring any particular form of religion, or prohibiting the free exercise thereof; or abridge the freedom of speech or of the press, or the right of the people peaceably to assemble and to petition the Government for a redress of grievances.
>
> SECTION 2.—No State shall make any law respecting an establishment of religion, or favoring any particular form of religion, or prohibiting the free exercise thereof; or abridge the freedom of speech or of the press, or the right of the people peaceably to assemble and to petition the Government for a redress of grievances. No religious test shall ever be required as a condition of suffrage, or as a qualification to any office or public trust, in any State; and no person shall ever in any State be deprived of any of his or her rights, privileges, or capacities, or disqualified for the performance of any public or private duty, or rendered incompetent to give evidence in any court of law or equity, in consequence of any opinion he or she may hold on the subject of religion.
>
> SECTION 3.—Congress shall have power to enforce the provisions of the second section of this Article by appropriate legislation.

The *Index* explained that the proposed amendment was necessary because the Constitution contained no provision prohibiting the states from restricting religious freedom, saying "this enlargement of the First Amendment, in order to secure to the people the full and unrestricted enjoyment of religious liberty."[7] Certainly, Abbot, the Liberals, and their National Liberal League had the right to advance such an agenda in their desire to modify church/state relations, but elected branches of Congress and the states also had the right to disagree with and refuse to adopt their proposal. Congress and the states saw this as an unworkable secular vision.

Congress and the states feared that such an amendment might tilt church/state relations too far towards the anti-religious, anti-Christian Liberals. Silly as it might seem, they feared that that kind of amendment, and the spirit which animated it, might one day make it unconstitutional:

- for a classroom library to contain books which deal with Christianity or for a teacher to be seen with a personal copy of the Bible at school. *Roberts v. Madigan,* 1990.
- for a Board of Education to "reference" God or "Biblical instruction" in any of its official writings related to standards for operation of schools. *State v. Whisner,* 1976.
- for a war memorial to be erected in the shape of a cross. *Lowe v. City of Eugene,* 1969.

---

7   Ibid., 21.

- for the Ten Commandments to hang on the walls of a classroom, even if they are purchased by private funds. *Stone v. Graham,* 1980.
- for a bill to be introduced by a legislator who had a religious purpose in mind, even though the wording may be constitutionally acceptable. *Wallace v. Jaffree,* 1985.
- for a graduation ceremony to contain an opening or closing prayer. *Graham v. Central Community School District,* 1985.
- for a city seal to depict religious heritage or any religious element of the community. *Robinson v. City of Edmond,* 1995.
- for a kindergarten class to ask during a school assembly whose birthday is celebrated on Christmas. *Florey v. Sioux Falls School District,* 1979.
- for a student to pray out loud over lunch. *Reed v. van Hoven,* 1965.
- for kindergarten students to recite: "We thank you for the birds that sing; We thank you [God] for everything," even though the word "God" is not uttered. *DeSpain v. DeKalb County Community School District,* 1967.
- for a public cemetery to have a planter in the shape of a cross because it might cause "emotional distress" and constitute an "injury-in-fact." *Warsaw v. Tehachapi,* 1990.

But, certainly, these were just "hypothetical fears" which could not result from federal actions. They chose instead to stay with the Founder's vision of church/state relations and did not alter the Constitution or Bill of Rights. Their rejection of this secular amendment and of Blaine's, especially in such close temporal proximity to the passage of the 14th Amendment, was proof positive that the 14th Amendment had not applied the First Amendment to the states. Their reactions "ensured" that the power of the federal government could not be brought against the states to force them to adopt the Liberals' secular agenda. Right?!

Prior to the Liberals' secular amendment, Congress and the states had similarly rejected an amendment they feared might tilt church/state relations too far toward the theocratic side. Starting in 1863, a small proportion of American Protestants, working through the National Reform Association, began introducing various forms of a Christian Amendment. They demanded a constitutional amendment to more explicitly recognize America's Christianity in the preamble of the US Constitution. Of course, Abbot, the Liberals, and the National Liberal League objected, saying,

> [i]t will be the overthrow of the Free Republic and the creation of a Christian Theocracy instead. It will be the formal abolition of the great principle of separation of Church and State, to which we owe the unparalleled civil liberty we enjoy. It will be the restoration to power and influence of the Christian clergy as the recognized priesthood of a Christian State.[8]

---

8   "The Proposed Christian Amendment," *Index*, 3 (no. 106): (Jan. 6, 1872).

But opposition to the Christian amendment proposal did not come only from the secularists; it was also not supported by the American church at large. The *Evangelist* viewed the National Reform Association's proposal as "a forlorn hope."[9] As even the *Index* reported, "the Protestant public ... to-day" was "[u]nprepared ... to carry out the plans" demanded by the NRA.[10]

CONGRESS DID NOT SING THE "SONG FOR LIBERALS"

The Christian amendment, like the secular amendment, failed spectacularly. Congress and the states chose to preserve the founding documents, resisting the temptation of both alternatives. For sure, they did not sing the "Song for Liberals":

We want no counsel from the priests,

No bishop's crook or gown,

No sanctimonious righteousness,

No curse or godly frown.

We want no Bibles in the schools,

No creeds nor doctrines there;

We want no superstition's tools

The children's minds to scare.

---

9   Daniel G. Strong, "Supreme Court Justice William Strong, 1808—1895: Jurisprudence, Christianity and Reform," (Ph.D. diss., Kent State University, 1985).

10   "The Proposed Christian Amendment," *Index*, 3 (no. 106): (Jan. 6, 1872).

We want the rights of liberty,

With reason's lamp to try

Each word and thought of other men

To solve our destiny.[11]

CRAFTING CONSTITUTIONAL WORDING

The wording of the Constitution and Bill of Rights were originally debated, discussed, proposed, written, redebated, rewritten, rejected, altered, rediscussed, and again rewritten until the delegates reached agreement on the founding documents. They had risked their lives, fortunes, and futures to win their independence and liberty, and, while making the nation's founding documents, were not about to rashly make a constitution whose wording was going to be easily susceptible to vicious interpretations from religious zealots on the one hand or from secular zealots on the other. They were well aware that hasty, vague language and careless sloganeering could be the avenue for the unscrupulous in power to wrest away what they so painfully won. They selected each word intentionally.

Regarding the meticulous attention necessary in forming constitutions and their amendments, the Presbyterian clergyman, Samuel Spear, who became the editor of the *Independent*, submits a clear warning. When President Grant proposed a constitutional amendment that would directly

---

11   "A Song for Liberals," in *The Truth Seeker Collection of Forms, Hymns, and Recitations. Original and Selected—For the Use of Liberals* (New York: Liberal & Scientific Publishing House, 1877), 377-378.

declare "Church and State forever separate and distinct," Spear objected, saying,

> [t]his language is altogether too general, too ambiguous, and too susceptible of *diverse constructions* to be of any practical service.... A mere general dogma on any subject will not do for a constitutional law. Making constitutions which are to be the basis of powers to be exercised, or restraints to be imposed and enforced, is a work that demands the utmost accuracy in the use of words.[12] (emphasis added)

The absence of exaggeration, metaphors, and other figures of speech should be noted. While these, especially metaphors, are of great use and force in making language colorful and poetic, they lack the precision and specificity needed for legal and governing discourse. The great English jurist Lord Mansfield warned, "nothing in law is so apt to mislead as a metaphor."[13] Also, Judge Benjamin N. Cardozo further warned, "Metaphors in law are to be narrowly watched, for starting as devices to liberate thought, they end by enslaving it."[14]

---

12   Samuel T. Spear, *Religion and the State* (New York: Dodd, Mead & Co. 1876), 22.

13   Wesley Newcomb Hohfeld, "Fundamental Legal Conceptions as Applied in Judicial Reasoning," *Yale Law Journal* 26, no. 4 (1916-1917): 711-712.

14   *Berkey v. Third Ave.*, Ry. Co., 244 N.Y. 84, 94, 155 N.E. 58, 61 (1926).

FOUR GOVERNMENTAL MODELS

In the twenty-first century, a society organizing a government can choose from four basic models. In the eighteenth century, the Founding Fathers could choose between three. The fourth model, to be addressed below—radical atheistic anti-religious and anti-clerical secularism—had not fully presented itself yet. It was in its incipiency in the French Revolution, prior to Robespierre's Reign of Terror. History shows that theocratic regimes had their abuses and "Inquisitions," but secular regimes had not yet implemented the most colossal case of political carnage in history. The planetary tragedy of the union of "atheism and State" cost the lives of between 85 million and 100 million people. The eighteenth century was before Stalin's Gulag Archipelago, Mao's Great Leap Forward and Cultural Revolution, Fidel Castro's Cuba, and Pol Pot's Khmer Rouge and Killing Fields. John Adams had warned Thomas Jefferson not to assume that the French Revolution was commensurate with the American Revolution.

THE THEOCRATIC MODEL

The first model of government is the theocratic model. In a theocracy the state submits to religion. There is no institutional separation between religion and government, and the government has no control over the functional interaction of the two. It is religious totalitarianism. The clergy or priests hold power over all religious and governmental issues. Examples from the past are ancient Egypt, China, Tibet, ancient Israel, and the Islamic caliphates of Rashidun,

Umayyad, Abbasid, and Ottoman. Theocracies can be found in various form of caesaropapism, where "Caesar" is also the supreme head of the church, the two forming a single power structure. In theocracies, there is no separation between "church" and state.

THE AMERICAN MODEL

The second is the American model. In it, the state does not submit to religion, nor does religion submit to the state. There is institutional separation but much functional interaction. Religion is allowed to influence government through democratic means, without the hostility of anti-religious animus. The church is seen as a legitimately cooperative force in the public square, struggling for influence alongside other forces, such as business, entertainment, education, sports, etc. The American model is a moderate model, and embraces a moderate understanding of "separation of church and state." In it, the state, while not hostile to religion, draws back from direct institutional involvement in religion and acknowledges the autonomy of religious institutions.

THE FRENCH MODEL

The third is the modern French model. In it, the state does not submit to religion, but religion is not afforded the same access to the public square as in the American model. There are residues of the anti-religious animus which were politically established during the French Revolution. There is institutional separation, but the functional interaction is attenuated. At best, there is a rather benign

251

attitude toward religion. Religion is viewed as a strictly private matter, and the state is considered to be the final arbiter of moral values. In France, religion is told to "ride in the back of the bus." Private religion is protected by law, but explicit religious symbols and expressions are barred from political life. In it, there is a stricter separation of church and state.

THE COMMUNIST MODEL

The fourth model is the one of the Soviet Union and the other communist countries. In it, religion submits to the state. There is total institutional separation and no functional interaction. In it, the relationship is anything but benign. This malevolent model evicts religion completely from public life, while also working to eradicate it. The "wall of separation between church and state" is a circular one built around the church. In it, there is the strictest version of separation of church and state.

THE PRESENT STRUGGLE IN AMERICA

The Founding Fathers constructed the American democratic experiment along the lines of the second model described above. The Founders knew the American Revolution was a pro-religious, pro-clergy event. They remembered how the "Black Robed Regiment," the American patriot preachers, were hated and feared by the British, and how they threw their religious support behind the American cause. But forces in America have for some time now been attempting to reshape the American model along the lines of the French model. Groups such as the American Civil Liberties Union and Americans for the Separation of Church and State drink from the cup of the French Revolution, not the American Revolution. These groups have the right to advocate for their desired changes, but changes they are. Their goal is a "return" to the founders' vision, but those founders are the ones of the French Revolution. Concerning their "history" of America's founding and Founders, their analysis is wrong, their history is wrong, and the exegesis is wrong. Their too general, too ambiguous, and too imprecise sloganeering have greatly damaged the American Founders' vision, and have insinuated into American jurisprudence views alien to those of the Founders.

America witnessed an increase in the attempt to move America closer to the French model during the Obama administration. In hostility towards religion, his administration lawyers openly used the courts to coerce religious institutions into suppressing their theological doctrines when they conflicted with secular liberal doctrines. As R. R. Reno said, "We're in the midst of climate change—one that is getting colder and colder towards religion."[15]

If you think that Obama's administration was not hostile towards religion, or that it was not advocating radical positions outside American political and legal norms, then consider this case. A former teacher filed an employment lawsuit claiming discrimination based on disability. Her employer, Hosanna-Tabor Evangelical Lutheran Church and School, fired her for violating the biblical injunction

---

15   R. R. Reno, at Hillsdale College February 20, 2013, National Leadership Seminar, Bonita Springs, Fl.

against Christians suing each other in court. American jurisprudence views such cases as Free Exercise covered under the First Amendment. This is known as the ministerial exemption.

However, Obama administration lawyers demanded "change"—they claimed that there should be no ministerial exemption. The 2012 Supreme Court decision revealed how shockingly radical Obama and his anti-religious foot soldiers were. The Court, in a rare instance of unanimity, ruled 9-0 in favor of religious freedom for the church based on the ministerial exemption. When so many Court decisions are 5-4 splits, that unanimity was a stark testimony to the President's anti-religious extremism. In this case, and in his attempt to force the Little Sisters of the Poor into secular submission, Obama revealed an animus like that found in the French approach to church-state relations. For him, religious values should succumb to legal coercion if found contrary to liberal secular views.

Pushing American governance back towards the Founders' American model, President Trump, three months into his administration, addressed religious leaders in the Rose Garden. Present among them were two of the sisters of the Little Sisters of the Poor. They had endured years of governmental harassment for objecting to the Obama-era contraception mandate which violated their religious doctrines. President Trump proclaimed, "Your long ordeal will be soon be over." President Trump's administration, within one year, brought to closure the majority of the religious conscience lawsuits which had stretched on for almost the entire duration of the Obama administration. But how

A History of Supreme Court Interpretation

long before Joe Biden revives governmental coercion of religion?

THE SECULAR IMPERATIVE

Another manifestation of the effort to bring America closer to the French model, demanding that religion "sit quietly in the back of the bus," can be seen in the secular logic of Federal Judge Vaughn Walker. In 2010, he overturned Proposition 8, the ballot measure that reversed the California Supreme Court's 2006 decision that homosexuals have a right to marry. His anti-religious logic stated, "The evidence shows conclusively that Proposition 8 enacts, without reason, a private moral view that same-sex couples are inferior to opposite-sex couples." That religious convictions were allowed to influence public policy is unacceptable in Judge Walker's church/state model. Earlier, Judge Anthony Kennedy noted in *Lawrence v. Texas* that moral censure of homosexuality has "been shaped by religious beliefs."[16]

Thus, the secular imperative here is that only secular-based "logic" and "decision-making" are allowed into the public square. Religious voters are to be disenfranchised by legal means and by ideological intimidation. The church must not acquiesce to this secular imperative. Religious voters must revolt against such intimidation.

---

16   Lawrence v. Texas, 539 U.S. 558.

THE PIETISTIC IMPERATIVE

While secular forces attempt to dissuade the religious from participating in the public square, pietism from within the church promotes the same. Though piety (right living) is a good thing, and one cannot be a Christian without it, pietism, on the other hand, is a defective view. As Francis Schaeffer stated,

> Pietism began as a healthy protest against formalism and a too abstract Christianity. But it had a deficient, "platonic" spirituality. It was platonic in the sense that Pietism made a sharp division between the "spiritual" and the "material" world—giving little, or no, importance to the "material" world.... Christianity and spirituality were shut up to a small, isolated part of life. The totality of reality was ignored by pietistic thinking.[17]

Aided by the "wall of separation," fabricated and erected by Justice Hugo Black in the *Everson v. Board of Education* decision (1947), the secularists imposed, from the outside, a "wall" dividing religion from much of its participation in the public square. The Pietists, from the inside, imposed a "wall" dividing religion from the same. The secularists said the public square was too important; the Pietists said it was too unimportant. In the sixteenth century, the Anabaptists' *Schleitheim Confession* proclaims "that it is not appropriate for a Christian to serve as a magistrate because

---

17   Francis Schaeffer, *The Complete Works of Francis A. Schaeffer: A Christian Manifesto* (CITY: Crossway Books, 1982), 424.

of these points: The government's magistracy is according to the flesh, but the Christians' is according to the Spirit; their houses and dwelling remain in this world, but the Christians' citizenship is in heaven."[18] In the seventeenth century, Roger Williams advanced the belief that the division between the spiritual and the worldly were so severe that they seemed totally irrelevant to each other. In 1797 a "Friend to the Clergy" admonished ministers, "You are not to profane the sacred desk by party rage, therefore, a less attention to politics, and a greater to the religion you profess, would be more congenial to the principles of the gospel, and consequently more useful to the people."[19]

A prominent Pietistic-type argument for keeping religion and politics separate appeared in 1800 in *A Solemn Address to Christians and Patriots* by Tunis Wortman. He wrote that "it is your duty, as Christians, to maintain the purity and independence of the church, to keep religion separate from politics, to prevent an union between the church and the state, and to preserve your clergy from temptation, corruption and reproach."[20]

---

18   The Schleitheim Confession of Faith, Michael Sattler, 1527
     trans. J. C. Wenger, *Mennonite Quarterly Review* xix, 4 (October,
     1945), 247-253.
19   "A Friend to the Clergy," "To the Association of Ministers in and
     about Cambridge," in ibid., vol. 29, no. 1728 (Oct. 12-16, 1797).
20   Tunis Wortman, *A Solemn Address to Christians and Patriots*
     (New York: 1800, in *American Political Sermons of the Founding
     Era, 1730-1805*, ed. Ellis Sandoz (Indianapolis: Liberty Press,
     1991).

THE PIETISTIC IMPERATIVE REFUTED

The Pietistic imperative was not embraced by all. One of the ministers refuting it was the Rev. John Mitchell Mason, advancing the right of "religion" to address itself to politics. Arguing that religion concerned all of life, including politics, he declared,

> And what is religion? Is it not an obligation to the service of God, founded on his authority, and extending to all relations personal and social? Yet religion has nothing to do with politics! Where did you learn this maxim? The Bible is full of directions for your behavior as citizens. It is plain, pointed, awful in its injunctions on rulers and ruled as such: yet religion has nothing to do with politics. You are commanded 'in ALL your ways to acknowledge him.' 'In EVERY THING, by prayer and supplication, with thanksgiving, to let your request be made known unto God,' 'And WHATSOEVER YE DO, IN WORD AND DEED, to do ALL IN THE NAME of the Lord Jesus.' Yet religion has nothing to do with politics! Most astonishing! And is there any part of your conduct in which you are, or wish to be, without law to God, and not under the law of Christ? ... Can you persuade yourselves that political men and measures are to undergo no review in the judgement to come? That all the passion and violence, the fraud and falsehood, and corruption which pervade the systems of party, and burst out

like a flood at the public elections, are to be
blotted from the catalogue of unchristian
deeds, because they are politics? Or that a
minister of the gospel may see his people, in
their political career, bid defiance to their God
in breaking through every moral restraint,
and keep a guiltless silence because religion
has nothing to do with politics?[21]

Many tried to deter the Rev. Alexander M'Leod from discussing public affairs in the pulpit. When he began his
career he was called to a church which had slave-owning
members. He maintained that they could not remain as
church members while owning slaves. His position was
elaborated in a sermon, "Negro Slavery Unjustifiable." He
took his rejection of the Pietistic imperative's separation
of religion and politics further in his discourse showing
that "Ministers have the right of discussing from the pulpit
those political questions which affect Christian morals."
He looked askance at Pietism's separation logic, for

the separation cannot be complete, unless all
Christians are secluded from every concern in
national politics: and the entire management
devolved upon those, who will not be tempted
to think of the bible, as the rule, as the principle,
according to which civilians should act: and
where would this end; but in the transfer of

---

21   John Mitchell Mason, *The Voice of Warning, to Christians, on
     the Ensuing Election of a President of the United States*, 35 (New
     York: 1800).

the undivided management of national affairs
into the hands of infidels.[22]

SECULARISTS GRANTED VETO POWER BY A SUPREME COURT DISASTER

For a hundred and fifty years, a delicate balance existed in
the United States regarding the role of religion in public
life. The approach to that role avoided the religious totalitarianisms found throughout history and in most Muslim
countries today. On the other hand, it avoided the secular totalitarianisms found in the French Revolution, China, Cuba, North Korea, and in the former Soviet Union.
Fortunately, in the US, the extreme versions of the secular imperative and the Pietistic imperative were avoided
by the fusion of the Protestant mentality, its cautious view
of human nature, and its reliance on separation of powers
and checks and balances. America's metaphysical dream of
government is summarized by Reinhold Niebuhr: "Man's
capacity for justice makes democracy possible, but man's
inclination to injustice makes democracy necessary."[23]

Then a disaster occurred. In 1947, the secularists were
given federal governmental veto power over the religious lives of millions of Americans and all the states. The

22 Alexander M'Leod, "Negro Slavery Unjustifiable"
    (Advertizement) (New York: 1802). Ibid. See Paul Patton Harris,
    "Alexander McLeod," in *Dictionary of American Biography* (New
    York: c. Scribner's Sons, 1943).
23 Reinhold Niebuhr, *The Children of Light and the Children of
    Darkness* (Chicago: University of Chicago Press, 2011 [reprint]),
    xxxii.

secularists' veto power was not acquired by a constitutional amendment, where the states, by democratic means, conscientiously relinquished vast areas of their autonomy and independence. Rather, that veto power was gifted to them by the Supreme Court's incompetent, or malicious, *Everson v. Board of Education* decision. The logic of that decision handed the secularists a cudgel with which to drive religion from its hundred-and-fifty-year role in the public square.

I will address this disastrous decision and its role in terminating the Paleo-Constitution and in inaugurating the Neo-Constitution and how that led to the removal of public school prayer. But before that, I want to show the foolishness of the untenable proposition that religion should stay out of politics.

RELIGION AND ITS ROLE IN THE PUBLIC SQUARE

Religion should have a role in the public square. But, like all the other public square participants, it can, if allowed, monopolize in dominating ways. Religion, as we know from history and experience, is not immune to the temptation to dominate every sphere of human life. It is for obvious reasons that much attention is now focused on Islam. Yet, religion's ambitions on monopolizing the public square is not limited to the jihadists. Religion is similarly tempted in India by the ideology of *hindutva*, by powerful groups in Russian Orthodoxy demanding a "monolithic unity of church and state," by some groups of Orthodox Jews in Israel calling for the ideal of a halakhic state.

Society's goal should not be a religious public square, or a secular public square, but a civil public square, where diverse ideas are proffered, debated, embraced, or rejected through democratic civil means.

THE REV. MARTIN LUTHER KING, JR. VERSUS THE SECULAR AND PIETISTIC IMPERATIVES

If the secular imperative demands that religious beliefs and religiously-motivated voices be dismissed from public life, how do they account for the Rev. Martin Luther King, Jr.'s role in America's public life? If the Pietistic imperative demands that the pulpit is no place to address "worldly" issues, how do they account for his "ministry"?

Does not the framing of these questions place both imperatives in an ideological quandary? Isn't this similar to the quandary the chief priests and the teachers of the law found themselves in when Jesus asked them, "Tell me, John's baptism—was it from heaven, or from men?" They knew if they said, "From heaven," He would ask, "Why didn't you believe him?" But if they said, "From men," they feared the people would stone them. Their final answer was, "We don't know where it was from."[24]

So how are secularists and Pietists going to fit "**Reverend**" King's role into their programs? If they embrace him and his methods, they must repudiate their respective imperatives. If they continue to embrace their respective imperatives, they must repudiate him. Their final answer may be, "We don't know what to do with him."

---

24   Matthew 21:24-27.

Because of the consequences of the disastrous Supreme Court decisions in Everson (1947) and Engels (1962), many in public education, fearing the wrath of the ACLU, steer clear of controversy by side-stepping King's religious motivations. He is regarded as a civil rights leader, but his religious influences are attenuated, to avoid violating the "separation of church and state" regime's lawsuits. They are frightened away from teaching historical facts by grave misunderstandings of the First Amendment.

Each Martin Luther King, Jr. Day, I would read to my young daughter and son King's "Letter from Birmingham City Jail." It is one of our nation's most important political and moral documents, constituting part of America's civil scriptures, along with the Declaration of Independence, the Constitution, the Bill of Rights, and Abraham Lincoln's Gettysburg Address. It deals with the issues of respect for the law, the church's obligations in the public square, and the grounds for justified civil disobedience. In it, King "mixes" religion and politics by references to the prophets of the eighth century B.C., their "thus saith the Lord," the Apostle Paul, the gospel of Jesus Christ, the Macedonian call, St. Augustine's claim that "an unjust law is no law at all," St. Thomas Aquinas, Martin Buber, "Shadrach, Meshach and Abednego's civil disobedience to Nebuchadnezzar," early Christian martyrs in the Roman Empire, Paul Tillich, "Love your enemies," Martin Luther, John Bunyan, the sacred values in our Judeo-Christian heritage, appeals to fellow clergymen and Christian brothers, the Southern Christian Leadership Conference, and the Alabama Christian Movement for Human Rights.

To further demonstrate King's utter disregard of the secular and Pietistic imperatives, consider his "A Knock at Midnight" sermon, preached from the "pulpit" of Mt. Zion Baptist Church in Cincinnati on June 11, 1967. In one excerpt he proclaimed:

> The church must be reminded once again that {it} is not to be the master or the servant of the state, but the conscience of the state…. As long as the church is a tool of the state it will be unable to provide even a modicum of bread for men at midnight. If the church does not recapture its prophetic zeal and cease to be an echo of the status-quo it will be relegated to an irrelevant social club with no moral or spiritual authority. If the church does not participate actively in the struggle for peace, economic and racial justice, it will forfeit the loyalty of millions and cause men everywhere to know that it is an institution whose will is atrophied.[25]

This excerpt embodies an approach to church/state relations which requires both institutional separation and functional interaction—something not possible where the church succumbs to the state or the state succumbs to the church. The church should not be the sole driver of the bus, nor should it be segregated quietly to the "back of the bus." The secular imperative will not allow the church to

---

25   Martin Luther King, Jr., "Draft of Chapter VI, A Knock at Midnight," accessed April 1, 2022, https://kinginstitute.stanford.edu/king-papers/documents/draft-chapter-vi-knock-midnight..

be the conscience, guide, or critic of the state, while the Pietistic imperative cloisters the church to private religious matters. Both produce the same results—a public square denuded of religious influence.

The secularists and Pietists do not understand the need for religion—specifically organized religion—participating in the public square as a limiting influence on government. As R. R. Reno puts it,

> Disorganized religion cannot limit government. A religion without commanding authority lacks the specificity and density of traditional faith strengthened by a creed and communal support in a church. As this weakens, government becomes the *saecula saeculorum*, the world without ends.... We need strong families and vibrant religious communities. Without them, Leviathan grows.[26]

THE SAFFRON REVOLUTION VERSUS THE SECULAR AND PIETISTIC IMPERATIVES

In Burma on August 28, 2007, eighty thousand Buddhist monks in saffron robes crowded the city streets in Sittwe to support efforts to move the government towards democracy and away from military rule. On September 5, tensions rose during a demonstration led by the monks in the city of Pakkoku. Regime soldiers used tear gas and fired warning shots attempting to break up the nonviolent protest. A

---

26   R. R. Reno, "How to Limit Government," *First Things*, no. 238 (December 2013): 4.

monk group, the All Burma Monks Alliance, demanded an apology for the violence and the release of all political prisoners and detained demonstrators.

A crowd of two thousand monks and civilians, on September 22, walked past a roadblock and gathered in front of Aung San Suu Kyi's house. The Burmese politician, author, and 1991 Nobel Peace Prize laureate had been under house arrest and it was the first time she had been seen in public since 2003. This was a clear display of unity between the pro-democratic movement and the monks. By September 24, more than one hundred thousand monks and civilians marched in Rangoon, with demonstrations taking place in every state in Burma.

On September 26, a massive crackdown began against the demonstrators. Regime soldiers raided monasteries, severely beating and arresting monks in Myitkyina, Kachin State. Four monks were beaten to death. A total of fifty-two monasteries were raided in the crackdown according to the Assistance Association of Political Prisoners.

Should the monks' Saffron Revolution not have occurred because it violated the "separation of temple and state"? Should the monks have refused to participate in the pro-democracy movement because that would have been "too worldly" an activity? Should monk "pulpits" have only been used to address private religious concerns? If I understand the secular and Pietistic imperatives correctly, they should have kept religion and government "forever separate" and the "wall of separation of temple and state high and impenetrable."

3,200 ANTI-SLAVERY SERMONS VERSUS THE SECULAR AND PIETISTIC IMPERATIVES

When in the mid-1850s the "Nebraska Bill" left open the possibility of slavery in the Kansas and Nebraska territories, Protestant ministers in New York and New England preached over 3,200 sermons in only six weeks. With no concern about violating the "wall of separation between church and state," more than 3,000 New England ministers signed the following memorial to Congress:

> The undersigned, clergymen of different denominations in New England, hereby, in the name of Almighty God, and in his presence, do solemnly protest against the passage of what is known as the Nebraska Bill, or any repeal or modification of the existing legal prohibitions of slavery in that part of our national domain which is proposed to organize into the territories of Nebraska and Kansas. We protest against it as a great moral wrong, as a breach of faith eminently unjust to the moral principles of the community, and subversive of all confidence in national engagements; as a measure of danger to the peace and even the existence of our beloved Union, and exposing us to the righteous judgments of the Almighty: and your protestants, as in duty bound, will ever pray.[27]

---

27 Phillip Hamburger, *Separation of Church and State* (Cambridge: Harvard University Press, 2002), 245.

Did the actions of these ministers transgress against the demands of the Secular and Pietistic imperatives? They most certainly did.

THE CHURCH'S ROLE IN THE COLLAPSE OF EASTERN EUROPEAN COMMUNISM VERSUS THE SECULAR AND PIETISTIC IMPERATIVES

Both the Protestant Church and the Catholic Church helped facilitate the 1989 collapse of communism in Eastern European countries. The reasons for that collapse are multi-faceted, but there is an undeniable role played by organized religion. Earlier, in 1980, the Catholic Church was conducive to the Solidarity uprising in Poland. It provided forums for the distribution of values and ideas which were different from those of the communists. Pope John Paul II gave the Polish people encouragement and support as they struggled for democracy. In 1981, persecuted Solidarity activists were given refuge by the Church. The modest victories achieved then against the communist juggernaut contributed to a cautious sense of efficacy for their cause, which was a contributing factor in the 1989 collapse.

Concerning Solidarity, Aleksandr Solzhenitsyn stated,

> It is the Communist ideology that, with its heavy steps, is crushing Poland, and let us admit it is not entirely alien to the socialists, though they are protesting vehemently: The ideology of any communism is based on the coercive power of the state. Let's not be

mistaken: Solidarity inspired itself not by socialism but by Christianity.[28]

Beginning in 1982, every Monday night at 5:00 people gathered for peace prayers at the Nikolai Church, a Protestant church in Leipzig, East Germany. In 1988, the peace prayers were seen as an opportunity to express their concerns. Attendance grew to nearly a thousand, and the peace prayer became very political. Juan J. Lopez explains,

> If people were critical of the regime and wanted to meet with like-minded individuals, they would either go to the prayers on Monday at 5:00 P.M. or go near the Nikolai Church at about 6:00 P.M. Hence the tradition of the peace prayers served as a mechanism of communication among people, but the crucial element was communication.[29]

On September 25, 1989, following one of the Nikolai Church peace prayers, the first of the pro-democracy demonstrations began. Soon after that initial protest of 5,000 people, the numbers exploded. Twenty thousand people participated after a peace prayer at another church on October 2. Seventy thousand demonstrated after another peace prayer on October 9. At that point, the repressive apparatus imploded, and the communist regime fell apart in a matter of weeks.

---

28 Aleksandr Solzhenitsyn, *Good Order: Right Answers to Contemporary Questions*, ed. by Brad Miner (New York: Simon and Schuster, 1995), 71.

29 Juan J. Lopez, *Democracy Delayed* (Baltimore: Johns Hopkins University Press, 2002), 25.

It is for obvious reasons that one of the first things a communist regime does is to coerce religion into subjection. They always move quickly to destroy churches and monasteries, appropriate their land, and imprison or execute ministers, bishops, and monks. They know that religion, especially organized religion, is their most formidable barrier to total domination of the public square, whether it is Catholicism in Poland, Buddhism in Tibet, Protestantism in East Germany, or Confucianism in China.

The historical fact that the Nikolai Church and its peace prayer meetings were the birthplace of the East German revolution looks like a clear violation of the secular and Pietistic imperatives. If Supreme Court Justice Hugo Black's "wall of separation between church and state" had existed in the mindset of the Nikolai Church in 1989, the "wall" separating East Germany from West Germany could still be there. Fortunately, that church was not intimidated by those two foolish imperatives.

WAS THE 1965 OR THE 1979 JERRY FALWELL CORRECT?

In March of 1965, Jerry Falwell preached a sermon, "Ministers and Marchers," chastising the clergy for their participation in the civil rights activity in Selma, Alabama, and other cities. He preached,

> Believing the Bible as I do, I would find it impossible to stop preaching the pure saving gospel of Jesus Christ, and begin doing anything else—including fighting communism, or participating in civil rights reforms.... Nowhere are we commissioned

to reform the externals. The gospel does not clean up the outside but rather regenerates the inside.[30]

This expresses the church/state relationship mindset he encountered in Bible school, saying later, "I was taught in Bible college, religion and politics don't mix."[31]

In June 1979, Jerry Falwell founded the Moral Majority, a prominent American political organization which mobilized the Christian Right, supported the Republican Party, and contributed to the election of three presidents. So, which Jerry Falwell was correct? The 1965 "Pietistic imperative" compliant Falwell, or the 1979 Falwell who rejected that imperative? I believe the 1979 Falwell was.

Here are two reasons which propelled Falwell away from a Fundamentalist "Separation from the World" doctrine, which included political involvement: 1. The increasing pace and degree of radical trends in the public square. 2. The influence in the 1970s of Francis Schaeffer, a knickers-wearing Presbyterian minister, intellectual giant, and prolific writer, who provided the theological and philosophical rationale which awoke much of the Protestant Church from its pietistic slumbers. Before Schaeffer, abortion was considered a "Catholic" issue. Early in their relationship, Jerry Falwell once said to Schaeffer, "That's a Catholic issue. It's nothing to do with us. Why would I

30   Jerry Falwell, *Ministers and Marchers* (sermon March 21, 1965, Thomas Road Baptist Church Lynchburg, Virginia), booklet, page 7.
31   God in America: "Of God and Caesar" NPR, Religion, Politics a Potent Mix for Jerry Falwell, June 30, 2006.

want to take a stand on that? I'm just a preacher. I want to talk about the Gospel, not social issues."[32] Schaeffer was instrumental in Falwell's abandonment of such pietistic notions and in understanding the need to address social, cultural, and political issues.

> I digress: Francis Schaeffer impacted me and many other Christians starting in the late 1970s. Having been a Christian for almost ten years, there was a creeping sense that Christianity had to relate to more of life than what seemed like a never-ending "pull up your spiritual socks" activity. Could Christianity contribute to other "non-spiritual" activities such as art, academia, politics, business, philosophy, literature, law, etc.? Or was it restricted to addressing personal piety? This scenario caused us a lot of spiritual and theological anxieties. Then, there was Schaeffer. He freed us from the limiting worldview imposed by the Pietistic imperative. On January 14, 1992, I wrote on the inside cover of my *The Complete Works of Francis A. Schaeffer* that Schaeffer had done for me what Martin Luther had done for the Renaissance artist Albrecht Dürer. In a letter to George Spalatin in 1520, Dürer wrote:
>
> > And help me God, that I might get to Dr. Martinus Luther, so that I might

---

32 "God in America: 'Of God and Caesar,'" PBS, accessed April 1, 2022, https://www.pbs.org/godinamerica/transcripts/hour-six.html.

> diligently picture him and etch him in copper for a lasting memorial of this Christian man who has helped me out of great anxieties.[33]
>
> Dürer's anxieties were related to the basic ideas of the Bible being the final authority for Christian doctrine and that salvation did not come through the addition of man's works but through Christ and His work only—ideas which were exploding into the Protestant Reformation with Luther as its champion. Schaeffer's message "helped me out of great anxieties."

REV. JERRY FALWELL AND REV. MARTIN LUTHER KING, JR. DID THE SAME THING

Falwell met much resistance from the advocates of the Secular imperative who objected to his insistence that religious people should bring their religious views into matters of public importance. However, if Falwell's activities are illegitimate, then doesn't it also mean the Rev. Martin Luther King, Jr.'s civil rights activities were also illegitimate? They both did the same thing—they sought to reform an errant American society by appealing to biblical truth. If Falwell "violated" the separation of church and state, then so did King.

---

33 Francis A. Schaeffer, *The Complete Works of Francis A. Schaeffer: A Christian Worldview*, Volume 5 (Westchester, Illinois: Crossway Books, 1982), 131.

Charles Krauthammer exposed the liberals' hypocrisy by saying,

> it is particularly hypocritical for liberals to profess outrage at the involvement of the Catholic Church in this political issue, when only a few decades ago much of the civil rights and antiwar movements was run out of the churches. When Martin Luther King Jr. invoked scripture in support of his vision of racial equality and when the American Catholic Bishops invoked Augustine in their pastoral letter opposing nuclear deterrence, not a liberal in the land protested that this constituted a violation of the separation of church and state.[34]

THE 1947 *EVERSON V. BOARD OF EDUCATION* SUPREME COURT DISASTER

Earlier I stated that the secularists were given federal government-sanctioned veto power over the lives of millions of Americans and all the States as a result of the 1947 *Everson* decision. This resulted from the ahistorical, torturous interpretation of the First Amendment's Establishment Clause. This Court decision, for the first time, "incorporated" this clause against the States. The decision did not remove prayer from public school—it was removed fifteen years later in the *Engels v. Vitale* decision. But *Engels* could

---

34 Charles Krauthammer, *Things That Matter: Three Decades of Passions, Pastimes and Politics* (New York: Crown Forum, 2013), 214.

not have occurred without the "new" jurisprudence fabricated in *Everson* by the Court's false interpretation, a result caused either by incompetence or maliciousness.

Survey articles concerning the Establishment Clause and most will state something like "the Establishment Clause prohibits the *government* from 'establishing' a religion." A few will provide a little more "explanation" by stating that "the clause has been applied to the states, and therefore operate against all levels of government. The clause prohibits the *government* from endorsing, supporting, or becoming too involved in religion and religious activities." It is true that the Establishment Clause and the Free Exercise Clause have been applied to the states (as well as most of the other clauses of the Bill of Rights). However, the question is, was it a *legitimate* decision for the Supreme Court to apply the Establishment Clause and the Free Exercise Clause to the states? Was that application the result of a logical, sequential, and justifiable line of constitutional reasoning? Or was that application the *illegitimate* result of erroneous reasoning, incorrect historical claims, judicial willfulness, tortuous constitutional interpretations, or amateurish exegetical fallacies?

My answer is that the application was *illegitimately* imposed on millions of Americans and on all the states through a false interpretation of the First Amendment embedded in the *Everson* decision. That false interpretation set in motion an anti-religious rationale which sanctioned much of what Francis Abbot and the Liberals wanted in 1874 with their constitutional amendment proposal. Their constitutional objectives failed spectacularly, mainly because their radical secular demands would lead to sobering consequences for organized religion. When the nation rejected their *amendment* process approach, they shifted to the *interpretation* process. Though they did not live to see the implementation of their goals, they were gifted to them posthumously by the disastrous *Everson* decision and its jurisprudential progeny (*Engels, Mapp, Aguilar, Lowe, Roberts, Warsaw, Ker, Klopfer,* etc.).

As mentioned before, the nation rejected attempts to tamper with church/state relations on the federal constitutional level, having rejected a religious amendment attempt to declare the United States a Christian nation on the one hand, and also rejecting a Liberal amendment attempt to constitutionalize secularism's hostility toward Christianity on the other. The nation simply did not want to tamper with constitutional language which had, for one hundred years, served to implement a church/state relationship the nation was pleased with. The nation also rejected the Liberals' claim that the 14th Amendment intended to apply the First Amendment to the states. Numerous Supreme Court decisions reinforced this rejection (*Slaughter-House Cases* of 1872 and *Hurtado v. California* of 1884).

However, all of that rejection—the rejection of secularizing our federal jurisprudence and basing it on the 14th Amendment—did not stop Justice Hugo Black from doing so in 1947. That *new* federal jurisprudence, and its consequences, invented by Black's *Everson* ahistorical rationale, was aptly condemned by Justice Scalia, when he declared:

> What secret knowledge, one must wonder, is breathed into lawyers when they become

Justices of this Court, that enables them to discern that a practice which the text of the Constitution does not clearly proscribe, and *which our people have regarded as constitutional for 200 years,* is in fact unconstitutional? ... The Court must be living in another world. Day by day, case by case, it is busy designing a Constitution for a country I do not recognize.[35] (emphasis added)

HOW PRAYER WAS REMOVED FROM PUBLIC SCHOOLS

The following is a timeline regarding church/state relationships and school prayer.

1788—US CONSTITUTION RATIFIED

It established a federal form of government with enumerated powers on the federal level, reserving all other powers to the states.

1791—BILL OF RIGHTS RATIFIED

The power to determine what constitutes religion was explicitly denied to the federal government. The first two clauses of the Bill of Rights stated that Congress shall make no law regarding the establishment of religion, and also that Congress could not prohibit the free exercise of state establishments of religion. The individual states could establish, disestablish, or reestablish an establishment of religion as they saw fit. The federal government could not

---

35   *Board of City Commissioners v. Umbehr,* 1996, Scalia dissenting.

dictate to the states the contours of their church/state relations. Eight of the States had establishments of religion at that time, and refused to ratify the Constitution without the written guarantee that their church/state relations would be determined on their own terms without federal interference.

1801—THE DANBURY BAPTIST LETTER TO PRESIDENT THOMAS JEFFERSON

The Baptist Association of Danbury, Connecticut, wrote to President Thomas Jefferson, asking him to use his influence to attempt to persuade the officially Congregationalist state of Connecticut to adopt more tolerant treatments of them and other dissenters. They knew the president had no federal governmental powers to dictate that the State do so, and their awareness of that is reflected in their letter, saying, "Sir, we are sensible that the President of the united States, is not the national Legislator, & also sensible that *the national government cannot destroy the Laws of each State*; but our hopes are strong that the sentiments of our beloved President ... " (emphasis added).[36] They acknowledged that the US Constitution had forbidden the federal government from forcing Connecticut to revise their establishment of religion and church/state relations. Notice

---

36   Letter from Dansbury Baptist to Thomas Jefferson, 7 October 1801, The Papers of Thomas Jefferson (Manuscript Division, Library of Congress), Series 1, Box 87, August 30, 1801-October 15, 1801: Presidential Papers Microfilm, Thomas Jefferson Papers (Manuscript Division, Library of Congress), Series 1, Reel 24, June 26, 1801-November 14, 1801.

that there are no appeals to Neo-Constitutional "First Amendment" rights.

1802—PRESIDENT THOMAS JEFFERSON'S REPLY TO THE DANBURY BAPTIST ASSOCIATION

In his reply, the President states, "I contemplate with sovereign reverence that the act of *the whole American people which declared that their legislature* should 'make no law respecting an establishment of religion, or prohibiting the free exercise thereof,' thus building a wall of separation between Church & State" (emphasis added).[37] The "whole American people" refers to the will of Americans at the federal level, not the citizens of the individual states on the state level. Jefferson underlines "their" in "their legislature," to emphasize the "federal" legislature, and did not say, "their legislatures," which would have included the state legislatures. As for the "wall of separation between Church and State," Jefferson's wall had the federal government on one side with the church and individual state governments on the other side.

---

37 Draft letter from Thomas Jefferson to Messrs. Nehemiah Dodge, Ephraim Robbins, and Stephen S. Nelson, a committee of the Danbury Baptist association in the state of Connecticut, 1 January 1802, The Papers of Thomas Jefferson (Manuscript Division, Library of Congress), Series 1, Box 89, December 2, 1801—January 1, 1802; Presidential Papers Microfilm, Thomas Jefferson Papers (Manuscript Division, Library of Congress) Series 1, Reel 25, November 15, 1801—March 31, 1802.

1804—PRESIDENT JEFFERSON'S LETTER TO ABIGAIL ADAMS

While not addressing religion, this letter further reveals his *jurisdictional* understanding of the Constitution. He responded to her by saying, "While we deny that Congress have a right to control the freedom of the press, we have ever asserted the right of the States, and their exclusive right, to do so."[38] Jefferson's "wall of separation" had the federal government on one side with the press and the States on the other. It was not whether or not there would be freedom of the press, or what the contours of that freedom would be, but a jurisdictional matter of who was going to determine that—according to Jefferson, it definitely was not within the jurisdiction of the federal government to dictate to the States what it would be.

1833—CHIEF JUSTICE JOHN MARSHALL AND THE BILL OF RIGHTS

Writing for a united Court in *Barrow v. City Council of Baltimore*, Chief Justice Marshall declared that freedoms guaranteed in the Bill of Rights "contain no expression indicating an intention to apply them to state governments."[39]

1833—JUSTICE JOSEPH STORY AND THE BILL OF RIGHTS

Justice Story, who twelve years later was a justice of the Court in the unanimous *Permoli* case, wrote in his *Commentaries on the Constitution of the United States* that the purpose of the First Amendment was to "exclude from the national government all power to act upon the subject of

---

38 Raoul Berger, *The Fourteenth Amendment and the Bill of Rights* (Norman: University of Oklahoma Press, 1989), 6.

39 *Barrow v. City of Baltimore*, 32 U.S. (7 Peters) 243, 250 (1833).

religion."[40] He goes on to say, "the whole power over the subject of religion is left exclusively to the state government, to be acted upon according to their own sense of justice, and the state constitutions."[41]

1845—JUSTICE JOHN CATRON AND THE BILL OF RIGHTS

In *Permoli v. Municipality No. 1 of the City of New Orleans*, a unanimous Court ruled to dismiss this religious liberty case because the Court lacked jurisdiction. Contrary to the defendant's position that his religious liberties were being infringed upon based on the First Amendment's Free Exercise Clause, the Court stated that it did not apply to the acts of state and local governments. The dismissed case states, "This Court has not jurisdiction, under the 25th section of the Judiciary Act, of a question whether an ordinance of New Orleans does or does not impair religious liberty. The Constitution of the United States makes no provision for protecting the citizens of the respective states in their religious liberties; this is left to the state constitutions and laws."[42]

1868—FOURTEENTH AMENDMENT TO THE UNITED STATES CONSTITUTION ADOPTED

The Fourteenth Amendment was proposed and adopted in response to issues related to former slaves. It made them

---

40   Joseph Story, *Commentaries on the Constitution of the United States* (Boston: Hilliard, Gray, 1833), 3:730, section 1873.

41   Joseph Story, *Commentaries on the Constitution of the United States* (Boston: Hillard, Gray, 1833), 3:730, section 1873.

42   *Permoli v. Municipality No. 1 of the City of New Orleans*, 44 U.S. (3 Howard)589, 609 (1845)

citizens of the United States and of the State wherein they resided. It required States to extend to former slaves their respective due process of law procedures and their respective equal protection procedures. Whatever the nature of the respective States' due process and equal protection was, it had to be applied to former slaves and descendants in the same way as all other citizens.

1870—FORMER NEW YORK JUDGE ELISHA P. HURLBUT'S PROPOSED CONSTITUTIONAL AMENDMENT

This amendment would have extended the First Amendment to the States. It would alter Article I of the Bill of Rights: "ART I. *Neither* congress *nor any state* shall make *any* law respecting an establishment of religion, or prohibiting the free exercise thereof; or abridge...."[43]

Hurlbut acknowledged the need for such an amendment, saying "The proposed amendment prohibits a *state* from establishing any religion, or prohibiting its free exercise. The writer has assumed, that there is nothing in the Constitution as it stands, which prevents a state from doing either."[44] Aware the Court could *strain* to reach other conclusions, and also aware of the impropriety of such an approach, he explains,

> There are ... clauses in the Constitution of the United States which might be *tortured* into a construction prohibitory of state establishment of religion, by a court which

---

43   E. P. Hurlbut, *A Secular View of Religion in the State and the Bible in the Public Schools* (Albany: 1870), 14.

44   Ibid., 5.

should *lean against it*; or might be held, as I think more properly by an impartial legal tribunal, not applicable to the case: such as the clauses which provide the privileges and immunities of the citizens of the several states shall be equal, and the United States shall guaranty to every state, a republican form of government.[45] (emphasis added)

Rejecting the "tortured" interpretational approach, Hurlbut did not consider the recently adopted Fourteenth Amendment to be a possible vehicle for an interpretation prohibiting state establishments. He advocated that "[it] is better that a Constitution should speak plainly than *hint* its meaning" (emphasis added).[46] He states again "that there is nothing in the Constitution as it stands, which forbids a *state* from establishing a religion."[47] Many of Hurlbut's contemporaries seemed to agree, demanding their own amendments. They held this was necessary because "the Constitution ... contains no provision prohibiting the several States from establishing a State religion, or requiring a religious test for office, or disqualifying witnesses in the courts on account of their religious opinions, or likewise restricting their religious liberty."[48]

---

45 Ibid., 5.
46 Ibid., 5.
47 Ibid., 5.
48 *Report of the Centennial Congress of Liberals, and Organization of the National Liberal League*, 12 (Boston: National Liberal League, 1876).

1873—THE SLAUGHTERHOUSE CASES AND THE BILL OF RIGHTS

In these cases, the plaintiffs claimed that the state of Louisiana had violated their constitutional rights protected by the Fourteenth Amendment's Privileges and Immunities Clause. Associate Justice Samuel Freeman Miller, writing for the majority, declared that the clause did not restrict the police powers of Louisiana because it was a protection of rights guaranteed by the United States, not the individual states. The Court rejected this attempt to apply the Bill of Rights to the States.

1874—A "SECULAR" CONSTITUTIONAL AMENDMENT IS PROPOSED

Francis Abbot and the National Liberal League objected to the nature of the US Constitution because it was not "secular" enough. They understood that without a constitutional amendment, the Constitution did not limit religion in the ways they preferred. Their amendment would require all the States to revolutionize their respective church/state relations in accord with their policy preferences. Section 2 of their proposal read, "No State shall make any law respecting an establishment of religion, or favoring any particular form of religion, or prohibiting the free exercise thereof; or abridging the freedom of speech or of the press..." Their proposal failed spectacularly. The nation rejected it. And, most importantly, it must be acknowledged that all of this occurred *post-Fourteenth Amendment*. If the Fourteenth Amendment had applied the First Amendment to the States, along with the other parts of the Bill of Rights, why was all this effort necessary? Why all the aspirations for something that our contemporary Court tells us they already had?

1875—REPRESENTATIVE BLAINE'S MORE MODEST CONSTITUTIONAL AMENDMENT IS PROPOSED

Representative James Blaine of Maine proposed an amendment which was less demanding than the failed one proposed by Abbot and the National Liberal League. He also believed the Constitution needed amending. He knew, like the secularists, that the Constitution did not limit the States. His proposal would alter the Constitution, bringing it in line with his policy preferences. He rewrote the First Amendment: "No state shall make any law respecting an establishment of religion or prohibiting the free exercise thereof; and no money raised by taxation in any State for the support of public schools, or derived from any public fund thereof, nor any public lands devoted thereto, shall ever be under the control of any religious sect, nor shall any money so raised or lands so devoted be divided between religious sects or denominations."[49] This amendment proposal also failed. Clearly Blaine, Abott, and the Secularists assumed the Fourteenth Amendment had not already applied the First Amendment to the States. Clearly, the Fourteenth Amendment was not intended to do what our contemporary Courts and Neo-Constitutionalism claim that it did.

---

49 *Congressional Record* 4(1): 205 H. R., Dec. 14, 1875.

1884—THE HURTADO *CASE AND THE BILL OF RIGHTS*

Hurtado v. California was another case where the plaintiff argued that the Fourteenth Amendment had applied the Bill of Rights to the states. The Court's 7-1 decision ruled that the Fourteenth Amendment was not intended to retroactively apply the Fifth Amendment to state criminal trials. Again, clearly, the Fifth Amendment applied only to federal criminal trials.

1897—THE CHICAGO, BURLINGTON & QUINCY *CASE AND THE BILL OF RIGHTS*

In a 7-1 decision, this Court ruled that the Due Process Clause requires states to grant just compensation when private property is taken for public use. The Court reasoned that the "just compensation" requirement of the Fifth Amendment, seen through the Due Process Clause of the Fourteenth Amendment, justified the application of the requirement to the states. *And so it begins!* The long march of judicial imperialism and usurpation is initiated with this decision. This marked the first time the Court applied a specific provision of the Bill of Rights to the states. Whatever its cause, either incompetence or malfeasance, this *false* interpretation punched a small hole in the constitutional dam that had protected the states and religion from the ever-threatening floods so inherent in centralized power. It was a precursor and initiator of future *false* interpretations, with the dam completely collapsing during the Warren Court. Interpretational error begets interpretational error—a small hole in the dam now becomes an uncontrollable torrent later. A major fallacy in this decision was that this Court disregarded the constitutional storyline—a century of constitutional behavior, rejected amendment proposals to apply the Bill of Rights to the states, and recent Court decisions dismissing attempts at the same. Just thirteen years earlier, the Court, in a 7-1 decision, had ruled in exactly the opposite direction.

> The 1897 Court in the *Chicago* decision had only three of the justices from the 1884 Court. There had also been a change in the Chief Justice. Of the three 1884 justices, the *lone dissenter* in the 1884 *Hurtado* decision was the *writer of the majority opinion* of the 1897 *Chicago* decision. It was almost a completely different Court. Perhaps this is part of the reason for the Court's schizophrenic decision-making in the *Chicago* case.

1920—THE NINETEENTH AMENDMENT AND THE BILL OF RIGHTS

A decades-long movement for women's right to vote was adopted August 18, 1920. An amendment for women's suffrage was first introduced to Congress in 1878. The proposal failed. It was not until May 21, 1919, that the House of Representatives passed such an amendment, with the Senate quickly following on June 4, 1919. The amendment then went to the States for ratification until it received the support of the necessary 36 States for its adoption. It went into effect on August 18, 1920.

If Neo-Constitutional jurisprudence is correct that the Fourteenth Amendment's Equal Protection Clause made such issues unconstitutional in 1868, then why did suffrage policy entrepreneurs not simply ask the Court to grant women the right to vote, and why did they not do that immediately after its adoption? Why did they think they had to still employ the old-fashioned, democratically legitimate Article V method for modifying the Constitution? Why did millions of supporters and at least 36 States not think of the much easier and less troublesome means of just persuading five Supreme Court justices to gift their policy preferences to them? Either millions of Americans and their legislators "forgot" that the Fourteenth Amendment had already constitutionalized such rights, or the Fourteenth Amendment did not do what present Neo-Constitutional jurisprudence *says* it did.

Of course, those millions of Americans had not "forgotten." They believed in a rock-solid, unchanging Constitution, one which did require Article V for its modification. They functioned in a pre-Living Constitution, pre-Doctrine of Incorporation, pre-Neo-Constitutional era. Those Americans knew that things such as women's suffrage and *the removal of prayer from all public schools* required an amendment.

Who can doubt that if suffrage was being addressed today, the Court would be the chosen instrument of change? As Antonin Scalia tells us, "The American people have been converted to belief in The Living Constitution, a 'morphing' document that means, from age to age, what it ought to mean.... This, of course, is the end of the Bill of Rights...."[50] The Living Constitutionalism promoted by

---

50   Antonin Scalia, *A Matter of Interpretation: Federal Courts and the Law* (New Jersey: Princeton University Press, 1997), 47.

non-originalists does not need a formally prescribed and democratically legitimate method for changing the Constitution—they can just ask liberal judges to "gift" to them their latest ideological fad, such as *Obergefell v. Hodges*. The era of formal amendments is over—that is, as long as non-originalists can successfully utilize Living Constitutionalism to ignore the Constitution's original intent. Originalism is under assault because the Constitution's original intent is an impediment to the Left's activist agenda.

1925—THE GITLOW *CASE AND THE BILL OF RIGHTS*

This Court ruled that the Fourteenth Amendment did apply to the states the fundamental "personal" freedoms in the Bill of Rights, declaring that "[f]or present purposes we may and do assume that freedom of speech and of the press—which are protected by the First Amendment from abridgement by Congress—are among the fundamental personal rights and 'liberties' protected by the due process clause of the Fourteenth Amendment from impairment by the States."[51] This tragic departure from the intention of Congress and the wisdom of prior Court decisions punched yet another hole in the constitutional dam.

1931—THE NEAR *CASE AND THE BILL OF RIGHTS*

In this case the Court began restricting the states by an unsystematic "incorporation" of the Bill of Rights, insisting that it was designed to apply to the states in some ways. More and larger holes were punched.

---

51   *Gitlow v. New York*, 268 U.S. 652.

1940—THE CANTWELL *CASE AND THE BILL OF RIGHTS*

The First Amendment's Free Exercise Clause was deemed by this Court to have been applied to the States by the Fourteenth Amendment. The appellant claimed his constitutional rights had been deprived by the State of Connecticut without due process of law in contravention of the Fourteenth Amendment. Part of this Court's reasoning was that "[t]he Fourteenth Amendment has rendered the legislatures of the states as incompetent as Congress to enact such laws."[52] But what strange reasoning—what an odd syllogism:

- The Founders knew the federal government was incompetent to enact such laws.
- The Court just realized, thanks to the Fourteenth Amendment, that the states are also incompetent to make such laws.
- Therefore, neither federal nor state governments shall make such laws.

Is this Court saying that no government entity is competent for the task? Yet, someone must determine what constitutes "such laws." For example, a law or decision had to be made as to whether the Little Sisters of the Poor must comply with the Obama-era contraceptive mandate. It turns out that, in *practice*, the actual and equally strange syllogism goes like this:

- The Founders knew the federal government was incompetent to enact such laws.

---

52   *Cantwell v. Connecticut*, 310 U.S. 296.

- The Court just realized, thanks to the Fourteenth Amendment, that the states are also incompetent to make such laws.
- Therefore, the federal government shall make such laws.

What a strangely handled syllogism?! What strange logic?! And how ironic that the Bill of Rights, which was explicitly designed to restrain the federal government, is now used by the federal government to restrict the States—exactly the opposite of its intended purpose. The Founders, as representatives of the several states, simply refused to grant to the federal government jurisdiction over what constituted "such laws." At the Constitutional Convention, they were not determining the scope and contours of "such laws," but who was given jurisdiction over that determination. The authority to do so was explicitly denied to the federal government and retained by the states. With this twisted decision, the Court further undermined the long-held understanding that the Bill of Rights was a limitation on federal authority, that it was a guarantee of federalism. This decision blasted another large hole in the dam.

1947—THE EVERSON *CASE AND THE BILL OF RIGHTS*

Seven years earlier, the First Amendment's Free Exercise Clause had been incorporated against the States. Now, it was time for the Establishment Clause. It was with this 5-4 decision that the Doctrine of Incorporation begins to harden into a matter of judicial practice, and provided the heretical interpretive apparatus which attempts to rationalize a jurisprudence allowing federal authority to spread like wildfire into countless areas of societal and economic activities. And it was with this act of incorporation that the greatest damage to the fabric of American life and spirit began, the greatest violence to the First Amendment's original intent, and the colossally arrogant ignoring of the clear council of history. This act of incorporation is the most fiercely resented of all the acts of incorporation due to the repugnant consequences to which it has led—the granting of veto power to secularists over the religious lives of millions of Americans and deeming unconstitutional practices regarded as constitutional for two hundred years. This decision set in motion the undemocratic secularizing of church/state relations by judicial fiat. What Hurlbut's 1870 amendment proposal could not do, and what Abbot and the National Liberal League's 1874 amendment proposal could not do, and what Blaine's 1875 amendment proposal could not do, and what the Court contemporaneous to the Fourteenth Amendment would not do, was gifted to anti-religious secularists. This decision did not remove prayer from public school. That despicable decision would come fifteen years later with the *Engel* decision. However, the heretical *Engel* conclusion could not have occurred without the heretical premises "constitutionalized" in the disastrous *Everson* decision.

1962/1963—THE ENGEL AND SCHEMPP CASES AND THE BILL OF RIGHTS

The legislatures of New York and Pennsylvania allowed public school prayer. However, the Court ruled in these two cases that school prayer was a violation of the

Establishment Clause, having been incorporated against the States fifteen years earlier. With these two decisions, school prayer *became* "unconstitutional" in *all* states. Over half of the States at that time allowed school prayer, which was a practice in public schools for two hundred years and is not proscribed by the US Constitution or the Bill of Rights. No due use of ordinary means of textual interpretation could ever have construed anything in them to prohibit such an entrenched practice. To construe so took a massive degree of what Jefferson had warned could happen. He cautioned the American interpretive community by saying,

> On every question of construction, carry ourselves back to the time when the Constitution was adopted, recollect the spirit manifested in the debates, and instead of trying what meaning may be *squeezed* out of the text, or *invented* against it, conform to the *probable* one in which it was passed.[53] (emphasis added)

Further he said,

> The germ of dissolution of our federal government is in ... the federal judiciary; an irresponsible body ... working like gravity by night and by day, gaining a little today and a little tomorrow, and advancing its noiseless

---

53   Thomas Jefferson, June 12, 1823, in a letter to Justice William Johnson. Thomas Jefferson, *Jefferson Writings*, Merrill D. Patterson, ed., (NY: Literary Classics of the United States, Inc., 1984), p. 1475.

step like a thief, over the *field of jurisdiction,* until all shall be *usurped* from the States.[54] (emphasis added)

If the *Everson/Engel/Schempp* decisions do not qualify for *squeezing, inventing against,* and *usurping,* then what would?

This timeline shows how the States crafted the Constitution and Bill of Rights (Paleo-Constitutionalism) to function as a restriction on the federal government and a guarantee of federalism, but how they began to function as a restriction on the States and an abandonment of federalism (Neo-Constitutionalism). How ironic that the entity intended to be restricted is the very entity which decided to restrict its restrictors—the teenagers who have been restricted to be home by 10:00 p.m. have freed themselves of this restriction and imposed a curfew on the parents! This illegitimate transformation, this hermeneutical sleight-of hand, ended with "constitutional" veto-power over the lives of millions of Americans being granted to anti-religious advocates, resulting in the removal of school prayer in all states. What secular policy entrepreneurs could not accomplish through democratic means, they accomplished through undemocratic means by way of the Court—their preferred method to this day.

---

54 Thomas Jefferson. 1821, in a letter to Mr. Hammond. Thomas Jefferson, *Thomas Jefferson on Democracy,* Saul K. Padover, ed., (NY: D. Appleton-Century Co., 1939), p. 1475.

CHAPTER 15

THREE FALLACIES REFUTED

O**N** S**EPTEMBER** 21, 1997, the billion-dollar missile cruiser, *Yorktown*, shuddered to a stop. The warship designed to survive the blast of mines and torpedoes was crippled by a zero. The engineers who had installed new computer software forgot to remove the zero which stayed hidden in the original code. The *Yorktown's* 80,000 horsepower became worthless when the computers tried to divide by zero. It took engineers two days to remove the zero and repair the engines. That zero was a small mistake, but it produced huge consequences.

An error or fallacy, even if it appears small, can result in appalling consequences when it is allowed to follow through with its self-perpetuating logic. Sometimes the small error is not recognized until it is too late, and only after its damage has occurred.

REFUTING JUSTICE HUGO BLACK'S "WALL OF SEPARATION BETWEEN CHURCH AND STATE"

In the disastrous 1947 *Everson* decision, Justice Black stated in the majority opinion that "The First Amendment has erected a wall between church and state. That wall must be kept high and impregnable. We could not approve the slightest breach." One of Black's errors is choosing to employ Jefferson's phrase in a way he did not intend for it to be used. It is clear in his letter to the Danbury Baptists that the wall Jefferson was referring to had the federal government on one side with the states and the church on the other side. Jefferson's wall protected the States and religion from federal encroachment. It was a wall which demarcated jurisdiction. Black's treatment of the "wall" moved it from Jefferson's placement to the unhistorical position, with the federal and state governments on one side and the church on the other (see Figure 3).

Figure 3

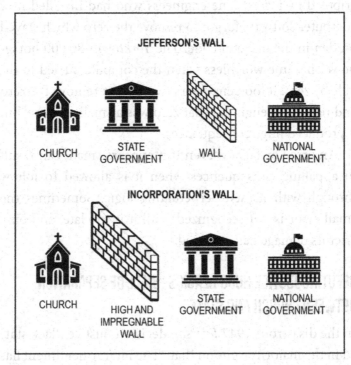

BARRY LYNN AND BLACK'S WALL

Black most certainly knew the original position of the "wall" intended by Jefferson. Yet, he does not make that clear, but capitalizes on Jefferson's prestige without acknowledging what he had actually meant. This is common practice today. Ultra-separationist Barry Lynn takes this conveniently ahistorical approach when employing the "wall" phrase. In *Piety and Politics*, he mentions "those who oppose and attack the wall of separation between church and state."[1] Yet Lynn never acknowledges how his use of Jefferson's phase is not the one intended by Jefferson. By the way, those attacking the "wall of separation between church and state" are attacking Black's "wall," the wall created by Incorporation, not Jefferson's.

Lynn quotes Justice Black's misguided rationale found in the 1947 disastrous *Everson* decision: "The clause against establishment of religion by law was intended to erect 'a wall of separation between Church and State.'"[2] Lynn's commentary declares, "*It's a sensible definition.* Had the Court itself fully adhered to it and the American people had its uniquely American significance explained to them, the nation would have spared a lot of heartache" (emphasis added).[3] In saying, "It's a sensible definition," Lynn is wrong. Black's "wall" is a Neo-Constitutional definition of Jefferson's Paleo-Constitutional "wall." They are using the prestige of pre-*Everson* terminology and words

---

1   Barry Lynn, *Piety and Politics: The Right-Wing Assault on Religious Freedom* (New York: Harmony Books, 2006), 12.
2   Ibid., 25.
3   Ibid., 25.

THE JOY OF INTERPRETATION

to "constitutionalize" post-*Everson* jurisprudence. They are defining two different "walls," and Black and Lynn are pretending there is no difference. This is an easy thing to do these days, since most Americans are oblivious to the distinction. Black's ahistorical definition has been so insinuated into contemporary American concepts of jurisprudence and constitutional history that the distinction now is nonexistent. Ask an American what "Congress shall make no law" means, and the majority will reflexively respond with something like, "It means government can't support or be involved with religion." Pressed further about "what government" and they will enthusiastically say, "All governments, of course"—a predictable response given the erosion of our understanding of federalism. When asked how "Congress shall make no law" now means "Alabama shall make no law," most are like the proverbial "deer in the headlights"—they are stunned by an obvious question that they have never paused to contemplate. As Woods and Gutzman have stated, "The received wisdom on America's recent constitutional history is, unfortunately, almost entirely wrong. That is why a sweeping re-assessment, one that lays bare exactly who killed the Constitution that the Founding Fathers bequeathed to us, is necessary."[4] And a "sweeping re-assessment" of our recent constitutional history is the very point of this chapter.

Lynn states, "Had the Court itself fully adhered to [a wall of separation between Church and State] ... the

---

4   Thomas E. Woods, Jr. and Kevin R. C. Gutman, *Who Killed the Constitution? The Fate of American Liberty from World War I to George W. Bush* (New York: Crown Forum, 2008), 2.

nation would have been spared a lot of heartache." Is Lynn claiming that the Court should have started doing in 1791 what the Court and Black did in 1947? Is he saying the 1791 Court should have immediately incorporated the Bill of Rights against the States? Is he saying that Chief Justice John Marshall was wrong in the 1833 *Barrow v. Baltimore* decision that the Bill of Rights was intended to be a restriction on the national government, not the States? Is he saying Justice Joseph Story was wrong in the 1845 *Permoli v. New Orleans* decision? Wrong that the nation rejected Judge Hurlbut's amendment in 1870? Wrong in rejecting Abbot's amendment in 1874? Wrong in rejecting Blaine's amendment in 1875? Is Lynn saying that the nation suffered because First Amendment judicial activism was unwittingly delayed by 156 years? Preposterous!

JUDGE CARDOZO'S WARNING ABOUT THE USE OF METAPHORS IN LAW

Another one of Black's errors in employing Jefferson's phrase is that he carelessly uses a metaphor, "wall of separation," in constructing constitutional doctrine. Metaphors were not employed by the Founding Fathers in writing the Constitution and Bill of Rights. They wisely employed explicit, literal language to construct these documents of ultimate authority. They knew that metaphors, while appropriately useful in other types of discourse, are not appropriate in legal discourse because of their imprecise nature. Make a mistake in interpreting a metaphor in one of Shakespeare's plays and it is unlikely to result in destabilizing a culture or a nation. Not so when interpreting legal documents of ultimate authority. As Judge Benjamin N. Cardozo warned, "Metaphors in law are to be narrowly watched, for starting as devices to liberate thought, they end often by *enslaving* it" (emphasis added). [5] And *enslaving* is exactly what Black's use of the metaphor has done. Most Americans are enslaved to conflating the First Amendment's Establishment Clause and the "wall" metaphor. The two are not the same, but people find it difficult to emancipate themselves from thinking in that uncritically received manner. That metaphor brings too many misleading dissimilarities into the discourse.

DANBURY BAPTISTS' ACKNOWLEDGMENT OF FEDERALISM

It is important to note that Jefferson was not writing constitutional law in the letter to the Danbury Baptists. From evidence in their letter to him, he knew they shared with him an understanding of federalism which allowed him to use his metaphor without much fear that it would be misconstrued—unlike what was misconstrued 145 years later by Black. As stated by Dreisbach,

> Both Jefferson and the Baptists understood that, as a matter of federalism, the nation's chief executive could not disturb church-state relations and policies that concerned religious liberty in the respective states. In their letter, the Baptists observed: 'Sir, we are sensible that the President of the united States, is not

---

5   *Berkey v. Third Avenue Railway Co.*, 244 Ny 84.

the national Legislator, & also sensible that the national government cannot destroy the Laws of each State.' Jefferson's 'wall,' strictly speaking, was a metaphoric construction of the First Amendment, which governed relation between religion and the *national* government.[6]

Never before had Jefferson's metaphor been used as an authoritative definition of the First Amendment. Americans who have unwittingly received a Neo-Constitutional understanding of constitutional history think that the eight state establishments of religion which existed at the time of the ratification of the Constitution were disestablished because the United States Supreme Court ruled that they violated the "wall of separation between church and State," which is "advocated" by the First Amendment. The last of the disestablishments of religion occurred in Massachusetts in 1833. All eight disestablishments occurred with no reference to a need for a "wall of separation," and without any Neo-Constitutional appeals to "First Amendment protections." Jefferson's "wall" metaphor simply was not an accurate enough metaphor to represent how the citizens of the States viewed their church/state relations. It never became the popular "bumper sticker" slogan so cherished by anti-religious advocates today. The disestablishments should have occurred, and they occurred in the legitimate way—by the democratic processes within the various

---

6   Daniel L. Dreisbach, *Thomas Jefferson and the Wall of Separation between Church and State* (New York: New York University Press, 2002), 50.

States and without textual violence to the Constitution and Bill of Rights. It was never conceived by any of those States that they were somehow in "violation" of federal authoritative documents. Could the Founding Fathers have "outlawed" establishments of religion during the Constitutional Convention? Certainly, it was "possible." But they did not—and advocates of Neo-Constitutionalism should stop pretending that they did.

REFUTING LIVING CONSTITUTIONALISM

THE FORMAL PRINCIPLE OF NEO-CONSTITUTIONALISM

Living Constitutionalism is the formal principle of Neo-Constitutionalism. It is an overarching theoretical presupposition which informs its goals and guides the methods of its practitioners and advocates. The Doctrine of Incorporation is the material principle of Neo-Constitutionalism. Neo-Constitutionalism could not exist without the radical results which are the consequences of the heretical Doctrine of Incorporation. And the Doctrine of Incorporation could not have developed without Living Constitutionalism.

The interpretive theory known as Living Constitutionalism arose out of the need for an interpretive method which could "rationalize" the textual violence perpetrated against the textual restraints of the Constitution and Bill of Rights—restraints designed to prevent the policy preferences of rogue judges. Living Constitutionalism is a desperate attempt to give a modicum of textual legitimacy to their vagrant Neo-Constitutionalism. The maxim which warns us that "insincerity is the enemy of sensible language" applies here, because no normal use of words, grammar, and language could have ever produced the "laws" that lead to the repugnant consequences resulting from this subjective theory.

NO CHRIST IN CHRISTMAS

One of those repugnant consequences of Living Constitutionalism was recently witnessed by my family. At Christmas, as we walked around the beautiful lakeside area at Cranes Roost Park in Altamonte Springs, Florida, we saw hundreds of decorations the city had installed for the holidays—dozens and dozens of snowflakes, elves, Santa Claus, reindeer, candy canes, Frostys, and Christmas trees. But, not one Christ! Not one manger! That may not have seemed so odd in San Francisco or Portland, Oregon, but this is in the Bible Belt. How could this have occurred? Because it "violates" the First Amendment's Establishment Clause—*that is, according to Neo-Constitutionalism*. And that because of the Doctrine of Incorporation, and that because of Living Constitutionalism. This trinity morphed the 150-year church/state relationship that had served America well into one where anti-religious advocates were granted veto power over the religious lives of millions of Americans. The same heretical jurisprudence which removed prayer from school also removed Christ from Christmas displays.

THE ACLU'S "SEARCH AND DESTROY" EFFORT

This is all part of the post-*Everson* "search and destroy" effort to dismantle the valuable heritage of public expressions of faith. This effort has put hundreds of millions of dollars into the coffers of the anti-religious group, the American Civil Liberties Union (ACLU). It is for good reason that they have been called "the Taliban of American liberal secularism." Without Neo-Constitutionalism, the ACLU could not have profited from their "search and destroy" lawsuits. Post-*Everson* jurisprudence is good for their business. Thousands of American cities, school districts, cemeteries, and courthouses have been coerced into abandoning practices they have regarded as constitutional for 200 years. George Will said,

> The ACLU is a political organization pursuing its agenda primarily through litigation rather than legislation—often an authoritarian shortcut around the democratic process.... It is impatient with ambiguity, and defends as a merely literal reading of the document various policies that bear no discernible relation to the intention of the authors.[7]

Few know the legal genealogy of this transformation, yet most know this—something is rotten in Denmark. This chapter will show the legal genealogy of this transformation.

The Living Constitution advocates that judicial interpretation should draw heavily from changing circumstances in

---

7   George Will, *The Morning After: American Successes and Excesses 1981-1986* (New York: The Free Press, 1986), 179.

society. Much less emphasis should be given to traditional approaches of interpreting texts, with their "slavish" devotion to the opinions of times dead and gone, to the limiting forces of textual context, to the rules of language and genre. Judicial decision-making should be "living," "creative," or "evolving." What the Constitution said yesterday is not necessarily what it means today. A changing society needs the "flexibility" the Living Constitution provides, without which society could snap, so they say.

THE LIVING CONSTITUTION KILLED THE COURT'S UNANIMITY

The Living Constitution has contributed to the destruction of the high degree of unanimity the Court once had. Before it, there existed a historical tradition of predominantly unanimous decisions. The ascendency of the Living Constitution coincides with the collapse of the Court's unanimity. Of course, correlation does not guarantee a cause-and-effect relationship between two factors; most issues are multi-determined. Of course, the Living Constitution is not the only factor in the collapse of the Court's high degree of unanimity, and scholars have produced several studies regarding the causes of this decline. They attribute some of the decline to the differences among the justices as to value systems, dissimilarity in major premise, chief justice leadership, diminishing of consensual norms, varying assumptions, contrasts in their social, political, and economic views, and to acts of Congress. But the role of the Living Constitution in undermining unanimity, and the accompanying diminishment of the authority and credibility of the Court's decisions, should be explored.

Would you drive your family across a bridge where engineers were of a 5-4 opinion that the bridge will not collapse? Of course not. Yet, the Court has driven the nation across a bridge into a radically different formation of church/state relations, into a 180-degree reversal of the function of the Bill of Rights, and into a revolutionary redrawing of jurisdictional domains, and has done so based on a proliferation of 5-4 opinions. The collapse of the Court's unanimity demonstrates that the Court only "thinks" these radical transformations might be constitutionally legitimate. The low degree of unanimity is directly proportional to our low degree of confidence that the nation is on the right constitutional track. Figure 4, from Drew Noble Lanier's *Of Time and Judicial Behavior: United States Supreme Court Agenda-Setting and Decision-Making, 1888-1997*, shows the disturbing collapse in unanimity.

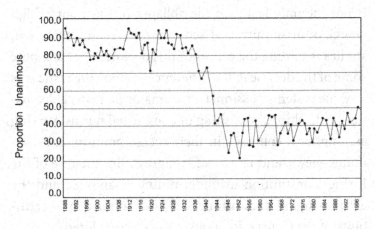

Figure 4.

CONCERNING UNANIMITY

PROPORTION OF UNANIMOUS DECISIONS OF THE UNITED STATES SUPREME COURT, 1888-1997

Most Americans are not surprised to hear that some monumental societal transformation was facilitated by a 5-4 Supreme Court decision, such as the 2013 *United States v. Windsor* decision which struck down Congress' 1996 Defense of Marriage Act, and the 2015 *Obergefell v. Hodges* decision legalizing gay marriage. Most assume that the 5-4 tradition is nothing new, that it was something which has always occurred. This is not true. Lanier's research found that

> There are several years in which no 5-4 decisions are announced. Three term years during Fuller's (1888, 1889, and 1892) and Taft's (1922, 1923, and 1929) tenures have no 5-4 decisions; the White Court has two years (1913 and 1915) with none of those decisions.[8]

Figure 4 shows that from 1888 to 1939, the Court justices shared a high degree of unanimity, and therefore had to have shared a high degree of solidarity in their assumptions, methods, and interpretive theories—a period of 83.35% unanimity. The chart also shows the rapid collapse of unanimity from 1940 to 1997—a period of 40.18% unanimity. That is a drop of 43.17% in unanimity. Americans need to know that this 5-4 situation has not always prevailed in Court decisions, and that, before the Living Constitution, the Court had a historical tradition of predominately unanimous decisions.

---

8   Drew Noble Lanier, *Of Time and Judicial Behavior: United States Supreme Court Agenda-Setting and Decision-Making, 1888-1997* (New Jersey: Associated University Presses, 2003), 123.

Lanier's research indicates that for the time period from 1888 to 1997, the highest point of unanimity for the Court was 95.4% in 1888, with the lowest being 21.7% in 1951—a drop of 73.7%. It was not until 1996 that unanimous decisions crested 50%, at 51.1%. The 50% level had not been reached since 1942 (56.4%), fifty-two years earlier. Clearly, something catastrophic interjected itself into the interpretational task the nation entrusted to the Court. Our history, rule of law, and social mores deserve better.

JUDGE HAND'S WARNING TO THE COURT CONCERNING THE IMPORTANCE OF UNANIMITY

Unanimous decisions increase the credibility and authority of the Court. Conversely, nonunanimous decisions diminish them. In 1958, Judge Billings Learned Hand warned the Court about the rise in nonunanimous decisions, calling them "disastrous" because they annul "the impact of the monolithic solidarity on which the authority of a bench of judges so largely depends."[9] Split votes jeopardize the prestige the Court needs in distinguishing itself from the presidency and the Congress, branches of government "sullied" by politics. The greater the number of nonunanimous decisions, the greater the chances the Court will be viewed as just another political body. And a political body it has become. The data in figure 5 indicates the thesis of Judge Bork's book, *The Tempting of America: The Political Seduction of the Law*, is correct. The abysmal level of

---

9   Billings Learned Hand, *The Bill of Rights* (Cambridge: Harvard University Press, 1958), 72-73.

nonunanimous decisions is the result of the abysmal level to which America has allowed the Court to be politicized.

Figure 5 shows the increase in nonunanimous decisions with at least one dissenting vote. After the advent of the Living Constitution, dissent became the new "norm." The visual effect of the chart is shocking.

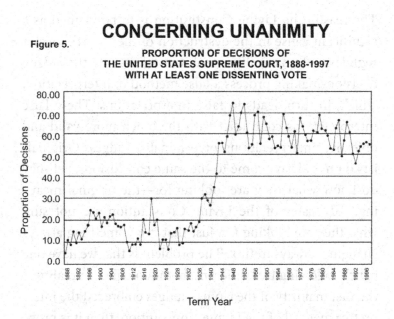

Figure 5.

CONCERNING UNANIMITY

PROPORTION OF DECISIONS OF
THE UNITED STATES SUPREME COURT, 1888-1997
WITH AT LEAST ONE DISSENTING VOTE

CHIEF JUSTICE REHNQUIST CRITICIZES THE COURT'S HOPELESSLY DIVIDED PLURALITIES

Regarding nonunanimous decisions, Chief Justice Rehnquist, in his refutation of First Amendment jurisprudence since the disastrous *Everson* decision, declared that

> it is impossible to build sound constitutional doctrine upon a mistaken understanding of constitutional history ... in the 38 years since

309

Everson our Establishment Clause cases have been *neither principled nor unified.* Our recent opinions, many of them *hopelessly divided pluralities,* have with *embarrassing candor* conceded that the 'wall of separation' is merely a 'blurred, indistinct, and variable barrier....'[10] (emphasis added)

The reason the Living Constitution is to be blamed as a significant cause in the destruction of the Court's former high level of unanimity is that it interjects into the judges' decision-making process a false method of interpretation, which, in turn, leads to false interpretations. These false interpretations contradict with the much more valid and objective interpretations of originalist judges. Originalists do not always come to the same conclusions, yet they do know what they are looking for—the original meaning. Advocates of the Living Constitution are not sure what they are looking for, just that it is something always changing, always in flux. The problem is that we have one bench following two different methodologies. In reality, if the vast majority of the Court's judges embraced the interpretive method of the Living Constitution, then it is probable that a high level of unanimity could be achieved once more—a disadvantage being that we would not have any Constitution left. Likewise, if the vast majority of the judges were originalists, as they were before the advent of the Living Constitution, a high level could again be achieved. *A bench divided against itself cannot stand.*

---

10   *Wallace v. Jaffree,* 472 U.S. 38.

The Living Constitution operates on the assumption that validity in interpretation is not possible, and that claims to "objectively correct" interpretations are arrogant illusions. Its advocates have made fruitful use of subjectivity—they certainly need it. And they need it because no ordinary, common-sense use of language and genre would produce their policy preferences. It should be remembered that *advocacy is only interested in itself.* It wants what it wants no matter what it destroys in the process—the rule of law be damned, validity be damned, objectivity be damned, the intent of the author be damned.

HIRSCH'S WARNINGS REGARDING THE "SENSIBLE BELIEF"

In 1967, Hirsch wrote,

> It is a task for the historian of culture to explain why there has been in the past four decades a heavy and largely victorious assault on the sensible belief that a text means what its author meant. In the earliest and most decisive wave of the attack (launched by Eliot, Pound, and their associates) the battleground was literary: the proposition that textual meaning is independent of the author's control.... [11]

While false methodologies are nothing new, the one Hirsch was refuting was new in that its founding presupposition was doubt: doubt that objectivity existed, doubt that texts could transmit the author's intent through space

---

11   E. D. Hirsch, Jr., *Validity in Interpretation* (New Haven: Yale University Press, 1967), 1.

and time, doubt that distances between the text and reader could be bridged, doubt of an independent reality, doubt that $1 + 2 = 3$ is "true," doubt of the modern view of science, doubt that a "true" interpretation was possible, doubt that a means existed to distinguish fact from fiction and myth from history, and doubt that universally valid interpretive principles are knowable.

Since Hirsch said "in the last four decades" in 1967, he was referring a beginning around the late 1920s or early 1930s. Most new philosophies take a while to percolate throughout a society. They begin with the intelligentsia and then spread out through the arts and academia, and then out to society at large. It took a while for the cancerous effects of "doubt" to metastasize from its abstract philosophical beginnings into concrete applications in everyday life. This cancer kills epistemological confidence in any truth-claim, creating a landscape littered with the wreckage of epistemological nihilism.

The assault Hirsch is addressing, the one against "the sensible belief that a text means what its author meant," began shortly before the Living Constitution started gaining traction as an alternative to originalism as a methodology for judicial decision-making. Judges influenced by the trendiness of this new method began synthesizing the subjectivity of T. S. Elliott, Ezra Pound, Martin Heidegger, and their associates into the decision-making process. Pauline Marie Rosenau writes,

> Critics allege that because post-modernists refuse either to apply established standards of inquiry or to be 'governed by preestablished

rules' (Lyotard 1984: 81) they are unable to evaluate intellectual production. Inspired by Heidegger post-modernists answer that there are no longer any rules or norms to guide inquiry, no overall validity, no universal, unequivocal basis for truth or taste.[12]

Rosenau goes on to say,

> In the end the problem with post-modern social science is that you can say anything you want, but so can everyone else. Some of what is said will be interesting and fascinating, but some will also be ridiculous and absurd. Post-modernism provides no means to distinguish between the two.[13]

BORK'S WARNING REGARDING THE NOMINATION OF LIVING CONSTITUTION-ALISTS

The Living Constitution is the new interpretive kid on the block. Prior to it, when originalism was the dominant interpretive method, the Court's decisions had a unanimity level, from 1888 to 1939, of 83.35%. After its advent, from 1940 to 1997, that level fell to 40.18%. When a bench of judges is composed of adherents to two different methodologies, unanimity cannot be sustained. *A board of judges divided against itself cannot stand.* It was the Living Constitution which embraced a heretical methodology which decimated the unanimity so important to the Court's

---

12 Pauline Marie Rosenau, *Post-Modernism and the Social Sciences* (New Jersey: Princeton University Press, 1992), 133.

13 Ibid., 137.

authority, credibility, and prestige. America could have avoided this if Judge Bork's advice had been followed. He advised, "No person should be nominated or confirmed who does not display both a grasp of and devotion to the philosophy of original understanding."[14] Amen to that!

The Living Constitution is opposed to the interpretive theory of originalism. Originalism demands that judges interpret the constitutional text based upon its original meaning. The grammar and facts of history are to govern interpretation, without interference from judges' policy preferences. As stated earlier, originalism embraced the "legal" model of decision-making—the Living Constitution embraces the "attitudinal" model. Originalists believe the Living Constitution undermines the entire purpose of a constitution. Antonin Scalia juxtaposed the "Written Constitution," where judges interpret the law, with the "Living Constitution," where judges make law.

Originalism and the Living Constitution are hermeneutical names of the two sides in our present culture's "interpretation war." James Davison Hunter describes the opposing sides in this war:

> One moral vision is predicated upon the assurance that the achievements and traditions of the past should serve as the foundation of communal life and guide us in negotiating today's and tomorrow's challenges. Though often tinged with nostalgia, this vision is misunderstood by those who label it as

---

14   Robert H. Bork, *The Tempting of America: The Political Seduction of the Law* (New York: The Free Press, 1990), 9.

reactionary. In fact, this vision is neither regressive nor static, but rather is both syncretic and dynamic. Nevertheless, the order of life sustained by this vision does seek deliberate continuity with the guiding principles inherited from the past. The goal of this vision is the reinvigoration and realization in our society of what traditionalists consider to be the noblest ideals and achievements of civilization.... Against this traditionalism is a moral vision that is ambivalent about the legacy of the past—it regards the past in part as a curiosity, in part an irrelevance, in part a useful point of reference, and in part a source of oppression.... Its aim is the further emancipation of the human spirit.[15]

Hunter does not go on to accurately describe the liberals' and the Left's intolerance. The "further emancipation of the human spirit" is actually an undemocratic cultural revolution which is facilitated with the help of the post-Doctrine of Incorporation Court. Contrary to the will of the people, that Court made it possible for them to protect pornography, redefine the family, limit school discipline, remove prayer from all public schools, create the right to abortion, create the right to gay marriage, and banish religion from public life. These Living Constitution "emancipations" were accomplished, as Judge Robert Bork tells

15   James Davison Hunter, "The American Culture War," in *The Limits of Social Cohesion*, ed. Peter L. Berger (Boulder: Westview Press, 1998), 2-3.

us, by the Court "prescribing a new constitutional law that is much more egalitarian and socially permissive than either the actual Constitution or the legislative opinion of the American public. *That, surely, is the point of the efforts*" (emphasis added).[16]

The Living Constitution is a direct assault on the Written Constitution's separation of powers: the legislative branch (makes the law), the executive branch (enforces the law), and the judicial branch (interprets the law). The Living Constitution and the subjective ambiguities it imposes on the interpretive enterprise allow the Court almost unlimited "options" in its decision-making activities. This leads to the Court's making of law, instead of interpreting of law—the usurpation of power intended for the legislative branch. It is an anti-constitutional activity. On the other hand, originalism embraces an objective approach to the interpretive enterprise. "The first and fundamental rule in interpretation of all instruments is, to construe them according to the sense of the terms, and the intention of the parties," declared Story.[17] Without this interpretive principle, the separation of powers cannot be maintained or the judiciary be democratically legitimate.

The Living Constitution's theory makes fruitful use of profound hermeneutical skepticism. It attempts to undermine our confidence that such a thing as true or valid constitutional interpretations are possible. Then, left with no

---

16   Robert H. Bork, *The Tempting of America: The Political
      Seduction of the Law* (New York: The Free Press, 1990), 6.
17   J. Story, *Commentaries on the Constitution of the United States vi*,
      Carolina Academic Press 1987, 1833.

objective means of arriving at the Founders' *intent*, we are left with *their* intent—what present judges say the meaning is. Similarly, the Bultmannians hold that the Bible's meaning is not fixed, but is a new revelation to each succeeding generation. Such sacred and legal hermeneutics claim that the meaning of a text is *what it means to us today*. This is certainly an anti-theological and an anti-constitutional activity. This should be rejected by the "People of the Book" and by the "People of the Constitution."

It should also be noted that the rise of Living Constitutionalism roughly parallels the rise of German and French postmodern philosophy and literary theories. The advocates of the Living Constitution have, in many ways, synthesized American jurisprudence with Martin Heidegger and Jacques Derrida. These postmodernists contend that there are no rules or procedures which we are obligated to follow, and this applies not only to hermeneutics, but to all disciplines whose pursuit is truth. They reject all notions of transcendent truth and all preoccupations with method. Their only method is an "anything goes" method.

JUSTICE BRENNAN'S PROFOUNDLY SKEPTICAL LEGAL HERMENEUTICS

The Living Constitution's profoundly skeptical hermeneutic was articulated by Justice William Brennan at Georgetown University on October 12, 1985. The following excerpts from his speech display this hermeneutic.

> There are those who find legitimacy in fidelity to what they call "the intention of the Framers." In its most doctrinaire incarnation, this view demands that Justices discern exactly

what the Framers thought about the question under consideration and simply follow that intention in resolving the case before them. It is a view that feigns self-effacing deference to the specific judgments of those who forged our original social compact.

But in truth it is little more than arrogance cloaked in humility. It is arrogant that from our vantage we can gauge accurately the intent of the Framers on application of principle to specific, contemporary questions. Apart from the problematic nature of the sources, our distance of two centuries cannot but work as a prism refracting all we perceive.... We current Justices read the Constitution in the only way we can: as 20th century Americans. We look to the history of the time of framing and to the intervening history of interpretation. But the ultimate question must be, what do the words of the text mean in our time? For the genius of the Constitution rests not in any static meaning it might have in a world that is dead and gone, but in the adaptability of its great principles to cope with current problems and current needs.[18]

Brennan claims the optimistic goal and method of originalism is "arrogance cloaked in humility." The goal of grasping the Framers' intent is unattainable? And there

---

18   Speech at Georgetown University, October 12, 1985. Reprinted in *The New Times* (October 13, 1985), 36.

exist no universally valid interpretive procedures by which
that intent can be recovered? Then why bother with a constitution at all? If efforts at interpretation are as invalid as
alchemy and astrology, why doesn't he resign and get out
of the interpreting business? If we are unable to confidently recover *intent*, how can we confidently recover *great
principles*? As for "our distance of two hundred years ...
refracting all we perceive," does that apply to *great principles*, or just *original intent*?

What could Brennan mean by "Apart from the problematic nature of the sources"? What is problematic about
the nature of the Constitution and Bill of Rights? We have
the autographs—that is, the actual, original texts. Not so
with many of the other important texts we *require* our students to study, such as Homer's *Odyssey*, Plato's *Republic*,
Aristotle's *The Nicomachean Ethics*, Herodotus' *Histories*,
and Marcus Aurelius' *Meditations*, to name a few. But these
texts come to us from copies of copies, and those from a
long line of other copies. We do not have any autographs
of these books, and the interval between the autographs
and the earliest extant copies of these are *many* hundreds
of years—for Plato, about 1,200 years. Now here are texts
with some authentic "problematic nature of the sources,"
yet we have enough philological confidence in these texts
for them to be a ubiquitous part of Western curriculum—
so much so that a person unfamiliar with these works is
considered culturally illiterate.

For our founding texts, the interval of time between the
composition of the texts and the earliest extant copies is
zero. The number of translations required for us to read

these texts is zero—thus having none of the translational complications inherent in works written in other languages. Those other texts were written thousands of miles from America, but these were written on our own soil. Again, what problematic nature might he be referring to?

JUSTICE BRENNAN'S DECAY RATE OF TEXTUALLY TRANSMITTED KNOWLEDGE

Brennan believes "our distance of two hundred years can only work as a prism refracting all we perceive." If his "two hundred years" are an unbridgeable temporal distance, then what about the wider implications of his hermeneutical skepticism for texts written two thousand years ago? As Hirsch said regarding hermeneutical skepticism, "At stake ultimately is the right of any humanistic discipline to claim genuine knowledge. Since all human studies, as Dilthey observed, are founded upon the interpretation of texts, valid interpretation is crucial to the validity of all subsequent inferences in those studies."[19]

If Brennen's claim is accurate, validity is lost after two hundred years. The decay rate of carbon-14 is such that its usefulness as a dating technique expires at around 50,000 years—the formula being $N(t) = N0e\ kt$. Brennan's textual decay rate—the rate at which a text can be useful in transmitting *intent* through space and time—arrives at 0% at two hundred years. Roughly speaking, using his decay rate, we have 18% less validity in determining what his intent was thirty-six years ago when he said, "Our distance of

---

19   E. D. Hirsch, Jr., *Validity in Interpretation* (New Haven: Yale University Press, 1967), viii.

two hundred years can only act as a prism refracting all we perceive"—since 200 years divided by the 36 years since he said it equals 18%.

Yet, Brennan does not explain how recovering *original intent* has a high decay rate, but the recovery of *great principles* has a very low decay rate. Somehow, texts are hampered when trying to transmit *original intent*, but not when transmitting *great principles*. In reality, his propositions boil down to this: what would hamper liberal/progressive policy preferences cannot be recovered, but what would promote those preferences can easily be recovered. Not surprisingly, *original intent* is traditional beliefs in limited government, enumerated powers, federalism, respect for American traditions, Judeo-Christian values, hermeneutical optimism, public expressions of faith, and separation of powers and checks and balances. And, again not surprisingly, *great principles* are unlimited government, rejection of enumerated powers, erosion of federalism, dismantling of American traditions, repudiation of Judeo-Christian values, hermeneutical skepticism, repression of public expressions of faith and renouncing the need for separation of powers and checks and balances.

How true that INSINCERITY IS THE ENEMY OF SENSIBLE LANGUAGE! The absurdities in Brennan's Georgetown lecture are the absurdities of the Living Constitution. What liberal theologians have done to the Bible is the same thing liberal judges have done to the Constitution—the hermeneutical skepticism employed by liberal theologians is the same as that of liberal judges. Because the Bible and the Constitution impose restrictions on liberal religious and political preferences, some means must be devised to preserve the symbol while eviscerating its meaning. The Living Constitution certainly does that to the Constitution and Bill of Rights. Keep the original copy of the Constitution and Bill of Rights safely displayed in the National Archives and just pay hypocritical homage to their meaning.

REFUTING THE DOCTRINE OF INCORPORATION: THE BILL OF RIGHTS IS LIKE POMPEII, AND INCORPORATION IS ITS VESUVIUS

WHAT IS THE DOCTRINE OF INCORPORATION?

The Doctrine of Incorporation is the gradual process by which the Supreme Court determines it is time to require the States to comply with some particular clause of the Bill of Rights. There are 28 clauses which compose the relevant eight amendments—Amendment I through VIII. (Refer to pages 230-233 for the list of these clauses and their labeling.) As of 2021, 23 of those 28 clauses have been incorporated (applied) against the States. The first clause to be incorporated against the States was the Taking of Private Property Clause (5-a) of Amendment V in 1897. The latest was the Excessive Fines Clause (8-b) of Amendment VIII in 2019.

The timeline in Figure 6 charts the gradual beginnings of the Doctrine of Incorporation, with the first case occurring twenty-eight years after its *alleged* genesis, the second case twenty-eight years after that. It took a total of fifty-six years for the Court to deliver those two cases—and we thought

TIMELINE OF INCORPORATION

Figure 6.

BILL OF RIGHTS CLAUSES INCORPORATED AGAINST THE STATES

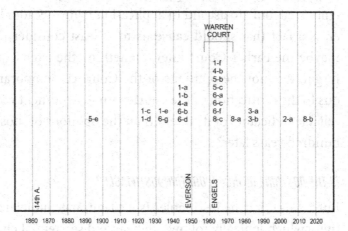

the US Postal Service was slow. A few more cases occurred, then five cases occurred in the 1940s when the Incorporation solidifies into a more defined interpretational theory, thanks to the Court and Justice Black in the 1947 *Everson* decision. The incorporation activity goes dormant in the 1950s, only to explode in the 1960s into a full-blown tsunami of judicial imperialism during the Warren Court—having realized Incorporation had given them sufficient "interpretive" cover to amend the Constitution at will. (It is for good reason the Warren Court has been named the most liberal Court in US history.) The 1980s saw two cases, no cases in the 1990s, one in the 2000s, and finally, one in the 2010s. The cases of Incorporation significantly declined, *mostly* because the Warren Court had incorporated almost everything, leaving the Burger Court only a few crumbs.

Practically the only clause left unincorporated against the States is the Dog Catcher Clause.

Observing the anemic pace at which Incorporation was embraced, only to ascend in application many decades later, is a fact that should cause us to at least consider that maybe the earlier Court knew something the later Court forgot. Are not the opinions of the Court contemporaneous to the ratification of the Fourteenth Amendment more reliable indicators of its intent than the opinions of those a hundred years later?

IS THE DOCTRINE OF INCORPORATION JUSTIFIABLE?

But is this doctrine justifiable? Is it a legitimate judicial activity which logically follows a linear and sequential chain of reasoning based on constitutional orthodoxy and history? Or is it the greatest manifestation of judicial usurpation in the history of the United States government?

The doctrine is not justifiable. It does not logically follow a chain of reasoning supporting its repugnant consequences. It is the greatest manifestation of judicial usurpation in the history of our federal government. And here is my case against it.

First, the American people have been told that the Fourteenth Amendment applied the Bill of Rights against the States. This is demonstrably false. What has applied the Bill of Rights to the States is the Neo-Constitutional Court *saying* "the Fourteenth Amendment applied the Bill of Rights to the States." The dividing line between the Paleo-Constitution and the Neo-Constitution was not drawn in 1868 with the Fourteenth Amendment, but was drawn when the Court began *saying* the Fourteenth Amendment did that. As Justice Felix Frankfurter once admonished the Court, "The relevant historical materials demonstrate conclusively that Congress and the members of the legislatures of the ratifying States, did not contemplate that the Fourteenth Amendment was a shorthand incorporation of the first eight amendments making them applicable as explicit restrictions upon the States."[20]

Regarding the function of the Bill of Rights, there are three opinions as to its function. One group, the most historically naïve, think the Bill of Rights has *always* functioned the way it does today—a list of citizens' rights to be protected against intrusion from all levels of government. Another group is aware that "something" transformed the Bill of Rights into a protection against all levels of government. They believe that "something" was the Fourteenth Amendment, and that "something" was the product of a legitimate constitutional development. The last group believes the Bill of Rights should function in the same way it did before the Court started using it in the way it is used in contemporary jurisprudence—it should still apply only as restrictions on the federal government. The jurisdictional function intended by the Founders should be the reigning one today.

The Fourteenth Amendment was adopted in 1868 to grant citizenship rights to former slaves. It required each state to extend to former slaves the same rights and protections it provided to other citizens. The manner in which

---

20   Raoul Berger, *The Fourteenth Amendment and the Bill of Rights* (Norman: University of Oklahoma Press, 1989), 8-9.

Michigan treated its white citizens is the way it must treat former slaves. The same goes for the other states. It did not prescribe how those various states should treat their citizens, just that it had to be the same within each state. There could not be a due process for one race, but a different one for another. The same held true of equal protection. The amendment did not allow the Court to prescribe the contours of each states' due process or equal protection, just that they had to be the same for all races.

When the legislatures of the States agreed to the adoption of the Fourteenth Amendment, they were agreeing to relinquish a small portion of their jurisdictional domain concerning citizenship—former slaves will be citizens as whites were. They did not agree to relinquish the massive amount of jurisdictional domain which has been usurped by the Court's squeezed exegesis of the Fourteenth Amendment.

Since about the 1930s, the Court has depicted the States as saying, "We agree to the Fourteenth Amendment, and understood that by agreeing to adopt it, we are consciously aware that we have agreed to allow the federal government to take any or all of our jurisdictional domains, and to take that jurisdiction at whatever time and for whatever occasion they deem appropriate. We trust the good intentions of the federal government and are confident they will take only when it is necessary. Though we as states share a long history of fierce independence and resistance to centralized power, we now renounce that long history of jurisdictional hoarding. We know one of the intentions of this amendment is to annul the *Dred Scott* decision, which blocked former slaves from citizenship, but we are looking forward to the many and unforeseen ways in which the federal government will lead us. We also have come to realize the federal government is better prepared than we are to determine how our citizens should be treated."

Is the above scenario likely? Is it at all plausible that the States would agree to something like this? Are we to believe they consciously gave a jurisdictional *blank check* to the federal government? As said earlier, a common interpretational fallacy is to ignore the storyline of an interpretive community's history. I doubt anyone familiar with the States' history in regards to independence and autonomy, when presented with this scenario, would conclude it to be plausible. This simply does not synchronize with the storyline of America.

Now, here is a more plausible scenario. The States were saying, "By adopting the Fourteenth Amendment, we are agreeing to relinquish a small portion of our jurisdictional domain in regards to the citizenship of former slaves. We are aware the intention of this amendment is to annul the *Dred Scott* decision, which had constitutionalized the denial of citizenship to slaves and free blacks. We do not casually relinquish our jurisdictional domains, domains of independence and autonomy which were fiercely won in the War of Independence. The adoption of this amendment must not be construed as a relinquishment of other unintended or unnamed jurisdictional domains. Our assent to the adoption of this amendment is not a reversal of our strong belief in federalism, and is not a reversal of our view of the Bill of Rights as being a limitation on federal powers only."

The former scenario is implausible, the latter plausible. The latter sounds like one which harmonizes with a common sense understanding of our history, traditions, and reputation. The implausibility that the former would harmonize with the storyline of the American States is one of the evidences that the Doctrine of Incorporation is an unjustified usurpation of jurisdictional domains which the States never intentionally, or unintentionally, relinquished to federal power. The later Court stole the checkbook and forged the signatures.

Second, the Doctrine of Incorporation was explicitly rejected by Congress three times in the 1870s. Multiple attempts were made through legislation to apply the Bill of Rights to the States. Congress rejected Judge Elisha P. Hurlbut's amendment proposal in 1870, two years *after* the ratification of the Fourteenth Amendment. Congress rejected Francis Abbot and the National Liberal League's amendment proposal in 1874, six years *after* the Fourteenth Amendment. And, for a third time, Congress rejected Representative James Blaine's amendment proposal in 1875, seven years *after* the Fourteenth Amendment. The *amendment* approach to modifying the Bill of Rights failed spectacularly.

Third, the Doctrine of Incorporation was rejected multiple times by the Court just subsequent to the ratification of the Fourteenth Amendment. As said before, the judicial opinions of those contemporaneous to that amendment would be better indicators of the intent of the amendment, and of the mindset of the States who adopted it. The Court rejected an 1873 attempt to claim the Fourteenth

Amendment was intended to apply the Bill of Rights to the States in the *Slaughterhouse Cases*. The Court decision rejected that claim. Again, in 1884, the Court rejected another attempt to claim the amendment applied to the States. In the *Hurtado Case*, the plaintiff argued that the Fourteenth Amendment had applied the Bill of Rights to the States. The Court's 7-1 decision ruled the amendment was not intended to apply the Fifth Amendment to state criminal trials. The interpretational approached failed, until 1897.

Fourth, the behavior of our nation revealed its *assumptions* as to how our governmental systems functioned. Orthopraxy is indicative of one's orthodoxy. In 1920, the nation *assumed* that a constitutional amendment was required for women to have the right to vote in every state. After a massive investment of time and energy, the nation adopted the Nineteenth Amendment, granting suffrage to women. But why the massive investment if this was actually granted to them by the Equal Protection Clause of the Fourteenth Amendment? Isn't it much easier to persuade five judges than millions of Americans and dozens of States? The advocates of Neo-Constitutionalism have certainly found that to be so. Under Paleo-Constitutionalism, women needed an amendment to achieve their goal. Under Neo-Constitutionalism, gay marriage advocates did not. Democratic means were once required—now only judicial means are required. Pre-Incorporation times were democratic—Incorporation times, undemocratic. Americans used to believe in a rock-solid Constitution, but Incorporation has made it clay in the hands of the Court. Pre-Incorporation jurisprudence and Incorporation jurisprudence is not a difference in degree, but a difference in kind. In Pre-Incorporation times, a willful judge had to cloak his bending of the law. In Incorporation, he now publicly announces that judges ought to construe the Constitution in ways they think best. As Justice Thurgood Marshall once said, "You do what you think is right and let the law catch up."

Fifth, the Doctrine of Incorporation was fabricated by the very entity which the Bill of Rights was intended to restrict. Had the States convened a Constitutional Convention where they adopted an amendment which explicitly said, "We consciously consent to the application of the Bill of Rights to ourselves and are willing to comply with the implications of such an action," then the Doctrine, wise or not, would at least have democratic legitimacy. But how can a doctrine that so radically transforms the governmental landscape of a nation have any legitimacy when its invention restricts the restrictors, and that by the restrictees. The teenagers have placed the parents on restriction!

Sixth, the Doctrine of Incorporation has contributed to the killing of the Court's institutional credibility by decimating unanimity. It allowed the Court to expand its judicial domain into many areas of highly controversial issues which are better resolved by state and local authorities. "The more of our rights we hand to judges, the less of them we keep within the kinds of social and political institutions that are accustomed to—and usually better at—optimizing competing values," declared Jamal Greene.[21] The theory

---

21   Jamal Greene, *How Rights Went Wrong* (New York: Houghton Mifflin Harcourt Publishing, 2021), 8.

of the Living Constitution loaded the gun—the Doctrine pulled the trigger. As addressed before, the Living Constitution is soil in which the Incorporation grew. Incorporation could never have grown in the soil of originalism. The doctrine *is* anti-originalism.

Very few Americans have heard of the doctrine, much less know what it is. But what millions of Americans do know is that there is something wrong with the federal ban on prayer in all public schools. They know something just isn't coherent about the ban on public religious symbols at Christmas. They may not be able to articulate that intuitive feeling of "something doesn't square here" shared by many millions, but they do look askance at the Court for having facilitated all this. Their "something doesn't square here" feeling was shared by Chief Justice Rehnquist when he said the Court's opinion "bristles with hostility to all things religious in public life." This was said in his dissent in the June 2000 *Santa Fe Independent School District v. Doe* case, when the Court struck down student-led prayer.

The Founders "bristled with friendliness to all things religious in public life," but this Court "bristles with hostility to all things religious in public life." And most Americans know who to blame for decades of anti-religious animus—the Court and the ACLU, which it has empowered. The doctrine has allowed the Court to stick its judicial nose into many jurisdictional domains of very controversial issues, ones which our Founders wisely knew would be better dealt with at state and local levels.

There is a large body of historical materials demonstrating that Congress, along with the ratifying States, never intended for the Fourteenth Amendment to be used as it is now being used in Supreme Court jurisprudence.

NEGATIVE RESULTS OF THE DOCTRINE OF INCORPORATION

The six clauses of the First Amendment were restrictions on the federal government, not the States. Throughout the history of Court decisions until around 1940, which includes the approximately seventy-two years after the adoption of the Fourteenth Amendment, the Court operated under the *Barrow* "assumption" that the Bill of Rights "contain no expression indicating an intention to apply them to the state governments" and under the *Permoli* "assumption" that "the Constitution makes no provision for protecting the citizens of the respective States in their religious liberties; this is left to the state constitutions and laws." The Court embraced a clear and definite "Doctrine of Non-Incorporation" from the time of the Constitutional Convention until many decades after the Fourteenth Amendment.

Figure 7 shows the percentage of the Court's agenda devoted to First Amendment cases. In the forty-six term years from 1888 to 1934, thirty-two term years recorded no First Amendment cases. Only once during those term years did the agenda's percentage crest 2%. In 1936 it reached 3.5%, eventually reaching 5.2% in 1942. During the 1950s, the Court's agenda began regularly exceeding 5%. It was 1965 before the cases reached 10% or more. Their agenda's highest percentage was reached in 1970 at 16.7%.

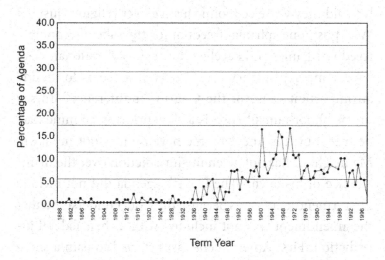

Figure 7.

FIRST AMENDMENT
DECISIONS

COMPOSITION OF THE AGENDA OF THE
UNITED STATES SUPREME COURT, 1888-1997

Why did the Court, before the 1940s, seem so unconcerned about First Amendment rights? Aren't these six clauses, especially the two religious clauses, listed "First" because of their importance? Why would the Court go decade after decade without giving them the priority we have witnessed now for the last 50+ years? Lanier attributes this lack of concern to the Court's engagement in "resolving economic issues."[22] Richard L. Pacelle, Jr. also attributes the almost non-existent percentage of cases to its commitment, before 1950, to "economic issues."[23]

22 Ibid., 78.
23 Richard L. Pacelle, Jr., *The Transformation of the Supreme Court's Agenda: From the New Deal to the Reagan Administration* (Boulder: Westview Press, 1991), 22.

But, could not the Court walk and chew gum at the same time? Could they not have relieved the "injustice" of Americans who were being denied their "First Amendment rights" and address economic issues simultaneously? Did they value economic justice over religious justice? Why postpone spiritual freedom for the sake of economic freedom? Lanier and Pacelle's "low priority" rationale does have some explanatory use. However, it seems to muddy an important cause of the Court's "indifference." To say my neighbor's uncut lawn is a "low priority" of mine may be true, but it is uncut by me because it is not my lawn. My neighbor has not given me jurisdiction over the maintenance of his lawn. The Court's agenda did not include First Amendment cases because the Court understood that the amendment was not included within their federal jurisdiction. First Amendment cases started to gain a share of their agenda only after the Living Constitution slowly began introducing inexcusable sloppiness into constitutional interpretation (i.e., the Court *saying* "the Fourteenth Amendment applied the Bill of Rights to the States"). This opened the door for the Doctrine of Incorporation to "legitimize" the Court's usurping of the States' jurisdictions—jurisdictions well established for almost one hundred and fifty years.

THE DOCTRINE OF INCORPORATION AND CIVIL LIBERTIES/RIGHTS DECISIONS

Figure 8 shows that the proportion of the Court's agenda involving civil rights began skyrocketing in the 1940s. As the Doctrine became implemented into the Court's decision-making rationale, more and more domains of

previously well-defined state jurisdictions were colonized by judicial fiat. The States did not consciously or willingly abdicate these jurisdictions—they were usurped.

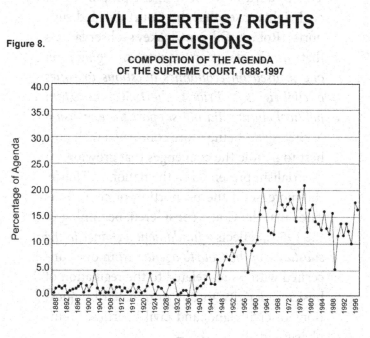

Figure 8.

CIVIL LIBERTIES / RIGHTS DECISIONS

COMPOSITION OF THE AGENDA OF THE SUPREME COURT, 1888-1997

Before Incorporation, the Court's agenda reached 5% or more only twice in the fifty-eight term years from 1888 to 1944 (in 1903 and 1944). Between 1925 and 1939, zero percent occurred five times (1925, 1929, 1933, 1937, and 1939). Beginning in 1945, civil rights cases became a regular part of the Court's agenda. A rapid increase began with 8.3% in 1947, 8.9% in 1950, 10.4% in 1952, 12.5% in 1955, and 18.5% in 1962. The highest percent was reached at 25.0% in 1978.

As with First Amendment cases, a shift in priorities is attributed to the unprecedented attention given to civil rights by the Court. Lanier states,

> This upward movement in the proportion of civil rights cases that the Court decided supports [Robert G.] McCloskey's observations that *the Court's priorities were changing from one focused on economics questions to issues of civil rights ... Prior to the 1950s, the extant political culture did not support the expansion of civil rights,* being more concerned with how best to handle the challenges that growing industrialism presented to the nation.... Hence, the increase in the proportion of civil rights cases that the Court considered, beginning in the 1950s, reflects a *fundamental change in the substance of the Court's agenda* from one concerned with issues related to the regulation of business activity to one dominated by questions of civil rights and civil liberties.[24] (emphasis added)

The advent of the Living Constitution and its progeny, the Doctrine of Incorporation, occurred at roughly the same time, and is at least one of the important causes of the skyrocketing of cases regarding the First Amendment, civil rights, and privacy. Two correlated events do not necessarily prove a cause-and-effect relationship, but Lanier's

---

24   Drew Noble Lanier, *Of Time and Judicial Behavior: United States Supreme Court Agenda-Setting and Decision-Making, 1888-1997* (New Jersey: Associated University Press, 2003), 76-77.

statement that "the Court's *priorities* were changing from one focused on economics questions to issues of civil rights" may be inferring a cause-and-effect relationship which is not the case. Isn't it possible that the extremely low, and sometimes non-existent, percentages reflected in Figures 7, 8, and 9 prior to the 1950s were because the Court *used* to understand that their jurisdiction did not include those issues? Shouldn't we interpret the data in these charts as "changes in jurisdiction," rather than "changes in priorities"? It should be remembered that the Bill of Rights is jurisdictional in nature, and nothing occurred between the Founding and now to justify how the Court transformed that nature—including the Court *saying* the Fourteenth Amendment did.

"Prior to the 1950s," Lanier said, "the extant political culture did not support the expansion of civil rights...." These types of statements seem to imply that no civil rights existed before the 1950s. I believe it would be more accurate to say "the extant political culture" did not want to remove these issues from the States' jurisdictions by transporting them into the domain of federal jurisdiction—jurisdictions defined in the Constitution and reconfirmed in the Bill of Rights—and that "the extant political culture," including the pre-1950s Court, knew things that the post-1950s Court forgot or ignored. The loss of the distinction between federal jurisdiction and state jurisdiction is our loss of the concept of federalism. This loss has allowed new non-historical notions to insinuate themselves into American governing assumptions.

Should the "fundamental change in the substance of the Court's agenda" be something we simply trust was a legitimate "change"? The charts definitely show a change in the agenda. But that does not automatically imply a benevolent, rational, evolutionary transition. The Doctrine of Incorporation removed the restrictions on federal jurisdiction, thus allowing the Court to breach the formerly well established "wall of separation between federal government and States."

THE DOCTRINE OF INCORPORATION AND PRIVACY DECISIONS

None of these charts display the complete arbitrariness of judicial imperialism than the one in Figure 9. A picture is worth a thousand words—so are charts. The chart shows in dazzling clarity the birth, out of thin air, of a new constitutional doctrine—a general "right to privacy" created in 1965 with the *Griswold v. Connecticut* decision. It was the result of judicial intercourse between its advocates, the Yale law school faculty, Planned Parenthood, and the ACLU, and its benefactor, the Court. This new doctrine was perfectly suited to enlist the Court on the side of those whose Sexual Revolution could not succeed in any other way. They needed new constitutional law created through the judiciary if their goals of social permissiveness were to succeed, because neither the Constitution nor the legislative opinion of the American public would deliver their permissive policy preferences. They had turned their efforts towards the judiciary as a result of their legislative failures. These advocates wanted a Court to make new major policy rather than continue to implement those duly

PRIVACY DECISIONS

Figure 9.

COMPOSITION OF THE AGENDA OF THE UNITED STATES SUPREME COURT, 1888-1997

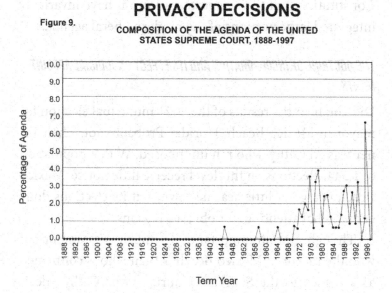

Term Year

constituted. And the Neo-Constitutional Court gave them what they wanted, and more.

As indicated in Figure 9, one would think the complete absence of cases throughout the Court's history might have served as an embarrassing rebuke to the claim that the Constitution and Bill of Rights provide for a "general right of privacy." Not so. Its advocates wanted one and the Court was glad to serve it up. Borrowing from Star Trek, their motto is: To boldly go where no Court has gone before.

This new "right" was, and still is, a loose cannon. We never know where it might fire next. Its meaning is undefined and its scope unexplained. It has been fifty-six years since its fabrication, and the Court still has not said how far this new constitutional right to privacy extends. In reality, it is a warrant fabricated by judges to do whatever they wish. These judges legislate policy in the name of the

339

Constitution, but their departures from it have invariably integrated large portions of the modern liberal agenda.

THE DOCTRINE OF INCORPORATION AND ITS EFFECT ON JUDICIAL APPOINT-MENTS

Did you hear the results of the 2021 municipal election for mayor in Mexico Beach, Florida? Probably not. The winner was Al Cathy, who ran unopposed. With a population of 1,544, elections on this level receive little notice. Mexico Beach is a great little seaside town, but its elections don't get national attention, for obvious reasons.

Though not unimportant, it's much less important who the mayor of Mexico Beach is than who is confirmed as a justice to the Supreme Court. Mayor Cathy's decisions affect 1,544 people; a Supreme Court justice's affect 329,000,000. However, in the pre-Incorporation era, it was much less important than now because a justice's decisions were much more limited in scope. While a Court justice's decisions have always affected all Americans, there were vastly fewer domains into which a justice could reach. Incorporation changed that. The judicial branch was never intended to become this important and be America's primary policymaker, thus transforming its role in the American political system. The hysterical frenzy which now surrounds Supreme Court nominations is one of the repugnant consequences of allowing the Supreme Court to colonize, as its own, vast areas of American civil life which the Founders wisely left to state and local decision-makers. In the pre-Incorporation era, the Constitution "meant what it said"—in the Incorporation era it "means what it *ought* to mean." At one time it was rock-solid—it is now clay in the hands of justices. Incorporation is to blame for much of that.

It's true that television and media have added to that hysterical frenzy, but the major contribution is that America has allowed the judiciary to become just another political body. Incorporation facilitated the Court's politicization, making it impossible to confine the judiciary's power to its proper role. It is just as important for the judiciary to be confined to its proper role as it is for the executive and legislative branches. Incorporation has made it theoretically and pragmatically impossible to objectively define the limit of the Court's legitimate authority.

There has been an *interpretational war* raging longer than conservatives were aware of. It took far too long for them to understand the implications of Incorporation. The liberals have known this for a long time. From the start, liberals understood the Court would be a willing ally in their "squeezing" and "inventing against" the Founders' intentions. As late as the 1990s, conservatives still thought nominees were to be evaluated on the bases of experience and legal knowledge. They were playing by the old standard, but liberals were playing by a new standard—the standard of ideology. No one, liberal or conservative, is pretending any longer to nominate using the old standard. But liberals started it. President George W. Bush saw the change. However, it was President Trump who saw clearly how to proceed, given the new realities of judicial nominations. He unapologetically made nominating originalists a major item in his agenda.

The patron saint of conservatism, Ronald Reagan, was operating by the old standard when he nominated Sandra Day O'Connor in 1981 and Anthony Kennedy in 1987. O'Connor received a confirmation vote of 99-0 and Kennedy 97-0. His two appointments began as moderates but drifted to the left during their tenure. As stated earlier, Incorporation destroyed the Court's decision-making unanimity. It has also destroyed the unanimity of the Senate's nominating process. When John Roberts became chief justice in 2005, his vote was 78-22, which was at that time considered a high degree of opposition. Here are the votes for the last seven appointments:

2005	Samuel Alito	58-42
2009	Sonia Sotomayor	68-31
2010	Elena Kagan	63-37
2017	Neil Gorsuch	54-45
2018	Brett Kavanaugh	50-48
2020	Amy Coney Barrett	52-48
2022	Ketanji Brown Jackson	53-47

Since conservatives have finally comprehended how the appointing of justices has changed, and now understand the damages caused by trying to play fair, the trend of high opposition in the voting pattern will continue for a long time. John Robert's "high" 22 opposition votes is now a thing of the past. Anything close to unanimity will not be reached in the foreseeable future. Until Americans return the Court's legitimate jurisdictional domains to those defined by the Founders, this abysmal division will persist.

The Court should *never* have become *this* important. It was never intended to be the primary force in American policy formation.

CHAPTER 16

A GRAMMATICAL LOOK AT THE ESTABLISHMENT CLAUSE AND FREE EXERCISE OF STATE-ESTABLISHMENTS OF RELIGION CLAUSE

WHY ARE WE SUCH bad readers and listeners? Try this. Ask ten people what "Congress shall make no law respecting the establishment of religion" means and I'll bet the family farm that all ten will say, "It means the *government* cannot do such-and-such." Then ask them what they mean by *government*. "Well, all government, of course!" they exclaim. Then you ask, "You mean the federal government and state governments?" "Certainly," they respond. At that point you ask, "But how can it be both federal and state governments when it clearly says, 'Congress shall make no law'?" Most will pause, puzzled, having been confronted with something so obvious, but so overlooked. They are not alone.

This is just one element of the received "wisdom" of American's recent constitutional history which is almost entirely wrong. How can a law which clearly states, "Congress shall make no law" be said to mean, "Michigan can make no law"? Isn't that odd? But conflating federal and state governments with "Congress" is something millions of Americans do without a second thought, and they are unaware how *the erosion of the concept of federalism* has caused that conflation. How can we be so bad at misreading this simple imperative? How did we miss this undeniable grammatical fact? Equating "all" government with "Congress" is something which has insinuated itself into our unexamined constitutional assumptions.

Stephen Mansfield's *Ten Torture Words* investigates the forces which have tortured "Congress shall make no law respecting the establishment of religion." His subtitle, *How the Founding Fathers Tried to Protect Religion in America ... and What's Happened Since,* is also what this chapter is about. He is correct about those ten words. But perhaps another book should be written titled *One Tortured Word,* that word being "Congress."

ESTABLISH MEANS ENDORSE?

The next element of the received "wisdom" of recent constitutional history concerns "establishment." This is the second most tortured word in the Establishment Clause. It has been so squeezed, mutilated, and tortured that it is now means "endorsement." But what does establishment mean? What did it mean when the Founders used it in the Establishment Clause? For its definition, the Founders didn't need to look far, nor did they need a dictionary. Of thirteen states at the time of the Constitutional Convention, nine had establishments of religion—that is 75% of the states, and, therefore, 75% of the delegates. The consensus of the convention was pro-establishment—that is, pro-state establishments of religion. What they were not supporters of was a federal establishment of religion. That is what the Establishment Clause and Free Exercise of State Establishments of Religion Clause of the First Amendment is about.

The ultra-separationist Barry Lynn would probably twist the last paragraph to say I'm a supporter of establishments of religion. I'm not! I oppose establishments of religion, both state and federal. It was a great thing when the last state, Massachusetts, finally disestablished its Congregational church establishment. It had been the state's official, tax-supported religion since the original settlement of the Puritan colony in the early seventeenth century. But it is a historical fallacy to portray the Founders as anti-establishment advocates. They weren't—they were anti-federal establishment advocates.

Establishment means to make a particular church the official state religion, to fund that church with state tax revenue, and empower that church with authority to intimidate or to discourage the activities of other, non-official, churches. Thankfully, establishments of religion ended a long time ago. However, it is hard to dislodge from our minds the Neo-Constitutional notion that all those disestablishments occurred because the citizens of those states rose up and demanded their "First Amendment" rights.

None of the legislative proceedings have any references to such rights. Those involved in the move to disestablish could never have imagined such an approach in the pursuit of their goal. Their Paleo-Constitutional minds would not have conceived it. They understood what the two establishment of religion clauses meant, and the two had no "US constitutional" relevance to their state policy preferences.

Establishment does not mean "endorse." After torturing the Establishment Clause by incorporating it against the States, the Court tortures it again by "expanding" establishment's meaning to include "endorse." But we should not get too distracted by the mincing of words over what establishment is, or whether it can also mean endorse. The point of the matter is this: whatever establishment or endorsement means, if it pertains to religion, the federal government was precluded from addressing it, and was required to leave religious matters to the States.

There are many things we know about the Establishment Clause that the Founders did not mean. Here are some:

1. It did not mean chaplains could not be hired by the federal government and their salaries paid by federal tax dollars.
2. It did not mean federal buildings could not be used for church services.
3. It did not mean Ten Commandments tablets were forbidden in federal buildings and courthouses.
4. It did not mean statues of clergymen, like Reverend Roger Williams, Reverend Peter Muhlenberg, and

Reverend Marcus Whiteman could not be displayed in federal buildings.

5. It did not mean the executive, legislative, and judicial branches could not open with prayer.
6. It did not mean Scripture could not be engraved on federal buildings.
7. It did not mean the military could not have a chaplaincy program.
8. It did not mean the military could not print Bibles or religious materials.

All of these fail to pass Justice O'Connor's "endorsement test."

IS IT THE FREE EXERCISE OF RELIGION CLAUSE OR THE FREE EXERCISE OF THE STATE-ESTABLISHMENT OF RELIGION CLAUSE?

The phrase, "or prohibiting the free exercise thereof," is commonly referred to as the Free Exercise Clause, and is usually meant as the Free Exercise of Religion Clause. As said earlier, in regards to biblical parables, a passage's real point can be obscured by a less-than-accurate title. The parable of the "Good" Samaritan is such a case. Jesus' real point in the parable is easier to grasp when the title is changed to the "Despised" Samaritan. The Samaritan was good, but Jesus' point was that he was despised. The same goes with the Free Exercise of Religion Clause.

The Free Exercise of Religion Clause is one of the commonly used titles. However, the actual clause is referring to "freedom of the state-establishment of religion." Yes, it includes "free exercise of religion," but the grammar most strongly suggests "free exercise of state-establishments of religion." It should be retitled the Free Exercise of State-Establishment of Religion Clause. Yes, that is too long, so let's just stay with Free Exercise Clause. But the point of this discussion is to show what the grammar and context are actually pointing to has been overlooked, which is, there can be no federal establishment of religion, and the federal government cannot prohibit state establishments of religion.

Hard as it is for our Neo-Constitutional ears to hear, this is what the evidence demonstrates.

The two clauses read, "Congress shall make no law respecting an establishment of religion, or prohibiting the free exercise thereof." Grammatically speaking, what is the "thereof"? It is a type of grammatical blank. Something goes in the blank. Something goes in "thereof." "Thereof" what? Is it "religion" or "establishment of religion"? Let's examine the grammar.

Grammatically, the subject is "Congress." The prepositional phrase is "shall make no law respecting." The object of the sentence is "an establishment of religion." It is what goes in the "thereof." The object is not "religion"; it is "state-establishment of religion." To refer to it as the Free Exercise of Religion Clause is incomplete. It is the Free Exercise of State-Establishment of Religion Clause, and retitling it this way reveals what the clause is actually saying, and reveals how misleading the former title is. As asked before, how is it that we are such bad readers? One reason this is being so badly misread is that we anticipate what we think it says, that is, what we have been told it says, without slowing down and actually reading it carefully for ourselves. We forget that "anticipation colors perception," and uncritically presume what we think it is going to say. If we can emancipate ourselves from what has insinuated itself into our received "wisdom" regarding these clauses, then we can read, for the first time, what the authors meant when they wrote them.

What the clause is saying is that the federal government cannot prohibit the States' establishments of religion. The States were free to establish, disestablish, or reestablish as they saw fit. And how do we know this? Other than the text itself, here are two examples which prove this.

First, the content of the correspondence between the Danbury Baptists and Thomas Jefferson shows us the constitutional reality of their day. As stated by Dreisbach,

> Both Jefferson and the Baptists understood that, as a matter of federalism, the nation's chief executive could not disturb church-state relations and policies that concerned religious liberty in the respective states. In their letter, the Baptists observed: "Sir, we are sensible that the President of the united States, is not the national Legislator, & also sensible that the national government cannot destroy the Laws of each State."[1]

---

1   Daniel L. Dreisbach, *Thomas Jefferson and the Wall of Separation between Church and State* (New York: New York University Press, 2002), 50.

The law which occasioned their correspondence was the Connecticut state law allowing the state establishment of the Congregationalist church.

Second, in 1870, former New York judge Elisha P. Hurlbut proposed a constitutional amendment which would have extended the First Amendment to the States. He proposed this because he knew there was nothing in the Constitution or Bill of Rights prohibiting the States from having religious establishments. Though all States had already disestablished, this would prevent them from reestablishing. Aware that the Court could *strain* to reach other conclusions, and also aware of the impropriety of such an approach, he explains,

> There are ... clauses in the Constitution of the United States which might be *tortured* into a construction prohibitory of state establishment of religion, by a court which should *lean against it*; or might be held, as I think more properly by an impartial legal tribunal, not applicable to the case: such as the clauses which provide the privileges and immunities of the citizens of the several states shall be equal, and the United States shall guaranty to every state, a republican form of government.[2] (emphasis added)

Rejecting the "tortured" interpretational approach, Hurlbut did not consider the recently adopted Fourteenth Amendment to be a possible vehicle for an interpretation

---

2   Phillip Hamburger, *Separation of Church and State* (Cambridge: Harvard University Press, 2002), 437.

prohibiting state establishments. He advocated that "[it] is better that a Constitution should speak plainly than *hint* its meaning" (emphasis added).[3] He states again "that there is nothing in the Constitution as it stands, which forbids a *state* from establishing a religion."[4] Many of Hurlbut's contemporaries seemed to agree, demanding their own amendments. They held this was necessary because "the Constitution ... contains no provision prohibiting the several States from establishing a State religion, or requiring a religious test for office, or disqualifying witnesses in the courts on account of their religious opinions, or likewise restricting their religious liberty."[5]

The First Amendment protects the States' establishments from having to compete against a federal establishment, and protects the States' establishments from being prohibited by the dictates of federal authority. All issues of religious establishments and of religious life were left to the citizens of the respective states to determine.

TO THE POINT—HOW PRAYER WAS REMOVED FROM PUBLIC SCHOOLS

The previous chapter was a survey of issues relevant to understanding the history of Supreme Court interpretation regarding this issue—*the changing of the Court's behavior through time regarding church/state relations, and how that change eventually led to the removal of prayer from all American public schools.* Everything in the chapter was

---

3   Ibid., 437.
4   Ibid., 437.
5   Ibid., 437-438.

included to help understand the genealogy of the removal of prayer from school. The goal of all of this is to investigate whether the change in the Court's decision-making is hermeneutically justified, or was it the product of "squeezing" or "inventing against the text."

THE GENEALOGY

Here is the genealogy of the removal of prayer.

1. After rereading the Bill of Rights, and after emancipating ourselves from the incorrect "received" history which has been insinuated into our Neo-Constitutional thinking, we discovered the original purpose for which it was intended—to serve as a restriction on federal powers, not state powers.

2. A careful exegetical and grammatical reading of the Establishment Clause and the Free Exercise Clause demonstrates how uncarefully and uncritically these clauses have been "read" to us. The Establishment Clause says Congress cannot create a federal establishment of religion—that's all it says. The Free Exercise Clause says the federal government cannot prohibit the States from having state establishments of religion or dictate religious practices observed in the States—that's all.

3. The Paleo-Constitutional Court issued a number of decisions declaring emphatically that the Bill of Rights was intended to serve as a restriction on federal powers and was not applicable to the States (*Barron v. Baltimore*, 1833 and *Permoli v. New Orleans*, 1845).

4. When the Fourteenth Amendment was adopted in 1868 it was understood to serve as an amendment to overturn the *Dred Scott* decision and to grant citizenship to former slaves. This was the understanding of the States which adopted it. It was not intended as a "blank check" written to the federal government to pillage their state jurisdictions.

5. Later, there were those who started claiming that the Fourteenth Amendment had incorporated the Bill of Rights against the States. This is proven wrong by the behavior of the States—they did not change their laws to conform to such claims. This is proven wrong by the numerous attempts to amend the Constitution to bring it in line with such policies, attempts which were all rejected by Congress. There would be no need for such amendments if the Fourteenth Amendment had already done what the amendments were intended to do. It was also proven wrong by Court decisions subsequent to the adoption of the Fourteenth Amendment (*Slaughterhouse Cases*, 1873, and *Hurtado*, 1884).

6. In 1897, the Court ignored the intent of the Fourteenth Amendment, the behavior of the States, Congress' rejection of multiple "incorporation" amendments, and the decisions of the Court contemporaneous with and just subsequent to the adoption of the amendment. In their *Chicago, Burlington, Quincy Railroad Co. v. City of Chicago* decision, the Court incorporated the fifth clause of the Fifth Amendment against the States. This mistaken

decision was the first step in a radical transformation of the American political landscape, making it possible for the Court to become the primary policymakers.

7. The adoption of the Nineteenth Amendment in 1920 granted women the right to vote. That amendment is evidence that the nation still understood that the constitutionally-prescribed method for amending the Constitution was valid and proper. If the Fourteenth Amendment did what the Court was about to begin "saying" it had done, then the amendment process could simply be circumvented and the Court could have just granted women the right to vote. The Nineteenth Amendment is an artifact from America's pre-Living Constitution and pre-Incorporation era. The *Obergefell* decision is an artifact of America's Living Constitution and Incorporation era.

8. The anemic pace at which the Court came to "discover" the amendment's "real" purpose serves as further evidence that the amendment was not what the later Court claims. It was not until 1925, twenty-eight years after the *Chicago* decision, that a second "incorporation discovery" was made.

9. The *Everson* decision in 1947 solidified the Doctrine of Incorporation into a fully developed, though heretical, theory of First Amendment jurisprudence. It incorporated the Establishment Clause against the States. This was the *crown jewel* of all Neo-Constitutional maleficence, and paved the way for the

removal of prayer from public schools fifteen years later in the *Engels* decision. With the *Everson* decision, the Court granted veto power to anti-religious advocates over the lives of millions of Americans and all fifty states. The Court had called a "Constitutional Convention," and had invited only nine delegates. Their "convention" repudiated Paleo-Constitutionalism, and enthroned Neo-Constitutionalism.

CHAPTER 17

IT IS TIME FOR A CONSTITUTIONAL REFORMATION

RETURNING TO ROOTS

There needs to be a Constitutional Reformation analogous to the sixteenth-century Christian Reformation. The Christian Reformation was an attempt to return the Church to its biblical roots. A Constitutional Reformation would return American to its constitutional roots. In the Christian Reformation, the Church was forced to rethink the method for interpreting the Christian Scriptures. A Constitutional Reformation would force Americans to rethink the method for interpreting American scripture.

In the sixteenth century, the accumulation of interpretive errors had stretched biblical theology to the breaking point. Finally, the selling of indulgences (the remission of temporal punishment due to sin) was the wildly unbiblical error that broke the camel's back. The accumulation of interpretive errors caused by Incorporation has been reaching the breaking point. The repugnant consequences of Incorporation are causing an urgent need for a

Constitutional Reformation. While medieval four-fold exegesis was the perennial interpretive heresy for the Church, Incorporation is the perennial interpretive heresy for the Constitution.

THREE "BILL OF RIGHTS" DOCTRINES

There are three doctrines of immense importance to Bill of Rights jurisprudence. One is in the past, one is present, and one is to come (hopefully).

THE DOCTRINE OF NON-INCORPORATION

The first doctrine is the Doctrine of Non-Incorporation. This was the Founders' doctrine which the Court operated on from the time of the Constitutional Convention until many decades after the adoption of the Fourteenth Amendment. As stated above, it faithfully represented the Founders' intention that the Bill of Rights was a restriction on federal powers only, and was not "incorporated" against the States. It operated on an originalist exegesis. This doctrine is a thing of the past.

THE DOCTRINE OF INCORPORATION

The second doctrine is the Doctrine of Incorporation. This is the doctrine invented by the Court against the Founders' intention for the Bill of Rights. It had its beginnings in the early twentieth century. It unfaithfully betrayed one hundred-thirty years of judicial precedence. It "incorporated" the Bill of Rights against the States. It operates on Living

Constitution exegesis. This doctrine is the one used by the Court presently.

THE DOCTRINE OF UN-INCORPORATION

The third doctrine is the Doctrine of Un-Incorporation. This is the doctrine which could return the function of the Bill of Rights to that intended by the Founders. This would reestablish the jurisdictional domains to those designed by the Founders. The federal government would be pushed back into the prescribed jurisdictions enumerated in the Constitution and Bill of Rights. The States would *reacquire* those jurisdictions they originally refused to grant to the federal government—jurisdictions "interpreted" away from them by a willful Court through the Doctrine of Incorporation. Like the Founders' Doctrine of Non-Incorporation, this doctrine operates on an originalist exegesis. This is the one which the Court should return to now.

SOLA SCRIPTURA AND *SOLA CONSTITUTIONA*

Sola scriptura (Scripture alone) was the motto of the Reformers and it stresses reliance on the Bible alone, rather than endless commentaries and traditions. *Sola constitutiona* (Constitution alone) should be the motto of a Constitutional Reformation.

Core biblical teachings had been buried under layers of "creative" approaches to interpretation (allegorical, tropological, anagogical, etc.). Core constitutional teachings have been buried under layers of "creative" approaches to interpretation (Living Constitution, Incorporation, expansivism, anti-textualism, etc.). Theologians and jurists must reject these devastatingly flawed approaches which obscure and mutilate the meaning of these authoritative texts. How did the sixteenth-century Church lose "justification by faith" and in the twenty-first century America lose "limited federal government"? One reason is the slow accumulation of mistakes, which, when compounded, can lead to conclusions wildly at odds with the original starting point. It is necessary from time to time to step back and take a fresh look at the original documents, and reanalyze their interpretive history.

The Apostle Peter warned about those who would "distort" the Scriptures and Thomas Jefferson warned about those "squeezing" and "inventing" against the Constitution. Both the "People of the Book" and the "People of the Constitution," and their ministers and judges, are responsible for defending against heresy.

Interpretational collapse can occur when documents of ultimate authority have been subjected to too much torture and unfaithful development, have been inflicted with too many unwarranted stretches and corruptions. The purpose of those documents can become so displaced and betrayed that the documents will either be officially abandoned, or, preferably, reformed.

A QUIXOTIC CALL—PROBABLY, FOR NOW

The call for reforming American jurisprudence away from the Doctrine of Incorporation by embracing the Doctrine of Un-Incorporation may be quixotic. Probably, for now. But it seemed quixotic that Martin Luther could have dislodged the scholastic theology and their medieval four-fold exegesis, both firmly entrenched in his time. Yet, against all odds, his revolutionary ideas successfully challenged the Roman Catholic Church in many ways, and set off religious and social changes still apparent today. If the hegemony of Incorporation were to be dislodged, it would not be the first time a hegemony collapsed. Things which sometimes seem unshakably strong turn out not to be—remember the former Soviet Union.

The Center for Constitutional Reformation was founded to advocate for Un-Incorporation. It is a nonprofit research and educational organization promoting the reform of much which has transpired in Supreme Court constitutional jurisprudence since the 1930s. CCR seeks to demonstrate the massive interpretational drift which has occurred and the causes of it. There is a great need to expose and reverse doctrinal impurities and the fallacious interpretive methodologies which produced them.

Today, much of what Americans embrace as legitimate constitutional wisdom is almost entirely wrong. That is why a sweeping reassessment is necessary to expose what went wrong and rediscover the Founding Fathers' Constitution.

We have six key objectives:

1. Rediscover the Founders' intents for the Constitution and Bill of Rights
2. Expose how far interpretational drift has moved us away from the Founders' intents
3. Reassess current 14th Amendment jurisprudence
4. Describe and refute the Doctrine of Incorporation
5. Advocate for specific reforms in interpretive methodologies and doctrines

6. Enhance Americans interpretive literacy in order to more quickly recognize error patterns and specious interpretations

More information regarding CCR can be found at constitutionalreformation.com.

PART FOUR

PART FOUR

EPILOGUE

INTERPRETATION HAS GIVEN ME great joy for several decades now. Its principles are beautiful and I am fascinated that writing can transmit knowledge through space and time. What an incredible thing that I can "hear" Plato, the Apostle Paul, Marcus Aurelius, Augustine, Martin Luther, Emily Dickinson, G. K. Chesterton, Margaret Thatcher, and J. R. R. Tolkien. But that is just one side of the coin.

The other side of the coin is the misery of witnessing the abuse of authors' objectives. It is distressing to observe the distortion of the Parable of the Good Samaritan by allegorization, the distortion of Christian theology by medieval four-fold exegesis, and the wholesale transformation of the Bill of Rights by the Doctrine of Incorporation.

It is also miserable to witness the assault on the objectivity of reading and writing by linguistic nihilists like Martin Heidegger, T. S. Elliot, Rudolph Bultmann, Barbara Johnson, and Jacques Derrida. It was their school of thought to which Hirsch asked, "why there has been in the past four decades a heavy and vicious assault on the sensible belief that a text means what its author meant"?[1] They reject the assumption that there exists universally valid principles of reading and writing—the primary presuppositions which make possible man's entire writing initiative. Absent those

---

1   E. D. Hirsch, *Validity in Interpretation* (New Haven: Yale, 1967), 1.

valid principles, writing, and reading is no more bona fide than alchemy or astrology. This book is an assault on linguistic nihilism, and an apologetic in support of the universally valid principles of writing and reading.

As a precursor to Scalia's call for training in legal hermeneutics, Johann Martin Chladenius, in his 1742 *Introduction to the Correct Interpretation of Reasonable Discourses and Writings*, instructed jurists and theologians to see "how important it is that a person first thoroughly acquaint himself with hermeneutics before making this discipline his life work.... A person who is well versed in theology and jurisprudence should firmly inculcate himself with the principles of interpretation."[2] I agree with Chladenius. However, this subject must not be consigned only to seminaries and law schools. The people sitting in *pews* and those affected by decisions of the *bench* should be armed with the knowledge and experience to spot when things go astray. We should remember Jesus' warning to "beware of false prophets," and we should also be aware of false jurists! But how can that be done if we are uninformed interpreters? "Think what punishment shall come upon us on account of this world, when we have not ourselves loved [the gift of literacy] in the least degree, or enabled others to do so."

---

2   Johann Martin Chladenius, *Introduction to Correct Interpretation of Reasonable Discourses and Writings* (Leipzig; 1742).

THERE ARE SEVERAL WAYS YOU CAN HELP ME GET THE WORD OUT ABOUT THE MESSAGE OF THIS BOOK...

- Post a 5-Star review on Amazon.
- Write about the book on your Facebook, Twitter, Instagram, LinkedIn – any social media you regularly use!
- If you blog, consider referencing the book, or publishing an excerpt from the book with a link back to my website. You have my permission to do this as long as you provide proper credit and backlinks.
- Recommend the book to friends – word-of-mouth is still the most effective form of advertising.
- Purchase additional copies to give away as gifts.

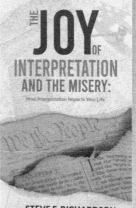

NEED A SPEAKER REGARDING BIBLICAL OR CONSTITUTIONAL INTERPRETATION?

The best way to connect with me is by email:
steverichardson1818@gmail.com